GIANTS CAST LONG SHADOWS

BY THE SAME AUTHOR :

Memoirs of a British Agent
Retreat From Glory
Return to Malaya
My Scottish Youth
Guns or Butter
Comes The Reckoning
The Marines Were There
Scotch
My Europe
Your England
Jan Masaryk
My Rod My Comfort
Friends Foes and Foreigners

GIANTS CAST
LONG SHADOWS

BY

SIR ROBERT BRUCE LOCKHART, K.C.M.G.

PUTNAM
42 GREAT RUSSELL STREET
LONDON

MADE AND PRINTED IN GREAT BRITAIN BY
MORRISON AND GIBB LIMITED, LONDON AND EDINBURGH

CONTENTS

BOOK I

THIS ENGLAND

' The dice have long been thrown when an epoch begins to discuss its own decadence.'

PIERRE REVERDY

CHAPTER ONE

Unhonoured Prophet

' When we are dead,
We do not need to ask
To be forgotten. Our dynamic past
Disperses with its self-appointed task,
Ends as all ardour must.

Yet if the hands of youth should ever rake
The ash of our sad time, it holds a friend,
Whose heart was in the cause all warmth will make
Its own until the end.'

Robert Vansittart, Envoi

I

I CANNOT remember exactly my first meeting with Robert Gilbert Vansittart. It must have been, I think, after 1928, because before that year I had been living abroad almost continuously from 1905. From the early 'thirties until the end of the Second World War and, indeed, until his death in February, 1957, I saw much of him and was constantly in touch with him. Of all the diplomatists of all countries, and of all the members of the Foreign Office, it was he whom I admired and whom I liked most. He was an inspiring figure, strong-minded, sure of himself, warm-hearted and generous in a hundred ways unknown to anyone but himself and the recipient of his kindness.

Although his mother was a Scot, he himself was the most typical of Englishmen, devoted to the English scenery, fond of most sports, and good at his books. At Eton he won the Modern Languages prize and was Captain of the Oppidans. After three years abroad, during which he learnt good German and impeccable French, he passed into the Diplomatic Service in 1902. In those days the Foreign Office and the Diplomatic Service were quite separate bodies and interchange between the two services was extremely rare.

His early training was admirably suited to prepare him for his great future. As a young attaché he was fortunate enough to be sent in 1903 to Paris for his first post. Four years later he was transferred to Teheran where he won the Persian Derby on a horse provided by Sir Percy Loraine, an all-round sportsman, a noted racing owner, a remarkably good linguist, and a great ambassador whose work in a country like Turkey has never been properly recognised by the politicians.

From Teheran ' Van ', as he was known to all who had even a nodding acquaintance with him, went to Stockholm in 1915. In the First World War the Swedish capital was one of the neutral windows on the conflict and was full, not only of British and German diplomats, but also of secret service agents and cloak-and-dagger men of both races. By 1920 he had become a Coun-sellor and Secretary to Lord Curzon, then Secretary of State for Foreign Affairs. That post is the one which usually leads to high promotion.

In 1928 he underwent a useful experience, which rarely comes to members of the Foreign Office. Now an Assistant Under-Secretary, he was appointed Principal Private Secretary to the Prime Minister. In this capacity he served both Stanley Baldwin and Ramsay MacDonald, and characteristically the optimistic Mr Baldwin called him ' Cassandra ', and gave him a K.C.B.

With a wealth of experience Van came back to the Foreign Office in 1930 as Permanent Under-Secretary of State. At that time military service in France had been reduced from three years to one year. Britain was unarmed. Germany, aided by American finance, had been allowed to re-arm, and under the influence of an Austrian-born megalomaniac the Nazi vote rose from 800,000 in 1928 to 6,500,000 in 1930.

What kind of man was this new Permanent Under-Secretary of State for Foreign Affairs ? By what methods was he to per-suade tired, and therefore lazy-minded, Ministers that within twelve years of the bloodiest conflict in history Britain was again in mortal peril, not only of war, but of almost certain defeat ?

He had many brilliant qualities. He was a poet who had written several books of verse. At least one volume, *The Singing Caravan*, went into three editions and was the only book which T. E. Lawrence always carried with him in the Arabian desert during the First World War. As a young Third Secretary of twenty-three he had written a play in French which ran for four months in Paris and then went on tour in the French provinces. He had a remarkably good memory, immense courage supported always by belief in his own judgment, and a pre-science, acquired by long experience, which amounted almost to genius.

Long before he came to the Foreign Office as Permanent Under-Secretary he had made up his mind that, thanks to American finance, Germany was the enemy, that a second war was coming and that, win or lose, we could not stand it. An intimate experience of two feeble Prime Ministers in Baldwin and Ramsay MacDonald gave him a contempt of most poli-ticians and, in his efforts to persuade them of the danger which threatened and of the necessity of re-arming, his technique was perhaps not as sound as his advice.

A civil servant can succeed in influencing Ministers only by remaining a civil servant. The late Lord Norwich, better known as Duff Cooper, who had been both a civil servant and a Minister, was a friend and firm supporter of Van, but he was quite adamant on the duties of the one and of the other. The Minister was responsible for policy. The civil servant provided the material which enabled the Minister to take his decision. Ministers did not relish direct advice from civil servants, who, if they wished to give advice, had to proffer it with such surgical delicacy that the Minister did not realise that it was advice. Duff Cooper was of course right, and over Munich felt himself so frustrated by one of the weakest Governments this country has ever had that he resigned.

His frustration, however, was minor in comparison with that of Vansittart who, receiving reports from ambassadors and Ministers all over Europe and, indeed, from all the world in-dicating the growing danger which he himself had realised from the beginning, found that Ministers paid no attention to his warnings. What he saw, others would not see, and he conceived it his duty to enforce his warning by admonitions and even by lobbying individual Ministers and ex-Ministers. During the neglectful 'thirties, which were the peak years of Van's career, it was he and Ralph Wigram who supplied Winston Churchill, then by no means a connoisseur of modern European history, with the

information which enabled him to speak so firmly and so pro-
phetically on the occasion of Munich. Van was rebuked by the
Government for giving information to a private individual !

Several of his former colleagues believe that his technique
was wrong and that he would have done better to bridle his
impatience. They feel that the contorted style of his minutes and
papers, full of paradoxes, quips and unrecognisable quotations,
irritated Ministers who perhaps grew tired of reading them,
whereas if they had brought themselves to study them they might
have seen the light, and the war might never have taken place.

There is a vestige of truth in this theory. He was a diplomat
of the old school and in his own posthumous book, *The Mist
Procession*, which does not do him justice, he makes it quite clear
that the civil servant and the ambassador whom he admired most
were Sir Eyre Crowe and Sir Francis Bertie. No one will deny
the appropriateness of Van's tribute to Crowe, that ' he was
greater than the men (Ministers) whom he served.' Van describes Bertie as ' the very last of the great ambassadors who was
wholly disinclined to scrape a second fiddle or to become one of
the mouthpieces which the Foreign Office and the Government
have now made their agents.'

Van may be right, but neither of those two men felt any
particular respect for Ministers. They did not regard themselves
as inferiors. Crowe was civil but not servile. Bertie was neither
civil nor servile.

During the 'thirties even his nearest friends likened Van to a
doctor whose patients were Ministers. It was said of him that
his diagnosis was always a hundred per cent right, that his
remedies were sometimes dangerous but effective, and that
his bedside manner was disastrous.

Van had beautiful manners and great charm. I am sure that he
was never rude to Ministers, but in his retirement he had little
respect for them apart from Churchill and Duff Cooper. He
was a man of great physical and moral courage who felt that he
had a momentous mission to fulfil. Time was all-important,
and when his warnings on the dangers to come fell on deaf ears
he became bitter, and complained, not so much against living
individuals, as against the politicians who had fire in their
tongues but none in their bellies.

Referring to the period after the First World War, he wrote : 'The politicians conceived themselves masters ; the next forty years testified to their conceit.' Of Balfour he said : ' I never knew A.J.B. to care for anything but Zionism.' It is true that in foreign affairs Balfour was inclined to take the opposite view of any proposal that was put up to him with the intention of obtaining his assent. In my own experience, I found that over the vexed problem of Russia in 1918, he would produce all the arguments in favour of intervention if one suggested an understanding with the Bolsheviks. Contrariwise, if one urged the necessity of intervention, he would advance the most formidable arguments against it. He was, however, more human than his colleagues have described him. When, as a result of our intervention in Russia, I was arrested and in some danger of my life, Mr Balfour, as he then was, sent a daily personal message to my wife during the period of my incarceration. He had, too, a sense of humour which endeared him to those who served him. Soon after the First World War, when the late Maurice Peterson went to Washington and New York as Private Secretary to Balfour, he brought back the best of all A.J.B. stories.

While he was sitting in Balfour's room discussing the agenda for the day, the telephone rang. Peterson answered it and, clapping his hand over the receiver, said to Balfour : " It's Otto Kahn. He wants to see you." Balfour replied gently : " Yes, tell him I'll call on him to-morrow at noon." Peterson at once protested : " Sir, you can't do that. You are here not only as Foreign Secretary, but as Head of an all-important British Mission. Otto Kahn is a Jewish banker. You cannot call on him. He must come here."

Balfour smiled mildly. " Mr Peterson," he said, " when you have reached my years, you will understand that, when you visit someone, you can leave when you like. When someone visits you, politeness makes you endure half-hours and even hours of boredom."

By senior Ministers of the Crown many things are taken for granted which are quite impossible to a civil servant. I doubt very much if by any other methods than his own Van could have persuaded Baldwin or Chamberlain, or the bulk of the Conservative Party, to arm.

True, Van could have intrigued and plotted, but plotting would have destroyed him and intrigue was not in his nature. Moreover, apart from Winston Churchill, whom Van kept well-informed, there was no one on either side of the House to support him. Labour was even more opposed to rearmament than the Conservatives in the City. Van was not given to gossip. He liked his home, and avoided as far as possible the invitations of the collectors of celebrities. If he went abroad by night, it was to play a little bridge at the St James' Club. In his posthumous book he admits that he should never have been a public servant, because he was never good at resisting the temptation to say what he thought.

Whatever defects there may have been in his technique, in his constant warnings by tongue and pen, in his long and sometimes tortuous despatches, the plain truth is that his policy was unpopular to both the political parties. Had he written like an angel and spoken like a cooing pigeon, he could have achieved no more or no less than he did. Cassandras are never popular and rarely heeded.

He was attacked violently both publicly and privately, and in the big finance houses of the City and in the more exclusive clubs one heard frequently the angry refrain : ' But for Van Hitler would be all right.' Van was probably hurt more deeply than one realised, but he bore no malice. He praised Ramsay MacDonald as a Foreign Secretary. He liked both Baldwin and Neville Chamberlain.

As the 'thirties advanced and the menace increased, Van began to interest himself in finding recruits to carry out the various activities of the Foreign Office in the event of war. By 1937 I was a free man in the sense that I was my own master, and Van was instrumental in arranging for me two long trips in Central Europe and the Balkans. My cover was as a lecturer for the British Council. This meant that I had to give a lecture on some harmless subject wherever I went, but my main task was to look up all the various people whom I had met during my ten years' stay in Central Europe after the First War, and to report to Van.

Two of the recruits whom I recommended strongly to him were John Wheeler-Bennett and Aubrey Morgan. Among their other distinctions, their knowledge of the United States was invaluable. In this book John Wheeler-Bennett has a chapter to himself, and so has Aubrey Morgan.

I do not say that other Permanent Under-Secretaries of State would not have picked John Wheeler-Bennett, for he had already a wide reputation for his knowledge of world affairs. Few, however, would have realised the qualities of Aubrey Morgan in one short interview, and none but Van would have put them in the right place and backed them consistently.

2

The supreme crisis in Van's career came in January, 1938. In the New Year's Honours List he was given a G.C.B. It was the anodyne to soften the blow that was to come. A few days later he was ' promoted ' from Permanent Under-Secretary to Diplomatic Adviser. The new post meant nothing or at the best very little. He was being muzzled, and he was well aware of the fact. He was hurt, and his first reaction was to resign and go into politics. He took a few days' leave to consider his position. On January 19 I went to see him at the Foreign Office. It was his first day at the Office in his new capacity of Diplomatic Adviser. There was bright sunshine till dusk and the air was balmy as on a good spring day. I did not congratulate him, but I felt hopefully that the blue sky was a happy portent.

My hope was vain. He was in his old room, but his waiting room had been taken away from him. He no longer received the foreign ambassadors. He had no Foreign Office official as his private secretary. I felt awkward, but he plunged straightaway into the matters which had always been his vital concern. We were arming at last, but we were still too complacent and too slow. We were progressing, but our enemies were making far greater speed. As for policy, we had made the impossible come true. By using violent language we had brought Germany and Italy together.

He made only one complaint in answer to my questions regarding his power to influence decisions in his new position. He said quite calmly : " Here I shall see no papers until they have been seen by others and action has been taken on them."

There were many people, including, not least, the editor of *The Times*, who wanted to shackle Van, but Mr Chamberlain as Prime Minister must bear the main responsibility. He regarded Van as too pro-French and too excitable. There were other Ministers in the Cabinet who were pro-German, in the sense that they wanted an understanding with Hitler. Moreover, Van sometimes differed from Anthony Eden's views, and this was embarrassing to the Foreign Secretary. Chamberlain thought that Eden was also excitable, and, wanting to tranquillise his relations with the Foreign Office and to make more elbow-room for Sir Horace Wilson, his own pet adviser, he had made this compromise.

The year 1938 must have been the most miserable twelve months in Van's career, and it was no consolation to him to find that virtually all his prophecies were coming true even on the very dates which he had predicted. At the end of January I made a ten weeks' inspection tour of the capitals of the Balkans and Central Europe. I saw Hitler march into Vienna, went straight on to Prague to see my Czech friends who knew their turn would be next, and finished up in Berlin to hear the tramping feet of Nazi soldiers and to be told by good German friends like Albrecht Bernstorff and Prittwitz that Hitler was determined to seize Czechoslovakia.

It was not until April that I saw Van again. He was in the deepest gloom, worried by the policy which had sent Nevile Henderson as ambassador to curry favour with the Nazis, and quite sure that every grab that Hitler made increased his prestige even with those Germans, including the senior officers, who thought him a mountebank. I have already said that Van's prescience amounted almost to genius. Here are three examples. On that 5th of April, 1938, he said that we could have stopped Hitler from taking the Rhineland without any protest from the German military leaders. They expected us to stop him. His unimpeded march into Vienna could also have been stopped without war. By not doing so, we encouraged the German generals to think that after all there was something to this fellow Hitler. In the autumn, Van said, it would be Czechoslovakia's turn. We would do nothing, and all Germany would regard Hitler as a genius. All three predictions were later proved true by the captured German documents.

I do not doubt that Van put his views before Ministers and
ex-Ministers both in writing and by word of mouth. Ex-Ministers
like Winston Churchill listened and learnt, but Ministers who
saw other despatches and received other advice took a colder
view of Van's proposals and prophecies and, so far from en-
couraging him, held him aloof. The more they tried to side-track
him, the more vehemently he pleaded his case in memoranda
that grew ever longer and more complicated. Van had not always
seen eye to eye with Anthony Eden, but when Halifax succeeded Eden the relationship between Foreign Secretary and
Diplomatic Adviser became more distant. Chamberlain was
dedicated to peace at almost any price. Van's insistence on the
imminence of danger was resented from a civil servant. It is to
be feared that his memoranda were regarded as boring and that
they were not read with the care that should have been given
to them.

It was well for Van that he was a man who could find peace
and consolation in his home-life. Both his marriages were very
happy. The first was ended by a double tragedy. His stepson,
to whom he was devoted, was killed in a lift, and Van's wife,
who never recovered from the shock, died a few weeks later.
His second marriage to Sareta, daughter of Henry Ward and
widow of Sir Colville Barclay, a former ambassador, was an
ideal union, for she understood him and knew how to interpret
his moods and to give him the praise which all men desire when
it is denied to them.

Throughout that summer I wrote at feverish pace a book on
Europe in which, thanks to Van's prescience, I prophesied that
there would be no war over Czechoslovakia. I wrote the book
of 100,000 words in just over eleven weeks, sent the final chapters
to my publishers on August 2nd, and the book was published
on September 30, two days after Munich. I arrived in London
on August 15 for the beginning of what was to be the final
Czechoslovak crisis and on the next day went straight to the
Foreign Office to see Vansittart. I found him at his most pessimistic as he saw all his forebodings coming true, and, as usual,
much concerned at the ignorance, lack of preparedness and too
comfortable attitude of people in this country. He blamed the
politicians of both parties and also the newspaper barons for

misleading the people. There was, he said, no possibility of a real settlement. Hitler was determined to make Czechoslovakia a vassal state of the German Reich. If he were allowed to do this—and he would do it quickly, he would go on. Poland, Rumania, Yugoslavia would fall into his maw. War or no war, Britain would become a second-class power.

During the Munich crisis I engaged myself to go back to the Foreign Office in the event of war, which Van predicted would begin within the next year. In July, 1939, he gave the exact date to Jack Wheeler-Bennett who was going with me to see Colijn, the Dutch Prime Minister, and the Kaiser, in Holland, and was then returning to the United States. Van said to him very seriously : " I advise you most strongly to be back in the United States by the end of August. I expect the final crash to come in the first days of September." Over a long period of years I cannot recall any prediction of his that was wide of the mark.

On our return from Holland I gave Van and Jack Wheeler-Bennett luncheon in the St James' Club. For once Van let himself go. He was not interested in our news of the Kaiser and was very sceptical about Colijn's optimism for peace. He told us that he had warned the Government for years. In this respect he had gone even farther than Eyre Crowe in the period before the First World War.

Now he was boycotted. His wife had been organising some charity and had numerous promises of help. Half of those who had promised to come stayed away. Remembering how in the England v. Scotland rugby match at Twickenham in March, 1924, Eddie Myers, the famous English three-quarter, received a bad kick on the head and began running with the ball towards his own goal posts, Van compared England to a rugger fifteen all running the wrong way, suffering from a form of mental concussion.

During the first twenty months of the war I saw less of him than usual. But two occasions remain fixed in my memory. While I was with him in his room in the Foreign Office, he rang for Miss Dougherty, his secretary, who served him faithfully to the end of his life. He asked her to make an appointment for him to see Lord Halifax, then Foreign Secretary. It was a Thursday afternoon during the ' phoney ' war, and the reply was slow in coming. Lord Halifax was going to Yorkshire on Friday. If the matter was urgent and important, he would see Van. If not, it would have to wait till Tuesday.

The other occasion was on Friday, June 27, 1941. By this time I had become a senior official of the Political Warfare Executive which dealt with all propaganda to enemy and enemy-occupied territories. I did not want the job and sought Van's advice. It was his last day in the Foreign Office, and for an hour I watched him clearing his desk and destroying his papers. He was utterly dejected, but he made only one complaint : that his post as Diplomatic Adviser had been a sheer waste of time. No one had sought his advice or paid any attention to his memoranda. He was an outsider in the Office in which no one else had known so much of the inside. As I went away, I felt that I had witnessed the failure of the one man who could have prevented the rise of Hitler and averted war.

3

When Van retired, Winston Churchill was not ungrateful. He made Van a Baron. But a public servant, once his career is over, can never come back

Throughout the war, Van took a keen interest in political warfare. It was perhaps just as well that we were good friends, for his views on Germany were rigid. Like Admiral A. B. Cunningham, Van believed that the only good Germans were dead Germans. He was therefore opposed to members of my staff like Richard Crossman, a brilliant propagandist, but not exactly amenable to official policy, who favoured a ' hope clause ' in our propaganda to Germany. Until the end of the war Ministers shirked the issue altogether, and ' unconditional surrender ' was the official policy towards Germany. It did not help our political warfare.

I must also admit that Goebbels and the German propagandists exploited Van's very proper dislike of German militarism in order to induce the German people to continue the war to the last gasp.

I have still in my possession a German poster four feet long by two and three-quarter feet wide, which has an excellent picture of Van, very smartly dressed in a grey Homburg hat and carrying an umbrella under his arm. At the top of the poster in large letters are the words ' *Ein Alter Bekannter* ' (An Old Acquaintance). Below in black ink follow two sentences : ' Vansittart, former Under-Secretary in the English Foreign Office, made in the House of Lords a hate-speech in which among other things he declared that England cannot win this war and cannot hope for a 100 per cent victory until at last the English people learn the truth. And this truth is that England must fight against the whole German nation and must utterly destroy it.'

Below in red ink on a black back-ground is a long tirade which begins : ' By this declaration this high-ranking freemason has again let the cat out of the bag,' and ending with the sentence : ' Vansittart and his kind have apparently not learnt that from the beginning the German people have adapted themselves to total warfare and are firmly resolved to fight this war to a victorious end. THEN WE CAN SPEAK AGAIN, HERR VANSITTART ! ' Obviously the Nazis recognised in Van the man who knew them best. As Anthony Eden said in 1958, drift is the demon of democracy. Van had no use for drift, although he was defeated by it in others.

After the war he spoke frequently, and always to the point, in the House of Lords and wrote vigorous letters to the newspapers. With the passing of the years he was seen less at the bridge tables in the St James' Club, and did most of his work in his beautiful home in Buckinghamshire. Soviet Russia, whose policy he described as ' keeping pots boiling everywhere ' was now the chief danger, but he still kept an eye on the Teutonic nation which he never trusted.

I, too, saw less of him, because I came less frequently to London, but we corresponded several times a year. We had a bond in that we both developed skin trouble towards the end of the war. He was a good letter-writer and gave me excellent advice which I should have accepted more frequently.

For Christmas of 1955 I wrote to him, not so much complaining, but regretting, that I might have done better if I had remained in the Foreign Service after the Second World War. Back came the reply and the healing salve :

' I am sure that you do not really regret not having accepted

Anthony's offer of an Embassy. I could never have faced one. My wife always said that I should die of *foie gras* and Château d'Yquem, and of fourteen meals a week in company! You, for your part, must reflect how furiously your skin would have protested.

'What a lot of things that one is sometimes tempted to regret appear quite certainly on reflection to have been better as they are. I have often thought so in my own case. Your references to Dawson's *Life* * have reminded me of some such things. I have not read it yet, but suppose that I must do so sometime or other. I suffered much at his hands, but grudges are an awful lack of *savoir vivre*, so I have never had one. I'm sure you haven't either.'

My last letter from him was dated January 19, 1957. I had complained to him of not being able to travel. He replied : ' I suppose this means for financial reasons, but travelling is a mixed pleasure if one has to do it on a strict allowance. For my part I cannot travel any more for an even worse reason—that I am too crippled by arthritis, which has become very painful. At least, thank goodness, the skin trouble has not returned to plague me.'

In just under four weeks he was dead. Ten years before, in 1947, he had said in a debate in the House of Lords : ' It almost breaks my heart when I think that I started life in a world inhabited by hope and am ending it in one inhibited by doubt of its own duration.'

In April of 1958 his posthumous book, *The Mist Procession* appeared. It was an interesting book, because everything that Van touched was alive, but it was not worthy of his great record, partly because he could not praise himself and partly because it was written in that contorted and sometimes obscure literary style which he affected and which irritated Ministers. Moreover, he began it late in life and did not live to finish it.

Of all the diplomats and ambassadors that I have met he was the most charming, the most generous, the most far-seeing, and the least ambitious. He thought only of his country and of the dangers which threatened it. In addition to his experience abroad, he was, during the 'thirties, the recipient of all official and secret

* Editor of *The Times* and one of Van's opponents.

information. If it is the sole duty of a civil servant to point out
to a Minister : on the one hand, you may do this, and, on the
other hand, you may do that, Van perhaps should not have
been a public servant. But in time of peril it is better to break
a lance against the vast ignorance of many Ministers and fail,
than to play for personal safety and a pension.

Van's good deeds are known only to those who were re-
cipients of his generosity. Widows of members of the Foreign
Service receive or used to receive no pension. There have been
Consuls and at least one ambassador who have died before their
time and left no money for their widows. Time and again it was
Van who came to the rescue.

Deeply to my regret I was unable to go to Van's funeral,
but I was gratified to learn that the Czechs whom he had always
defended did not forget to honour him.

With Lady Vansittart's permission I quote her letter to me a
few days after the funeral :

' Thank you so much for your very kind letter of sympathy
and for all you say about Van. He was so fond of you and, as
you say, he was so loyal and so reliable.

' Thank you for speaking of Van in your broadcast to
Czechoslovakia. The free Czechs sent a beautiful wreath. It lay
alone on Van's coffin in the village church where we took him
on the night before the funeral. The other flowers had not yet
arrived, and I know he would have been pleased to have the
Czech flowers with him to the end.'

This is an age of biographers, and here is a rewarding opportunity for a young man to write, before it is too late, the life of
a civil servant whose like this country will never see again.
Van did not wish or expect to be remembered. Nevertheless,
he belongs to the Churchill legend, for in 1928 Churchill as
Chancellor of the Exchequer reduced our expenditure on defence
and as late as 1930 was not convinced that war was coming.
It was Van who warned him, and it is right that the man who
foresaw the danger so clearly should have his place in the history
of his country. He, like Sir Eyre Crowe, was greater than all
but one of the men whom he served.

CHAPTER TWO

Dining Out in the 'Thirties

'Little gossip, blithe and hale,
Tattling many a broken tale.'

FROM the ages of seventeen-and-a-half to forty-one I was more or less permanently abroad. I was therefore friendless and forlorn when in the autumn of 1928 I came to London to work for Lord Beaverbrook. At Stornoway House and at Cherkley Court, his residences, I met British and Dominion Prime Ministers, politicians of all countries, great bankers, painters, foreign celebrities, Hollywood tycoons, and every man, woman and child who ever filled the front page of the *Daily Express*. It was an exciting and rewarding experience. But, unlike Mr Eammon Andrews, my conscience said to me ' This is *Not* Your Life ', and in one sense conscience was right. I was always in the presence. I was like the little boys of whom our grandfathers used to say : ' Children should be seen and not heard ', the only difference being that I had to listen and not be heard.

For a wider experience of London life I owe much to four hostesses who seemed to make a special custom of mixing titled people with authors, actors, artists, musicians and even journalists. They were Lady Colefax, Lady Cunard, Mrs Beckett, and Mrs Greville. I soon learnt to call Lady Colefax, Sybil, Lady Cunard, Emerald, and even Mrs Beckett, Muriel, but, although I knew her well enough and was asked to go to Polesden Lacey to stay with her, I never dared to call Mrs Greville, ' Maggie '.

Sybil Colefax was the kindest of the four, for she was not a gossip, and English gossip has to have a razor edge of unkindness. Short and rather plump with well-set dark eyes, she had the energy and drive of a modern jet engine. Not a great talker herself, she took the utmost pains to make her guests at ease and to ensure that the right lions roared at the right time.

Argyll House in King's Road, Chelsea, was her home until the end of 1936. It was a charming house, especially in summer, for it had at the back a pleasant garden. Here she entertained several times a week both for luncheon and for dinner. Her husband, Arthur Colefax, was a barrister who, as a specialist in insurance matters, could have made a fortune, but in the First World War he took a war job. I liked him, because his main topic of conversation was fishing.

Sybil ran the whole house, and sent out her invitations on ordinary postcards which she wrote in bed in the morning. The writing was often illegible, so that even her oldest friends had to telephone her to discover what the right time and the right day were. This did not worry Sybil in the least. Her energy carried her through everything. I never saw her ill-tempered or even irritated. Her guests ranged from King Edward VIII and Mrs Simpson, future Prime Ministers like Winston Churchill and famous writers and musicians, to humble journalists and people whom she really liked.

The conversation at her table varied greatly and depended largely on the age of the chief speaker. At Argyll House I met many ghosts of the past, including George Moore and Max Beerbohm. At Argyll House, too, I met Mrs Simpson for the first time on April 2, 1935. The conversation was more or less a monologue by Austen Chamberlain who was not a good talker. However, he told a number of stories, including one about the first Lord Rosebery, who used to be a member of a club which had no guests and at which Ministers and other members could speak as freely as they liked without any risk of being quoted. In due course a member with a famous name became secretary. He was known to keep a famous diary. Lord Rosebery ceased coming. Eventually the diarist-secretary died, and Lord Rosebery came back to the club. He was silent throughout the meal. The members, whose curiosity was whetted, thought he was preparing an oration, and all waited for the silver voice. At last someone ventured a few words in praise of the late secretary. Then Lord Rosebery opened his lips : " Gentlemen," he said, " now that the late secretary is dead and the obsequies have been decently performed, we can talk again."

It was also on this occasion that Austen told us that King

George V had snubbed him severely for daring to suggest an Order of Merit for someone ; the O.M. being the Sovereign's sole prerogative, and on this subject George V, at least, took no hints from Ministers or anyone else. Shortly after this, I was again lunching at Argyll House, and someone mentioned Chamberlain's story about the O.M. H. G. Wells and Somerset Maugham were present. Diplomatically Maugham kept silent, but H. G. Wells made an outburst.

" I may be called a snob," he said, " but I've too much pride to take an Order which has been given to Hardy and Galsworthy."

Poor H.G. ! The 'thirties tried him severely. He foresaw clearly the Nazi danger which so many failed to see. He became a prophet and a pamphleteer, and his new style of book did not sell as well as the great novels of his youth and middle age. I remember another outburst at Argyll House on August 11, 1936. Among others Sir Alexander Cadogan, then soon to be head of the Foreign Office, and Sir John Maffey were present. 'H.G.', goaded perhaps by the presence of so-called experts, launched out into a tirade about the future of Britain. We were, he said, already a third-rate Power, but were unwilling to admit it. Palmerston, Britain's last great Foreign Secretary, had always backed the Left. Since the National Government came in, we were backing the Right. Our money was now on the Fascists in Spain. We were backing the Nazis in Central Europe. In Spain we should lose Gibraltar. In Central Europe we should lose Austria and Czechoslovakia.

He was on the whole a true prophet, but he had a knack of rubbing even his best friends the wrong way, and in any event the English rarely want to hear unpleasant things.

I have already told in *Your England* how, when at a large party in Argyll House at which King Edward VIII was present, Arthur Rubenstein played and the guests continued talking, but became interested when Noel Coward sat down at the piano and sang !

What I remember best and most gratefully were the small parties where there were unforgettable and unrehearsed surprises as, for example, on one August night in 1934 when Francis Toye sat down at the piano and began to play the musical comedy and music hall songs of thirty years before. Up jumped Gertie Lawrence and sang to us all. She knew all the words and had learnt them as a child from her mother. I met her five years later in Boston. She was a charming woman, completely natural and without any of the frills and flummery which so many people seem to acquire with success.

In the autumn of 1936 Sybil Colefax was ill and underwent an operation which sapped her strength considerably. She moved into a smaller, but most attractive, house in Lord North Street. Her husband was dead, and she was now straitened in circumstances. Entertaining was her life's work, and she could not live without it.

As the European crisis drew nearer, there was a noticeable change in the guests. Politicians and members of the Foreign Office tended to replace the literary and artistic intelligentsia. Favourite authors, however, still came and were almost certain to see one of their books in the basket of new books which she kept at the entrance of the small drawing-room upstairs. Both before and during the war she did an excellent job in bringing leading American journalists like Ed Murrow into touch with British politicians and diplomatists.

During the 'phoney' war I still kept in touch with her and went occasionally to the 'ordinary' which she kept at the Dorchester Hotel and at which each guest paid his or her own way. When the war really started, I had a regular sixteen hours day of work, and there was no time for social life.

After the war she became frailer and frailer, and her health was further undermined by an accident. She died in 1950. She was a woman of great courage who succeeded in what she wanted to do, and, although there were people who laughed and even sneered at her, she left not an enemy among the vast number of people whom she invited to her table.

So much has already been written about Lady Cunard and Mrs Greville by much better authorities than myself, notably Lady Diana Cooper on Lady Cunard, and Sir Osbert Sitwell on Mrs Greville, that there is little new that I can write about them. Indeed, I have told some of my own experiences in their company in *Your England*. I liked Emerald Cunard, although she had a sharper tongue and a greater hunger for gossip than Sybil Colefax. When Emerald, ' Maggie ' Greville, and Lady Oxford were tearing, say, Sir John Simon to pieces, not a shred of clothing was left to cover his nakedness.

Of the three women ' Maggie ' Greville was by far the strongest character. She was kind to me, but inwardly I trembled before her. Like myself she was a Scot, but not even Edward I of England was such a hammer of some Scots as she was. Her father was William McEwan, the head of the famous firm of brewers and one of the richest men in the country. When his first wife died, he was lonely and took unto himself his Scottish housekeeper whom he eventually married. Their daughter was ' Maggie '.

Edinburgh society, which with little reason gives itself great airs, was shocked and the McEwans were ostracised. ' Maggie ', who was given the best schooling, came to London, married Ronald Greville, and by sheer strength of character became a formidable and attractive figure in the highest circles in London. In her new position she could give vent to her likes and dislikes. Edinburgh society, when it visited London, felt the razor-sharp edge of her displeasure.

She had great qualities. She was devoted to her father and cared for him tenderly in his old age. Osbert Sitwell, whose writing I admire and whose opinion I respect, says that she was clever. I do not doubt that she was, in many matters, but she was not clever in politics. She fell for Hitler, went to at least one Nazi rally, and was treated by the Nazis as if she were royalty. She was always the first person whom Ribbentrop went to see on his visits to London in 1934 and 1935.

What she had in abundance was courage. She was afraid of no one and, no matter who was present, she never watered down her opinions.

If she was not clever in foreign affairs, she was a shrewd judge of men and, I imagine, of women. Quite apart from her favourite story, always brilliantly acted, of how Sir John Simon bit the poker when she refused him, she told me seriously that she would have married John, but not John and his children. Talking of Hoesch, the attractive German ambassador, who later died of a heart attack in the German Embassy in London, she praised his beautiful manners and his charming kindness, then she turned to me as one Scot to another non-Edinburgh Scot and said cynically : " if you or I ever lost our position Hoesch would never lift a finger and never want to see us again." I do not doubt that she was right. She had the same appraisal of Lord Tyrrell who was so nice to everyone but whom she advised me never to trust for one moment.

She was no social climber. She got there not so much by her marriage as by her own merits. She had principles and, like most strong-minded people, had rather rigid likes and dislikes. She would not meet Mrs Corrigan, an American lady who in the 'thirties spent much of her time in London and was lavish in her hospitality. When I asked her why she was so unkind to someone whom she had never met, she replied : " To be known in the States as an English woman who doesn't go to Mrs Corrigan's parties is to be placed on a pedestal."

" I like pedestals," she added.

When someone else asked her why she didn't go to Mrs Corrigan's parties, she replied tartly : " I'm never hungry enough."

Muriel Beckett, wife of Rupert Beckett, banker and owner of the *Yorkshire Post*, differed greatly from the hostesses whom I have mentioned. She was a Paget, a grand-daughter of the fourth Lord Anglesey, and had her own circle of friends. She also had favourites, whom she took up for some whim or other and whose welfare she did her best and kindest to promote. From 1936 until the war crisis I was fortunate enough to enjoy her friendship and her patronage. I was first asked to her country house, The Camp, at Sunningdale, to be catechised about my books. Having survived the examination, I was made a member of her inner circle.

She was a great admirer of Lloyd George, and I remember very vividly my first luncheon-party at her house in Hyde Park Gardens. There were only eight of us altogether, and L.G., Robert Horne, and myself were the only men. L.G. had an enemy at the table in Lady Pembroke, who had never met him but, as a staunch Conservative, was prepared to be cold to him. Quite unaware of this hostility, L.G. kept the whole table thrilled with story after story. The best one was of J. H. Thomas, the famous leader of the railwaymen and, according to L.G., ' the one unsinkable ship that Britain ever built.' The miners had not supported ' Jimmie ' in a railway strike. Later, the miners struck, and their leaders came to see ' Jimmie.' He gave them all his sympathy. All would be well, but of course he would have to consult the railwaymen.

Jimmie then summons the railwaymen and tells them they must support their mining pals. Then he adds : " Of course you remember how I pulled off a pretty good wages agreement for you last time and, if we join this miners' strike, we might lose all that we gained." The railwaymen voted against the strike.

The next day Jimmie is back in his London office. Pleased with himself, he lights a cigar and pours himself a whisky and soda. The telephone rings. The miners' leaders are on their way to see him.

Jimmie hides the whisky in his cupboard and throws his cigar out of the window. When the miners are shown in, they find him with his head buried in his hands over the table. He looks up. " Boys," he says, " me bloody 'eart is broke. Me boys have gone back on me."

I had the good fortune to hear L.G.'s conversation on quite a number of occasions, and as a raconteur he had few equals in any country.

Lady Pembroke was thrilled by him. When the women left the room L.G. did not remember who she was. I told him, and at once he went upstairs, talked to her about Carnarvonshire and the Pagets, and chaffed her for ratting to the Conservatives. In Carnarvon there had been two big families : the Pagets and the Wynnes. The Pagets—and Bea Pembroke was a Paget—had been Radicals.

That same summer I was staying with Muriel Beckett at her Sunningdale house. The other guests were Tommy Rosslyn and the Taubers. On the Sunday Muriel drove us all to Churt to spend the afternoon with L.G. When L.G. was writing his memoirs, I had been several times to Churt, usually to bring Russians like Kerensky whom L.G. wished to question. There had been big changes since my last visit : a new wing with a cinema theatre and several new treasures.

The weather was the best that England can produce on those
rare occasions of a real English summer, and while L.G. was
showing his garden to his guests and talking politics all the time,
I nearly choked with suppressed laughter when I spotted a very
tubby Tauber running about now on one side behind L.G.
and now on the other, tripping over the border of the path,
and working a cine-camera in much the same manner as a pre-
revolution Russian assassin used to look for an opportunity to
launch his bomb at the right moment.

At tea-time L.G. was full of reminiscences. I reminded him
of his first (and perhaps only) salmon which he caught on the
Ewe in Ross-shire in 1921. At once he reacted. It was a very
important event, he said, because the Irish troubles were coming
to a head, and L.G. called the first and only British Cabinet
meeting north of the Tweed. It was held in the Inverness Town
Hall on September 7, 1931. The Irish Treaty was signed in
December, and Muriel Beckett had a photograph of L.G. discussing the meeting with the King and the Mackintosh at Moy
Hall.

Muriel told L.G. that King George V had seen this photograph a few months before his death. She had intended to ask
him to sign it, but had refrained from doing so because L.G.'s
speeches before the election of 1935 had been so bad. " That
was an awful mess you made, L.G.," she said. Back like a flash
came the answer : " Not so big a mess as your P.M. landed us
all in six months after."

He showed us all the treasures of his library. As he went along
the shelves, he stopped before two of my books. " Ah," he said,
" here is Lockhart, just where he ought to be, next to Hitler,
Ludendorff and the other rascals."

He also showed us the copy of *Macbeth* found by his daughter
Lady Carey Evans in the Caledonian Market with the signature
of William George, L.G.'s father, on the fly-leaf. I wonder how
many people there are to-day who, being in the same circumstances, save their money to read Shakespeare. The answer is
probably very few of them are in such circumstances as was
William George at one time, and that to-day they prefer to
look rather than to read.

What interested me most of all was the book which belonged

to Robespierre and which had still a piece of blood-stained leather from the table on which he was laid after trying to shoot himself in the Hotel de Ville the evening before he was guillotined.

It was given to L.G. in 1916 by ' Le petit Père Combes ', then a member of the Cabinet of ex-Prime Ministers of France. It was called the ' Cabinet of the Pyramids ' because all its members were so old.

Clemenceau was invited to join it. " *Ah! non!* " he said, " *je suis trop jeune.* "

He was then seventy-five !

L.G., Winston Churchill, Clemenceau, Lenin and Trotsky ! If the world survives, Lenin may well outlast the others in fame, but of the five I would prefer to have served Georges Clemenceau.

Richard Tauber was another favourite of Mrs Beckett, and I got to know both him and his wife at The Camp. Later, we crossed the Atlantic together in the *Aquitania* in January, 1939. He had a nervous temperament and, like many singers, had expanded lungs and a big chest. In other respects, he was gentle and almost as naïve as a child. At The Camp he did not hesitate to say how proud he was to be singing Caruso's great part in *Pagliacci.* He was just as enthusiastic about the new Lehar operetta which Cochrane was to put on in March, 1937. He was proud, not because he was to sing the leading role, but because Lehar was coming over from Vienna to conduct the opening per-formance. At other moments he seemed to be asleep while Muriel Beckett played most of the famous Tauber records. Then when a jazz tune came on, he would wake up and say : " Ah ! that's nice."

He was very much under the influence and care of his wife, the former actress, Diana Napier. I found her attractive, but just as temperamental as her husband whom she watched as a partridge mother guards her chick. " Richard," she would say, " you're talking too much ; we can't hear ourselves speak for the echo of your voice," and Richard would reply gently and affectionately : " Well, my sweet, we live from that echo, don't we ? "

Later, Diana saved him from certain death. On March 10, 1938, Diana was at Antibes. Richard rang her up to say that his throat

was bad and that he was going by Orient Express to Vienna in
order to see his doctor. Having heard from Geoffrey Lloyd
that the situation in Austria looked very ominous, she hired a
fast car and arrived at Milan on March 11 half an hour before
the train went. There was a scene on the platform. Tauber,
himself a Viennese, insisted that all would be well and that
Schussnigg, the Austrian Chancellor, was master of the situation.
Diana won. Four days later Hitler marched into Vienna, and
Richard was so put out that for three days he sat in his room
and refused to speak or to eat. He was on the verge of hysteria,
and Diana went in despair to her doctor who told her : " You
must wake him up violently ; shake him and slap his cheeks."
She did as she was told. At first Richard was furious, but he
was cured. He went to Rome and sang before the Queen of
Italy. He had one of his greatest triumphs, and all was well.

I had seen Tauber on the stage before I ever met him, and
heard him sing " You are my Heart's Delight " in Berlin long
before it reached London.

A Tauber story was again provided by Muriel Beckett in that
splendid summer of 1936. On July 26 I went to her London
house to dine and to hear Tauber sing. It was a Sunday evening,
and I had been told that it would be a small party with not more
than six people. When I got there I found a huge party headed
by Princess Helena Victoria, the Duchess of Portland, the
Londonderrys, the Pembrokes, Lord Anglesey, Lord Hambleden
and several others, including, not least, Sir Thomas Beecham.
Presumably the Taubers had also been told that it was to be a
small party, for he had not brought an accompanist with him.
Within a few seconds of his arrival I could see that he was
worried and his first reaction was to send for his accompanist.

When dinner was over, Tauber's accompanist had not been
found, and, as the party had to go on, Tauber had to sing to the
accompaniment of Mr Hart-Davis who did nobly. Mrs Beckett,
however, was not satisfied and begged Sir Thomas Beecham
to help Tauber out. As Sir Thomas walked from the audience
to the piano stool, the Duchess of Portland said in a loud
whisper heard by all near her : " Who's that ? Is he Tauber's
man ? "

Tauber, petrified by Sir Thomas's presence, was not in his

best form and after singing Schubert's *Ständchen*, a Grieg song. and ' *Das Blaue Himmelbett* ' from *Frasquita*, he dried up.

I felt sorry for him. I, too, had had a difficult time, for I had sat next to Lady Londonderry at dinner and had been harangued by Lord Londonderry after dinner, and both of them were pro-German and I was pro-Czech. But for me at least the Duchess's remark made the evening.

CHAPTER THREE

Diplomat and Author

' Blest with each talent, and each art to please.'

I FIRST met Harold Nicolson at the end of 1918 soon after my
return from the dismal failure of my mission to the first
Bolshevik Government. He was one of the very few people
in the Foreign Office who were kind to me at that time. As I did
not know him then, I have never forgotten his friendly gesture.
I repaid it nearly eleven years later in bad coinage when I suggested to Lord Beaverbrook that Harold would be the ideal
person to write and edit the ' Londoner's Diary ' of the *Evening
Standard*.

The truth is that I had a personal desire to go to Berlin where
Harold was Counsellor at our Embassy. I never imagined for one
moment that he would accept Lord Beaverbrook's offer of a
hard chair in Shoe Lane. However, his brilliant wife, better known
by her maiden name as the author, V. Sackville West, found no
glamour in diplomatic luncheons and dinners and longed to
escape from them. Moreover, Harold himself was not entirely
happy. His *Some People*, published in 1927, had given him public
fame, but had not pleased Sir William Tyrrell (afterwards Lord
Tyrrell) who was then all-powerful in the Foreign Office. To my
surprise Harold did not refuse the offer, and I left Berlin in
triumph, but with a slightly troubled mind lest I had deprived
the Foreign Office of one of its most promising diplomatists.

Harold, who joined the *Evening Standard* in September 1929,
was not happy in Fleet Street and left it in June, 1931. I felt
conscience-stricken, but he has always told me that he has never
regretted abandoning the sinecure of diplomacy for the risks of
a literary career. During those twenty-one months in Shoe Lane
I got to know him well. Since then I have seen him more or less
regularly, and have learnt to appreciate his virtues and his failings.
His greatest weakness is an incurable shyness which is not at

first discernible and which some people are inclined to regard as arrogance. His virtues are many. They include a brilliant mind, an immense capacity for work, speed in everything that he undertakes, and an almost unequalled command of his time. He is the only man I know who with unfailing regularity answers every letter on the same day on which he receives it. As he used to say to me when I groaned under my own burdens, " there is time for everything if one cares to make it." Like many clever people he gives better advice to others than he sometimes gives to himself. I owe him much, because it was he who first urged me to leave Fleet Street and pointed out that a book on my Russian experiences would provide the way of escape.

Since those early days I have always admired him without deviation or the slightest envy, unless perhaps it be for his early boyhood which has always seemed to me to be enchanting and therefore romantically enviable. I should like to have been born in Tehran, to remember Buda-Pest as a boy of eight, to have taken Constantinople and Sofia in my progress to the formative years in Tangier, and to have spent my Oxford vacations in Madrid and St Petersburg. Above all, I should like to have had a diplomat for my father and to have studied the *va-et-vient* of most of the Embassies of Europe.

According to Harold the reality was not so alluring as my dreams. In Buda-Pest he nearly died of typhoid and remembers only seeing red devils dancing before him in his delirium. Constantinople was better. There were wild dogs in the streets, and he recalls seeing the sinister Sultan Abdul Hamid driving to the Selamlik. The memories of Sofia are clearer. There were long rides with Bourchier, the famous *Times* correspondent and surely the first journalist to figure on a postage stamp. There was also the murder of Stambuloff, in itself excitement enough for a young boy living in that tranquil age ; and to the Legation another historical figure, in Prince Ferdinand, came to dine. He was not yet a King, for Bulgaria was still a principality. Later, he was to be known as ' Foxy ' Ferdinand, caused great trouble to the Allies in the First World War, was deposed, and to-day is forgotten except perhaps by bird-lovers, for he was a great ornithologist.

The ten years in Tangier ended in 1905. By then Harold spoke excellent French and German and had picked up some Spanish. With the vigilant interest which fathers of those days took in the education of their sons, Harold's father did not allow him to learn Arabic as he contended that the language, as spoken in Tangier, was a debased dialect.

Harold's memories of Tangier, then so primitive that there was not a wheeled vehicle in the place, are affectionate. Nevertheless, it was not his home. In those days diplomats had no home except England and, although they did not see it very often, they took the greatest care to ensure that their children were educated there. Harold endured this ordeal, and endured is the right word. Soon after his father went as Minister to Tangier, Harold was sent to a private school in Folkestone. He hated every minute of it. After the warm houses of the Continent, he was cold, underfed, and bullied by the headmaster.

Wellington was a little better, but not a happy or spiritual place until he reached the Sixth Form and came under the influence of Bertram Pollock who was, I think, the first man to be appointed a headmaster before he was thirty. Both as Master of Wellington and as a teacher Pollock could not only inspire clever boys but also command their admiration. Although Harold has been a Governor of Wellington, I think that his only happy memories of his school are centred in Pollock. Indeed, when I knew him first he was antagonistic to the whole idea of public schools. He disliked games ; still less did he admire the public school worship of rugger and cricket gods. Later, however, he sent both his sons to Eton.

His period at Balliol, of which college he is to-day an honorary Fellow, coincided with his father's tenure of the Madrid and St Petersburg Embassies. It was in the St Petersburg Embassy that he took part in the most exciting physical exploit of his life. In those days Embassy staffs were tiny. There were no stenographers and no clerks. All the typing and coding and decoding of telegrams were done by young and not so very young diplomats who had received the most expensive education that Britain could supply, and in St Petersburg the Counsellor and the whole Embassy staff were comfortably accommodated in two-and-a-quarter rooms, the quarter being a kind of cubicle in which sat the Head of the Chancery.

During one of Harold's visits to his father, there was a scare about security. One or two Embassies had been burgled, not for loot but for cypher codes. There were indications that someone had tried to enter the Chancery, which was easy of access because, in addition to the main entrance, there was a small passage behind the Chancery which led into the Counsellor's room and from there into the main rooms where were the safes and the cyphers. The ambassador was anxious, and Nevile Henderson, then a powerful man, and Harold volunteered to sit up all night for a week.

For two nights nothing happened, but on the third night between two and three a.m., when the two young men were nearly asleep, they heard sounds. Taking off their shoes, they crept towards the Chancery. The steps ceased but there was a candle-light and a slight noise of rumbling as if someone was moving books. The two men had no arms, but Henderson had a Foreign Office bag which he had filled with a red box. As they reached the entrance to the Chancery, they saw a figure with a candle moving cautiously down the back passage to the Counsellor's room. Nevile Henderson went first, jumped on the back of the intruder, and crashed man and candle to the ground. As the man seemed stunned, Nevile and Harold re-lit the candle and, holding it down towards their victim's face, nearly fainted themselves. The burglar was Harold's father and Henderson's ambassador. He was not amused.

Harold himself entered the diplomatic service in 1909, and of the twenty years of his official career ten were spent abroad and ten in the Foreign Office. His posts abroad were in Madrid, Constantinople, Tehran and Berlin, and in none of them did he spend more than three years. His most important work, therefore, was done in the Foreign Office during the First World War and again from 1920 to 1925. He also attended the Peace Conference and for nine months from October, 1919, to June, 1920, assisted at the birth pains of the League of Nations.

In the Foreign Office he was brilliant. Given a line of policy to follow, he could develop the theme and produce a draft in better language and with greater speed than any public servant of our times. A man of high ideals and firm principles, he could have been the perfect ' number one ' to any Foreign Secretary or Prime Minister. Judging from his subsequent political career, I do not think that he would have been a great leader of men, partly because he went into the rough scrimmage of politics too late in his career, and partly because he is too shy and gentle, although in argument he can sometimes get very hot under the collar.

He himself enjoyed his years in Tehran and Berlin and for years has nursed a clinging regret that he never went to China. My own view is that in the Foreign Office he was busier and therefore happier and more useful to his country than anywhere else, and, although he has never regretted his literary career, I remember, and noticed at the time, that it was to the Foreign Office that he wished to return after the first disillusionment of Fleet Street and Shoe Lane.

Certainly the ' Office ' gave him wonderful material and scope for the literary career which was to make him famous in all civilised countries. It is to the Foreign Office that he and we owe the biography of Lord Carnock, his father, his *Peacemaking*, the entertaining and very human picture of Lord Curzon in *Some People*, and his *Diplomacy* which was the most remunerative of all his books because of its wide sale in virtually all countries.

The literary career was always in his mind, and once he decided on it he gave to it all his best powers, his full time and that zealous determination of which the generation preceding his and mine assured us that if we had it in sufficient measure we could be anything we wanted to be. He confesses to a novel begun in Madrid in 1910 but never finished, and, if he ever told me what was in it, I have forgotten what he said.

The most remarkable trait in his character is his quite exceptional capacity for work. I should say that of all the people in the Foreign Office during the First World War he wrote more drafts and accomplished more work than anyone else. At the same time he managed to do an immense amount of serious reading. I have always marvelled how he gets through so much in every day. It is not done by working the long hours which are often the penalty of lack of organisation. Harold is well served by an excellent memory and a very orderly mind. Like William Strang (now Lord Strang), he finishes all the tasks of the day, and at the end of it his desk is tidy.

It is an enviable triumph of mind over matter, for Harold is no ascetic and is fond of good food, likes his glass of wine, and is what used to be called a good clubman. He owes something of his good talk and literary knowledge to his talented wife who, I always think, understands him better than anyone else.

If Harold was uncomfortable in Shoe Lane, his next venture was to be perhaps the most melancholy period in his career. He threw in his lot with a small group of disgruntled Labourites, of whom Sir Oswald Mosley, not yet a Fascist, was the leader. Harold, who had always had an ambition to enter politics, accepted the editorship of the group's weekly periodical called *Action*. I lunched alone with him at Boulestin's soon after the periodical was launched. The first number had sold 175,000 copies, but Harold was worried and complained bitterly of the wear and tear of journalism. He looked tired and unhappy, and became himself again only when he began to talk of the group's Parliamentary prospects at the next election. Apart from ' Tom ' Mosley, he was optimistic of the success of several others and thought that he himself had an outside chance of a seat as a member for the combined universities. From the start *Action* lacked what its name stood for, and the best column in it was Vita Sackville-West's gardening notes. Circulation fell quickly, and Harold wisely got out before Mosley became a Fascist.

From this semi-disaster he recovered quickly. He was to review books, to contribute a weekly column to the *Spectator* and to write articles for American and foreign newspapers, but never again was he to sit in a Fleet Street chair or engage in daily journalism. The itch to become a member of the House of Commons remained. Otherwise, he was free and could devote himself entirely to his literary career. Apart from the unfinished novel in 1910, the career had started in earnest in 1921, and it is a wonderful testimony to his intensive reading, much of it accomplished when he was working long hours in the Foreign Office, that four out of his first five books were studies of Verlaine, Tennyson, Byron and Swinburne. All were written between 1920 and 1925. *Some People*, his first big popular success, appeared in 1927.

During the 'thirties, the only period in my life in which I saw much of London life, hardly a week passed without our meeting. He helped me greatly with my first book, *British Agent*, which, largely thanks to him, started a new fashion in personal history. We gave each other advice. His was good. He urged me to leave Fleet Street, and I shuffled and boggled until 1937 when it was too late. I advised him not to undertake to do the biography of Dwight Morrow unless he had a completely free hand. It was, I think, good advice, but he did not take it and did not have a free hand. Too many relations and friends of the American were still living, and Harold could not get straight answers to his questions. Was Morrow a selfish man? he would ask, and the American's friends would say that selflessness was his greatest virtue. Only J. P. Morgan junior told Harold what he thought was the truth: ' Morrow unselfish? Why, he'd have murdered his children if they'd stood in his way.'

I also heard much about Harold from other people. London gossip is more acid than the gossip of any other capital, and I remember a large luncheon party at Lady Colefax's house in December, 1934. Several authors were present, but not Harold. Suddenly the conversation died away. Mr Somerset Maugham was talking and held the table. He was praising Harold as a writer and praising him highly. He declared that no professional novelist could describe a person's exterior better than Harold Nicolson. This was high commendation from a superb word-painter of exteriors—who had once told me that if I wished to create verisimilitude I must always study the exteriors of people: the colour of their suit and tie, whether their nails were manicured or not, and what kind of collar they wore.

Harold deserved the praise, but a few months later he was again restless. He had been forced to go over to the States again about his Morrow book. The great house of Morgan had expected the book to be a eulogy not only of Dwight Morrow, but of Morgans. When they learnt that Morrow was a hero indeed, but a hero who was never very happy in Morgans, the partners brought pressure on Harold. He had his way, but he toned down some of the strictures on the financiers.

Although he was firmly supported by Lindbergh, Morrow's son-in-law, he was restless. He is and always has been a man of high principle, and anything in the nature of writing a book

more or less to order troubled his conscience. And when a
Scottish conscience is active, the possessor of it is miserable.
In spite of his English upbringing, his forebears, as the spelling
of the name shows, were McNicols from Skye. They came to
Edinburgh, acquired an estate at Carnock, sided with the Stuarts
in 1745 and were driven into exile. Harold's grandfather was
brought up in Belgium. His father, the first Lord Carnock,
was a Scot of Scots and was always amazed that Sir Edward
Grey, his chief at the Foreign Office, was so difficult to understand although he was born so close to the Scottish border.
I remember, too, a Russian story of his sister who, then a girl
of seven, was riding in the Summer Garden in St Petersburg
when her father was ambassador there. She was stopped by
the Grand Duke Vladimir who said to her : " You are English,
I suppose." She sat up straight on her saddle and replied firmly :
" *Non, Altesse, je suis Écossaise.*"

Scots are, or used to be, ambitious. The real cause of Harold's
unhappy restlessness was the fact that at forty-eight he had no
place in public life. A club man, he wanted to be a member of
the greatest club in the world. Hitherto, perhaps because he was
never a real Party man, he could not get into the House of
Commons. He had first sought adoption as a Conservative
candidate for Sevenoaks, but was unsuccessful. In the election of
1935, he won Leicester for National Labour.

As a member of the House of Commons he did all the right
things, spoke well on foreign affairs, opposed Munich, was
highly critical of the Labour and Left-wing intellectuals who
prevented us from arming three years sooner, and attacked
Neville Chamberlain for neglecting the advice of his experts
like Vansittart who was consistently right and listening to Sir
Horace Wilson ' whose advice was never inconvenient '. Many,
too, will remember his brilliant broadcast on September 26, 1938,
immediately after Hitler's hysterical speech in the *Sportpalast*
in Berlin.

In spite of his interest in the House of Commons, he was as
active as ever in other enterprises. 1938 was a particularly busy
year. He had been reviewing books regularly for the *Daily
Telegraph*. He delivered the Clarke lectures at Cambridge.
He had written a long and authoritative article for the 150th

anniversary of Byron and he had made his first appearance on
television, for which he had received the meagre fee of five
guineas. After March, 1939, he and I were convinced that war
was inevitable. Already in September, 1938, I had agreed to go
back to the Foreign Office in the event of war. My publisher
was very strongly against this and used every argument to dis-
suade me. Other people would take my place with readers;
I should lose my public. I went to Harold. I remember his words
to this day : ' Stick to the F.O. even if you are obscure, rather
than take an unworthy job.'

Harold's first job in the war was one of his speediest and most
valuable efforts. Early in October I went to see him in his
brother's rooms in the Temple. His hair was ruffled. His table
was strewn with paper. He had just finished a ' Penguin ' of
40,000 words in ten days, 7,000 words of which had been written
that day. This most useful book was vitally important to the
English people, who had been misled by the politicians of both
Parties. It was called *Why Britain is at War*. Although it was a
book written for the compelling hour, it has its moral and its
lesson even for to-day.

I had hoped that during the war he and I would work together
in the Political Intelligence Department of the Foreign Office.
This, however, was not to be, for it was decided that Members
of Parliament could not work as ordinary officials in Government
departments. Under Neville Chamberlain, Harold got no ministerial job. But when Winston Churchill came into power, he
rewarded Duff Cooper and Harold by making the former
Minister of Information, and Harold Parliamentary Under-
Secretary. From the beginning of the war both Duff and Harold
had been members of a small but important group whose main
object was to make Mr Churchill Prime Minister as the only
means of saving the country.

On a majority of only 80 Harold remained a Member of
Parliament for the ten crucially important years from 1935–1945.
It would be fair to say that, although he found the moral
standards, especially in regard to truth, of the House of Commons
were much below those of the Foreign Office, he thoroughly
enjoyed his life as a Member of Parliament.

I have asked him more than once how far his Parliamentary

occupations interfered with his literary career. Soon after he left the *Evening Standard* in July, 1931, he had unfolded to me a plan for a Proustian autobiography in ten volumes, each of which would cover a period of roughly five years and would have, apart from himself, a leading figure in each period. Within a month of his becoming an M.P. in 1935, I realised that he was taking his new Parliamentary duties very seriously. I felt sad and reminded him of his great literary plan. He said without any apparent regret that he would have to abandon it. Literature demanded that he should be frank. The kind of frankness that it demanded would damage his political prospects.

Quite recently I put the question to him brutally: "Years ago we discussed your wish to write an autobiographical picture of your times. The ambition was killed by your going into politics. Would it be fair to say that your interest in the House of Commons interfered with your literary career?"

He replied: "It was rather that the impulse waned, since what I had envisaged was being done better by other people. In a sense *Helen's Tower* and *The Desire to Please* were experiments or instalments of that work. Of course being in the House left me less time. But I managed to go on writing just the same. I have never regretted going into the House of Commons."

In one sense the answer is undoubtedly accurate. With all his knowledge of foreign affairs Harold would never have been at peace with his conscience unless he had been at the centre of events during the war. It is true that his experience of the House of Commons contributed to his knowledge of people and events. On the other hand, he liked the House and, after his defeat in the 1945 election, sought to return to it, standing unsuccessfully as a Labour candidate at East Croydon. He is still a member of the Labour Party. The plain truth is that he was not, and never will be, a good candidate, for he is far too fair to his opponents and unsuited by nature and character to be a voting machine in the causes of any Party. His ten years in the House were the most critical in our history, and he was right to be there. He would, I think, have wasted his valuable time had he gone back after 1945.

Inevitably, I did not see him as much as I should have liked. He broadcast and was, indeed, one of the very best broadcasters.

He kept in touch with literature and journalism by reviewing for the *Daily Telegraph* and writing a weekly article for the *Spectator*. Above all, he was deeply interested in his Parliamentary work. I was with him three days after Labour's great victory in July, 1945. He was miserable. He had lost not only his seat but also his chambers in the Temple, and his left eye was puffy and swollen from the sting of a wasp. He told me that he would sooner give up anything than the House of Commons.

Fortunately—at least in my opinion—his optimism revived quickly with the full return to his literary work. In March, 1948, he gave up his reviewing for the *Daily Telegraph* in order to become the leading reviewer of the *Observer*. At the end of 1952 he wrote his last *Marginal Comment* for the *Spectator*, a weekly column which he had written for fourteen years.

It was necessary for him to curtail his journalistic work. Through the influence of Sir Alan Lascelles, a friend from his Oxford days, Harold had been given an exacting duty which was to keep him busy for three years. He had been chosen to write the life of King George V. Wisely he set a new style in royal biographies, for he made it his task to combine biography with the history of King George's period. When the book appeared in August, 1952, it not only received the highest praise, but, in spite of its price, was *the* book of the autumn.

In the New Year's Honours List of 1953 Harold was given a K.C.V.O. While he was writing the life of King George V, I saw less of him than usual, but I was the main witness of one remarkable instance of his powers of concentration. On the first of April, 1950, he and I went to see the Boat Race in Sir John Anderson's launch *The Viscountess*, Sir John then being Chairman of the Port of London Authority. We sat on deck in cold, inclement weather, with a strong wind which made the Thames quite choppy. For most of the time Harold talked exclusively on two subjects: his biography of the King, over which he had received so much help from Queen Mary, and Maurice Paleologue, the French diplomat, whom he disliked greatly. When he had exhausted both subjects, he had one look at the two boats. I do not think he knew who won until we went below for drinks and sandwiches.

He is a great worker partly because he likes work better than anything else in life, but mainly because he does not over-load his mind with too many subjects. The books which he reviews are read conscientiously, but he makes, or, until recently, used to make, a point of reading every day some book which has nothing to do with his work. When he lived in Neville Terrace he used to read a Loeb classic in the tube on his journeys to and from Clubland, and I have come on him dining all alone in the Beefsteak with *Plutarch's Lives* open before him in the original Greek.

Among his virtues is his affection for his sons, both of whom regard him more as a friend than as a father. Although good-tempered and kind-hearted, he can turn red with anger when he thinks one or other of them has been treated unfairly, as, for instance, the adverse attitude of the Bournemouth Conservative Association towards his son Nigel when he opposed the attack on Suez. In matters of principle he has a fastidious conscience. Towards the end of the war he brought me the Russian edition of *Peacemaking*, which appeared in Britain in 1939. The Russian edition had a long preface by Maisky. The Soviet Publishing Department was prepared to pay a proper remuneration for it. What ought he to do ? he asked. " Take what you've earned," I said. " The Russians are our Allies." " Yes," said Harold, " but the Russian Publishing Department is the same as the Soviet Government."

He does not like old age and would like to go on living and learning. I envy him his perennial freshness of mind. I think he retains it because throughout the years he has kept in touch with youth. As a critic he has written recently that old men should not reprove youth. Malicious critics say that he does this in order that youth should not say unkind things about him. This is quite untrue. Ever since he began to review books nearly thirty years ago, he has fired one or two broadsides at authors who were affluent beyond their worth, but he has never been anything but kind to the first book of a young writer. As for the so-called angry young men of to-day, they have respect neither for cajolery nor for abuse from the elderly. They want to step into the shoes of the successful. They are in favour of the painless extermination of the over-sixties.

I do not think that Harold will perish under the axe of these modern Malthusians. Indeed, it is not improbable that they will be forgotten before he has finished writing books, for he still carries several in his head and is now engaged on a book on the Eighteenth Century.

He stands high in the esteem of all cultured people in the world, is an honorary Doctor of Literature in half a dozen European cities, and has few equals as a raconteur. His niche in the history of literature is secure for two reasons. He is a fine scholar and he has written serious books in which he has something new to say on whatever subject he has chosen. He is that rarest being in literature—an author who has always been himself. For that reason he is likely to outlive in reputation many authors of his period who have had more readers and who have won greater temporary fame during their life-time.

CHAPTER FOUR

Admirable Crichton

' The days of our youth are the days of our glory.'

IN club circles in these islands, where sport is the main topic
of conversation, someone is sure to start a late evening by
asking who was the greatest amateur all-round games-player of
all time. The starter in this game leans forward and hurls his
question like a defiance, for, of course, he has his own favourite
on the tip of his tongue and has great difficulty in holding it back.
Yet his real joy is to keep it until the others have spoken and
then, like a card-player, to pull out the trump which he thinks
will win the game.

No one ever agrees, but certain names come up regularly in
this type of discussion. One of the first favourites is sure to be
C. B. Fry, and his claims are strong, though he had to work hard
to make himself a great batsman. Close to C. B. Fry comes
S. M. J. Woods, who played rugby football for England and
cricket for Australia, and R. E. Foster, who was the best all-
rounder of the famous Fosters. Another fit to be mentioned
is Max Woosnam who represented Cambridge at Association
football, golf, lawn-tennis and tennis. If there are some ancient
M.C.C. members present, they will bring out the giants of the
distant past : C. J. Ottaway and the Hon. Alfred Lyttleton,
both of whom won Blues for athletics, cricket, Association
football, rackets and tennis, and C. P. Wilson who played for
England both at rugby and Association football and won a
Cambridge Blue for cricket, soccer and bicycling. At this point
some stickler for facts goes to the library to fetch the book of
records in order to discover who has won the largest number
of Blues and half-Blues. On his return he announces that the
record number of representations by an individual Oxford or
Cambridge undergraduate is sixteen by K. C. Gandar-Dower
for Cambridge between 1928 and 1931. The sports at which he

represented Cambridge were Eton fives, Rugby fives, lawn tennis, tennis, squash rackets and billiards !

This information invariably causes a big slump in the value of numbers of ' Blues ', and younger members present, who know nothing before the days of Erroll Holmes, H. G. Owen-Smith and B. H. Valentine, pick up their courage and put forward the claims of Peter May or M. J. K. Smith. This, however, is the age of specialisation, and, on the whole, the young man of to-day who plays too many games is likely not to excel in any one of them.

The idyllic days of the all-rounder were before the First World War, and it is in the decade from 1900 to 1910 that I have my own favourite. His name is Kenneth Grant Macleod and he was born on February 2, 1888. He came to Fettes in 1899 and entered Glencorse House, where he had as his housemaster K. P. Wilson, a fine athlete and a brother of the C. P. Wilson already mentioned. He was then only eleven and must have been one of the youngest boys ever to come to Fettes.

Unlike housemaster's sons like the Fosters, ' K.G. ' or ' Grunt ' (Grant), as he was called at school, had no particular advantages in the way of coaching. He had two elder brothers, Donald and Lewis, who by their own contemporaries at Fettes were considered outstanding athletes. Donald's career was ended at school when he crashed into a goal-post in a school match against Edinburgh Academy. His knee never recovered sufficiently to enable him to play rugger again, but it was good enough to take him into the trenches in the First World War, in which he was killed. ' L.M.'s ' life ended after a kick in a match at Cambridge. The doctors diagnosed the cause of death as appendicitis, but I think the father, a rich tobacco importer, never believed it. He never liked rugby football and was no games player. The Macleod boys believed him when he said he was good at billiards—until he bought a billiard table. If genius or talent for games is inherited, it came to the Macleod boys from their mother who was a useful tennis player and very fast on her feet.

' K.G.' was an exact contemporary of mine at Fettes and I had the hard task of playing against him and the grim pleasure of playing with him. He was not by any means an outsize in boys. Indeed, both in weight and height he was lighter and shorter than the more powerful ' L.M.' No one ever saw him practising rigorously to improve his skill. He seemed to have a natural genius for any game. In his time, Fettes rugger was at its best. Scotland was then comfortably ahead of the other three Home countries in wins, and the Scotland and Cambridge fifteens had on occasions as many as six Fettesians in them.

' K.G.' made his debut in the Fettes XV in 1902–3. For virtually the whole season he was still under fifteen, and those were the days when rich Glaswegians sent their sons to Fettes to learn rugger and to stay till nineteen or even twenty in order to get into the XV and then go on to Pembroke College, Cambridge. During the three years from 1902–3 to 1904–5 in which ' K.G.' played, Fettes never lost a school match. In his second year, to a total of 260 points scored by the team, ' K.G.' himself contributed 123 points made up of 28 by dropped goals, 51 by tries, and 44 by placed goals. In his last year no school scored a point against Fettes. No club defeated the school, and the only defeat sustained by Fettes was at the hands and feet of the Scottish XV who were having a practice before the match against Wales.

In that year Scotland were a poor side, and there was much clamour in the newspapers and in the clubs for ' K.G.'s ' inclusion. It has often been written and said that the Scottish Union selected him and that Dr Heard, the headmaster of Fettes, refused to allow him to play. The facts are a little different. My father, who was for several years a member of the Union, told me many times what actually happened. The canny Scottish Union put a question to Dr Heard : ' If a member of the present Fettes XV were chosen for Scotland, would he be allowed to play ? ' The answer was ' no '.

Perhaps the most remarkable feature of ' K.G.'s ' rugger career at Fettes was that at the end of it he was only a fortnight or so over seventeen and just missed being the youngest boy in the XV. The youngest player in the side was George Cunningham (now Sir George and formerly Captain of Oxford and Scotland at rugby football) who was playing in his first season and whose birthday was just over a month later than ' K.G.'s '.

Fettes cricket was never internationally of the same standard as Fettes rugby football, but, having always a good leaven of English boys, the school was well ahead of the other Scottish public schools. During his school career ' K.G.' was not the best cricketer at Fettes. This honour must go to Gerald Turner, a younger brother of A. J. Turner, the Essex cricketer. ' K.G.', however, was very useful indeed as an all-rounder and set up a record which even M. R. Jardine, the greatest of all schoolboy cricketers at Fettes, could not accomplish. He got his colours for cricket when he was under fourteen and a half.

In athletics he distinguished himself in various ways without any apparent practice or special effort. When he was just fifteen, he established the then school record for the high jump with a height of 5 ft. 5½ inches. He was then in the junior class. When just sixteen he won six out of the twelve open events at the school sports. His best performances were the ' 100 ' in a yard inside ten and four-fifths seconds, and a throw of 103 yards 2 ft. 9 ins. with a cricket ball. I doubt if he had more than one trial practice. In his last year, when he was just seventeen, he set up a new record for the ' 200 ' with a time of twenty and four-fifths seconds. He also did a long jump of 20 ft. 7½ inches. As usual, he carried off most of the open events.

At school he excelled at all other games which were played. He was a first-class hockey player, of whose services Scotland would have been glad. Without liking the game, he headed the Fives Ten. But it was at soccer that he really stirred the waiters and domestic staff. In those days Fettes played house-games twice a week. Rugger was barred, and only hockey or soccer were played. I preferred soccer, which I am sure was an excellent training for rugger, and we had matches against the waiters, the masters and I think an eleven of Hearts' reserves. ' K.G.' was the school star, and there was a rumour, I think in a local evening newspaper, that Manchester City had invited him for a trial. I have never checked the accuracy of this story, but, if ' K.G.' had been interested, I am quite certain that he would have made the grade.

K. G. Macleod was seventeen and six months old when he left Fettes at the end of July, 1905. In November he was playing for Scotland at Inverleith against the famous first ' All Blacks ' from New Zealand. This was the match which gave the then rather mean Scottish Rugby Union a lesson in three vices : ignorance, arrogance and avarice. In arranging the match before their arrival in Britain, the New Zealanders asked for a guarantee. It was quite a small sum, but, as Scotland were then cock of the Rugby world, the Scottish Rugby Union turned up their noses. Who on earth would give a guarantee to these people ? In all probability they will have been beaten ten times before they come here, and no one will want to see them. A guarantee ? Certainly not. They can have the whole gate.

When the day arrived, all Scotland was at Inverleith to see the visitors. Scotland gave a very good display and were leading by 7 points to 6 seven minutes before ' no side '. Then L. M. Macleod sliced a drop at goal. The New Zealand backs swept down the field and carried off not only the victory but a bumper gate. There were six Fettesians in the Scottish side, two of them more or less straight from school. The seventeen-year-old K. G. Macleod won high praise, and on more than one occasion his speed saved a certain try.

A month later Macleod was playing alongside his brother in the first of four appearances for Cambridge against Oxford. Eight Fettesians, six for Cambridge and two for Oxford, played in this match, and with the increased competition from other schools to-day this record is likely to stand for a long time.

Cambridge won, and ' K.G.' made a creditable appearance in what was a very closely contested match. A year later, now eighteen, he was in Glasgow playing for Scotland against the South Africans and scored what most people who saw it considered the most dramatic try of all time. Fast as he was on the running track, ' K.G.' was relatively faster on the football field because he could get into full speed a yard or two sooner than anyone else. With the game still in the balance Pat Munro, the famous Oxford and Scotland half-back, punted a long diagonal kick from one side of the field to the other and ' K.G.', who was playing wing three-quarter on that day, saw his chance, caught the ball full-pitch at his highest speed and left the very fast Springbok's back division standing. Scotland was the only Home country to beat the Springboks, and ' K.G.'s ' try clinched the victory.

His great year was 1908. On February 2 he celebrated his

twentieth birthday. On March 23 he was playing his last international rugger match. It was played at Inverleith and the enemy
was England. ' K.G.' was playing centre with Hugh Martin, the
Oxford ' flyer ', as his wing, and Scotland won by 16 points to
10. In the opinion of most critics it was the best game ' K.G.' ever
played. The comment of *The Times* was that ' had Martin only
been more certain in the taking of his passes from Macleod
England must have had a bad beating '. Hamish Stuart, the
E. W. Swanton of those days, let himself go in *Sporting Life* :
' It should be observed that the match was a very severe test of
class and was essentially a game in which only the greatest could
touch greatness. That is why Macleod's superb display must
remain historic.'

A week later at Queen's Club ' K.G.' won the ' 100 ' for
Cambridge against L. C. Hull, the crack Rhodes Scholar sprinter
from Michigan University. In the three years that he ran the
' 100 ' for Cambridge he was never beaten, although he had a
dead-heat with N. G. Chavasse in 1907.

George Lyttelton, President of the Athletic Team in 1906,
tells a good story against both ' K.G.' and himself. As a Fresh-
man who received almost too much praise, ' K.G.' was afraid
of no one. Lyttelton, who saw in him at once the sprinter needed
to win the ' 100 ', was horrified to learn that ' K.G.' was going
to play rugger for Scotland against England a week before the
Sports. He addressed the young man sternly : " Look here,
Macleod, what's this I hear about your playing for Scotland at
rugger ? You just can't do that kind of thing up here."

" Can't I," said ' K.G.', and, as Lyttelton says to-day, he could.
All the same there was sense in Lyttelton's remark. In 1906
' K.G.' ran the ' 100 ' with a nasty bruise received in the rugger
international a few days earlier.

In July, 1908, he established a new record by being the first
Scottish schoolboy to get a cricket Blue at Cambridge. In a
low-scoring match Cambridge were beaten by two wickets.
' K.G.'s ' 21 was third top score in Cambridge's first innings.
It was not a great debut, but he was just about the best fielder
in the two elevens.

He got his cricket Blue in a remarkable manner. In 1906 he
was playing for the Fettesian-Lorettonians against the Old

Reptonians who had then almost a full side of first-class cricketers. 'K.G.' played a wonderful innings and saved the Fettesian-Lorettonians from disgrace. R. A. Young was playing for the Old Reptonians, and, when he became captain of the Cambridge XI in 1908, he remembered that innings and said to Grant : " I'll want you for cricket this term."

' K.G.' replied, " Are you serious ? "

"Yes," said Young, "if you'll promise to give serious attention to your cricket, I'll give you a full try-out."

' K.G.' made a 100 for the Quidnuncs and got a trial for the University. His first match was against Lancashire, his own county, and he got runs and his Blue followed in due course.

He learnt all his cricket, he told me, from men like A. C. Maclaren, who taught him to use his feet, to run out, but not to hit against the spin. As ' K.G.' was a fine hitter Maclaren did not mind his lifting the ball. He had to unlearn all he learnt at Fettes where he used to hit the school pro out of the ground and the pro would say reprovingly, " bad shot, keep the ball on the ground."

On December 12, 1908, at Queen's Club he played his last rugger match for Cambridge. Every member of the Oxford back division was an international or future international, and there were two internationals and two future internationals in the Oxford pack. Cambridge were good forward, but weak behind, apart from C. C. G. Wright and, of course, ' K.G.' himself. The betting was heavy on Oxford.

It was, however, a disappointing match. It started in a fog which got worse. The Cambridge forwards dominated the game, but in the back division Vassall for Oxford and Wright for Cambridge broke down with old injuries and were more or less passengers. Wright was ' K.G.'s ' wing, and on both sides the back play was spoilt. With the score at a goal each, ' K.G.' made stupendous efforts to win the match by prodigious drop-kicks from almost every part of the field. One went very close, and in the gathering fog one mighty kick from inside his own half might have gone over, for it was dead straight—but no one could see. And on a bad day a draw was perhaps the fairest result. *The Times*, writing of ' K.G.', said : ' This was his last University match, and it may be said that Cambridge has probably never produced a finer three-quarter.'

It was not only his last University match. It was his last game
of rugger. His father had a perhaps not unnatural anxiety lest his
youngest son might be maimed or taken from him by this
dangerous game. He was a business man and he made a business
offer. ' Give up this wretched game, and you can do whatever
you like for the rest of your life.'

' K.G.' who was far from stupid, but not much given to hard
mental work, surrendered. His admirers, who were legion, were
sad, and I was one of them. Rugby football was, I think, the
perfection of his genius as a games-player. Englishmen may
rank Poulton higher as a centre three-quarter, but my own
view will always be that, if ' K.G.' had played for Wales or the
Springboks in 1906 he would have stood out pre-eminently
as the greatest of all three-quarters. I am not alone in this
view. Sir George Cunningham, who gave Ronald Poulton his
Blue, has told me more than once that, great runner though
Poulton was, ' K.G.' was the greatest three-quarter he had ever
seen.

' K.G.' was not an easy man for a half-back to play to or
play under. At Fettes he had received the most extraordinary
hero-worship not only from the school, but from the Press.
In those days, before the headmasters intervened, the school
championship had a big following among the public, and the
evening papers commented on the school matches with a
long report on Saturdays and gossip comment on Fridays and
Mondays. ' K.G.' was the idol of the reporters who described
him lyrically as ' the poetry of motion '.

Inevitably the hero-worship went a little to his head. As a
centre three-quarter he liked to be fed. Throughout the season
of 1904-5 at school I got cursed heartily on many occasions if
our forwards were not getting the ball every time. The halves
got the blame, and Arthur Gallie and I had to listen to a refrain :
' Get that ruddy ball back.' We did not mind. Indeed, it made
me fiercer, and for the rest of the game tears of rage filled my
eyes. When the match was over and won, all was well and all
was forgotten.

' K.G.' was an attacking player from the first day that he put
on a Fettes jersey and must have been the first Scottish three-
quarter to tell a Scottish captain, in those days always a forward,

to let the ball out on his own goal line. The occasion of this experiment was in Dublin when with only five or six minutes to go, Ireland were leading Scotland by 16 points to 6 and were still battering the Scottish line. There was a scrum, and 'K.G.' grunted to Louis Greig: "Let's have that ball out." Greig nearly fainted and shrugged his shoulders. "Go on," said 'K.G.' Out came the ball. 'K.G.' got it on his own line, was up to the Irish full-back in a flash with Hugh Martin at his side, and Scotland scored the try and kicked the goal.

Ireland won of course, but the Scottish mania for forward play and for never letting the ball out unless they were within their opponents' 'twenty-five' lost the match. 'K.G.' has told me more than once how difficult he found it to adapt himself to Scotland's game when he was at Cambridge. All the talent of a great past was still there, but Scottish rugger was already beginning to be ruined by conservatism.

To-day most people forget how young Grant Macleod was. In spite of all his skill as a games-player, the most remarkable thing about him is that he finished his whole rugger career before he was twenty-one. Many enthusiasts still refuse to believe this fact; they still insist on betting, but I now refuse to take their money.

Although he was not so famous as a cricketer, 'K.G.' was a very useful all-rounder and, as a hard-hitting bat, was a great favourite with the Lancashire crowd. His best performance was for Lancashire v. Yorkshire at Sheffield in 1911. The match was for Rhodes's benefit and, when things were going badly for Lancashire, 'K.G.' saved the situation with a brilliant innings of 121. With typical Macleod indifference to any kind of nervousness he got his century from 94 by hitting Wilfred Rhodes for 6.

His best hitting performance was at Bath in 1909 against Somerset. He got a 100 in sixty-three minutes and was run out for 128 after hitting eight sixes and eleven fours!

In the opinion of many cricket lovers, however, his most sensational and effective contribution to the game was in a Lancashire v. Warwickshire match. Lancashire were in grave trouble with the body-line bowling of Frank Foster, who was then at his best and most dangerous, swinging the ball very fast,

right into the batsman's body, with four or five short legs close
in. When the first five batsmen were out for a low score, Lancashire looked set for defeat. In came Grant Macleod with different
ideas. Taking a careful look at the fielders clustered round his
legs, he prepared to face Foster. As the first swung in to him,
' K.G.' turned in to the wicket and threw his bat over the first
short-leg's head. The second ball was treated in this manner.
This time the bat hurtled farther and hit the second leg-slip on
the shins.

The game stopped. The umpires were consulted. ' K.G.',
who had faced bigger troubles on the football field than this
contretemps, tackled the Warwickshire captain in the most practical way : ' You stop that man Foster bowling at my body
and I'll stop throwing my bat at your fielders.' The Warwickshire
captain agreed, and ' K.G.' went on to make 70 runs and saved
Lancashire.

As he had no superior as a fieldsman and was also a useful
change bowler, he also played for the Gentlemen at Lord's
and altogether had a very pleasant life right up to the First
World War. I was not to see him again until 1926 when we met,
of all places, in Strathspey. During the war he had been threatened
with tuberculosis as the result of a gas attack. He had been sent
up to Strathspey to recuperate, had liked the place, and had
taken a house above Dulnain-Bridge with a superb view of the
Spey and the Cairngorms. I soon discovered from the local
experts that he was just about the best shot and the best salmon
and trout fisher in the Central Highlands. I do not think that he
had done any shooting or fishing until he came to Strathspey.

For some years he spent the winter in Switzerland and inevitably became a crack curler, playing for Scotland v. Switzerland
in the final at Murren and being beaten by one shot.

He has now lived in South Africa for over twenty years,
and still plays golf two or three times a week but, as he had a
' coronary ' four years ago, he takes things easily. Six or seven
years ago I ran into Bobby Locke who told me that for one
round ' K.G.' was as good as any amateur in South Africa and
a tough match for any professional. ' K.G.' strenuously denies
this. Bobby Locke's praise comes from one round when Locke
was in the Air Force and out of practice. He rang up ' K.G.' to

bring a partner along and he would play their best ball. ' K.G.'
and his partner went mad from the first tee, dove-tailed mar-
vellously, and never lost a hole. He was for a time a fictitious
' plus one ', but he has never taken golf seriously, although he
won the Seniors' Championship of South Africa. For him serious
golf is too like work.

As an all-rounder I put him top because his genius for games
was such that he could excel at almost any game with a speed
and an ease that games-players must envy. Moreover, he has,
or had, the priceless gift of never knowing when he is beaten.
To-day he plays bridge and likes racing. He has mellowed
greatly, is a most generous host to all his friends, and has a
charming South African wife. As both have been married before,
' K.G.' three times and she once, they are known jocularly among
their friends as Mr and Mrs Bluebeard.

CHAPTER FIVE

Royal Biographer

'Courage is the thing.'

IN one of his best-known aphorisms Leo Tolstoy says: 'Nothing weakens a strong man so much as the hope that he can find salvation and happiness through other means than his own effort.' Of all men that I have known, John Wheeler-Bennett, my proven friend of over thirty years' standing, has always relied on his own effort and has shown the greatest courage and determination in conquering over long years difficulties which might have ruined or impaired the value of his life. As it is, he has lived to serve his country in several ways well known to the public and in many others just as important but less manifest.

He was fortunate in his birth, for his father was rich and his forebears, all of Anglo-Saxon stock, came from both Europe and the New World. His maternal grandfather was a United Empire loyalist who died in Halifax, Nova Scotia. His maternal grandmother was a Virginian and her cousin was General A. P. Hill who was a noted commander in what we call the war between the North and the South, but Americans, especially Southerners, know only as 'The War between the States'. Jack's second home-town is Charlottesville. He has lectured at its charming university. It was from Charlottesville that he brought his delightful Virginian wife to England. In Virginia Jack feels himself a Southerner. Having spent part of an early spring with him there, I would say that life in Virginia is not unlike the England of a hundred years ago with a superb climate which would put the best English summer day to shame.

Jack was born at Keston in Kent—of which county his father subsequently became High Sheriff—on October 13, 1902, and in due course went through the usual educational routine of the English upper-class male. As a youngster he went to Wellington

House, Westgate-on-Sea, where he was head-boy, before going to Malvern, a school famous for the Fosters, the most gifted games-playing family in the history of sport. The father was a Malvern master and produced a large family of athletes. The boys who were all excellent cricketers, rackets players and soccer geniuses, went to Malvern, and when Worcestershire was admitted to first-class cricket, for almost a generation the new county was known as ' Fostershire '.

Like several other schools, Malvern is more famous for games than for scholarship, and its two best-known literary men are H. de Vere Stacpoole and Dikran Kouyoumdjan, better known as Michael Arlen. Both were best-sellers in their time.

As Jack Wheeler-Bennett was an intellectual, he did not find Malvern very stimulating. There was a good deal of bullying. Although he has always liked cricket, he had undergone a period of youthful illnesses which had retarded the powerful physique which he has to-day.

His chief contemporaries at Malvern were Rajindra Sinhji, nephew of the famous Ranjit Sinhji, brother of the equally famous Duleep Sinhji, and Commander-in-Chief of the Indian Army; Michael Arlen; and Erroll Holmes, all-round athlete and Test Match cricketer. Of these three Jack liked Holmes best, who was his fag. When I was last at Garsington, Jack's lovely home near Oxford, I found in the bookcase in my bed-room a book entitled *Flanelled Foolishness* by Erroll Holmes, published by Hollis and Carter. On the title page in the author's handwriting was the dedication : ' To Jack Wheeler-Bennett, a great historian, from an indifferent cricketer.' In the course of my life I met all three quite apart from Jack. I was impressed by Rajindra Sinhji. I received from Michael Arlen excellent advice which, alas, I did not take. I found Erroll Holmes a most modest and pleasant man with plenty of good talk and not a boast in his vocabulary.

At Malvern Jack reached the History Sixth when he was sixteen. He was too young for the war which, however, hit him most cruelly. During the holidays in Kent a German Taube dropped a bomb close to him, and the blast blew him downstairs, made him a nervous wreck and left him speechless. When he began to recover, he had for a long time a very troublesome stammer.

He had wanted to enter the diplomatic service, but this career was now closed to him on account of his ill-health. Jack was born when his father was over sixty, and there was not quite the same companionship between father and son as there is to-day between fathers of forty-five and sons of twenty-two. Moreover, his father had spent much of his life in Canada, wanted Jack to go into business, and was accustomed to getting his own way. Jack was determined to be an historian and, in spite of his charm and gentle manner, there is no one who can drive him when he has once made up his mind. He was determined to write and became a free-lance journalist. Gradually his father relented, and Jack was able to travel. He visited Canada, Australia and New Zealand.

At this time Jack went through what he now calls a period of youthful illusions. He joined the League of Nations Union and sat at the feet of Mr Gladstone Murray, the Canadian who did so much for British Broadcasting in its early days. It was the inevitable process towards becoming a political expert and a Conservative by conviction, not merely by tradition.

Jack's father died in 1926 and Jack himself was not only rich but on his own. He had already set up at his own expense the special Information Service of the Royal Institute of International Affairs. It remains to this day the most useful service of the Institute.

He was now able to travel freely. Between 1927 and 1931 he went twice to Korea and twice across Siberia by train to Moscow, where he saw in the Marx-Engels Institute the busts of the three English heroes of Communism : Thomas More, Oliver Cromwell, and Bernard Shaw ! He also went twice to the Far East and visited Singapore and the British North Borneo Company, serving as special assistant to General Sir Neil Malcolm who had become almost a foster-father to him.

Jack also spent a considerable time almost every year in Germany. He rode in steeplechases and enjoyed himself, but he also began to study seriously the re-creation of the German army under Seeckt. In this work he received great help from Sir Neil who had been Head of the British Military Mission in Berlin. Through him Jack was able to meet the leading German politicians, including Stresemann, Luther, Mueller, Papen,

Schleicher and Bruening, who became a close friend. During all this period Jack's stammer was still a hindrance both to his conversation and his mastery of foreign languages. Yet he persevered with remarkable courage and, as the long years passed, he won through.

I am not quite sure, nor is he, when we first met. The earliest mention of him in my diaries is August 22, 1929. The entry states: 'Lunched with Lewis Namier, Kisch, and Wheeler-Bennett at Les Lauriers and discussed Zionism. Kisch gave up a brilliant military career to join the Zionist organisation and Namier has just been appointed its political secretary.' Les Lauriers was the predecessor of Quaglino's Apéritif in Jermyn Street. Lewis Namier, a staunch and helpful friend of many years' standing, became an admirer of Jack's work, and I recall his tribute to *Wooden Titan*, Jack's life of Hindenburg, when it appeared in 1936: 'This is the best biography written for a long time. It is brilliantly done and very valuable.'

Jack deserves all his successes, for there is no historian who takes so much trouble to check all his evidence. I remember vividly his account of his visit to Trotsky in Mexico in 1937 when Jack was writing *Brest-Litovsk, The Forgotten Peace*. He wanted some information from the temperamental Trotsky and had a most rewarding interview. When he asked Trotsky about Stalin, Trotsky flew into a passion and, throwing his arms up to the skies, roared: " Where was Stalin at the Battle of Kazan ? Muddling about with minorities in the Commissariat of Nationalities ! " Although I had known him best of all the Bolsheviks, and had received both courtesy and abuse from him, he was no kinder to me when Jack mentioned my name. I was a deceiver and a crook.

After that first meeting with Jack in 1929 I saw a great deal of him. He was living then in Albany, and to his luncheons and dinner came diplomats like Jan Masaryk, Albrecht Bernstorff, and Richard Kühlmann, foreign correspondents of all countries, German politicians like Bruening and von Rheinbaben, French diplomats like Roland de Margerie, and, indeed, anyone who had made some contribution to the study of foreign affairs. In his preface to *The Pipe Dream of Peace*, the late Hubert Knickerbocker, best of all American foreign correspondents of my time, wrote in 1936 : 'He (Wheeler-Bennett) has been present at almost all the famous 'turning points' in post-war history. . . . Not from his study but from the spot, Mr Wheeler-Bennett has watched the forces that have whirled Europe into the race that never ends except in war. . . . He is personally acquainted with virtually every Minister of importance and State executive in Europe. His indefatigable travels from capital to capital precede or parallel the historical moments which punctuate his chronicles. Not a few of these moments have been influenced by the information which he has exchanged with the prime movers of European politics. . . . It is this knowledge that makes his judgment so sound.'

There is not an exaggerated word in this eulogy. Unlike our modern historian-journalists or journalist-historians who write glibly on present-day affairs before even the facts are known, John Wheeler-Bennett never accepts a statement from anyone, even if it is someone speaking of some past incident in which he himself may have been concerned. He always checks all unseen incidents. To make doubly sure, he goes to the sources for all his information, and no journey is ever too far for him. He is fortunate in being able to travel, but he is relentless in his pursuit of the truth.

I had a good insight into his methods when he was writing *Brest-Litovsk, The Forgotten Peace*, for after a long period of service in Russia I had been sent back by the War Cabinet at the beginning of 1918 to enter into relations with the Bolsheviks and to do my best to prevent them from making a separate peace with the Germans. In the 'thirties I was therefore consulted by Jack, and I gave him such help as I could. But I was one of many whom he sounded, and I have no doubt that all my information was subjected to a double or triple check. Not content with bearding Trotsky in his stronghold in Mexico, Jack interrogated the leading Germans who were at Brest-Litovsk. Kühlmann he knew well, but the man who dominated the proceedings and gave the real information was General Hoff-mann, probably the best of all German strategists in the First World War.

All through the 'thirties John Wheeler-Bennett was not only travelling, but also working like a student who has to pass an examination or die. Although he was making great progress in conquering the stammer, his general health suffered from the long hours which he worked.

In 1937 he went to Virginia to recuperate from what might have been a break-down. But even there he did not or could not rest entirely. He went back to his beloved Charlottesville, and the next I heard of him was that he had been appointed Lecturer in International Law and Relations at the University of Virginia. And, with short returns to London, there he remained until 1939.

As I was lecturing in the States in the winter of that year, I not only saw him in New York but also had the great pleasure of staying with him twice in his Charlottesville house. In New York he was most helpful to me, for he arranged a luncheon for me with Paul Scheffer and Kurt Riezler. Paul Scheffer I had just met before, but did not know well. Kurt Riezler was an old acquaintance. When I was head of the British Mission in Moscow in 1918, Riezler was the German Counsellor and was present when Blumkin, a member of the Soviet Che-ka, assassinated the German ambassador in the German Embassy. Riezler was anti-Nazi, and long before Munich he and Albrecht Bernstorff gave us warning after warning that Hitler intended to go to war. At our New York luncheon on March 13, 1939, both Scheffer and Riezler were very pessimistic. In their view Hitler not only intended but would be forced to go to war. Otherwise his régime would collapse. Two days later Hitler marched into Prague and established his headquarters in the famous Hradčany.

This luncheon was another minor example of Jack's remarkable flair for assembling people concerned with a country or situation which is about to explode an historical event. At that time the Americans themselves were very critical of Chamberlain's England, but had no intention of fighting themselves.

At his Charlottesville house Jack was the most thoughtful of hosts. If I were tolerably well-off, I think I should like to live in Virginia and, preferably, in Charlottesville. The ghost of Jefferson haunts it. He planned and built the lovely classic University. His house at Monticello stands on a hill with a superb view for miles around in every direction. Jefferson, who was his own architect, was keen on gadgets of all kinds : 2

weather-cock clock to show him which way the wind was
blowing without his having to move his chair; another clock
which marked the days of the week as well as the hours of the
day; and a telescope room so that he could watch at every
moment of the day the progress of his beloved university. Like
the younger Pitt, he died in debt.

In 1939 Eduard Beneš, driven from his country by Hitler,
came to the University of Virginia. Jack took him to Jefferson's
tomb, and on it Beneš placed a wreath. He took a look at the
surrounding scene and, though not given to lyrical ecstasy, he
gave utterance. "Where," he said, "are your wooden dogs?
Everyone tells me that the forests of Virginia are full of wooden-
dogs." He meant dog-wood!

In that early spring of 1939 the atmosphere of Virginia was
wonderful. One seemed to be in an England before the American
War of Independence. There was a strong Episcopalian tradition.
The Virginians were charming and hospitable if you were taken
into their circle. Compared with the Americans of the North
they were poor, but cultured and proud of their lineage. In
Virginia there was no room for Yankees. There 'the war' was
still the war between the States. If in conversation one meant
'The Great War', one had to give the dates of 1914–18.

In his lectures on international relations Jack did his best to
instil the danger of the Nazi peril into the minds of his students.
He had with him a number of records of Nazi speeches and he
played them for the benefit of his seminar. On being asked what
he thought of the speeches, one student replied : " I can't understand the language, but it sounds beastly. That last record of
Hitler just made me feel as if I'd like to go out and kill a couple
of Yanks."

When I came back to Charlottesville towards the end of March,
everything was in bloom and the whole countryside was a riot
of forsythia with a carpet of periwinkles on the ground. My
lecture tour was over, and after the strain I let myself go. I
drank mint juleps, basked in a sun which raised the temperature
in the shade to nearly 80 degrees Fahrenheit, and feasted my
eyes on the lovely Virginian mountains, rightly called The Blue
Ridge. I drove over them with Jack on our way to Lexington
where I was shown Lee's tomb which to Virginians is what the

Cenotaph is to us, and also the Virginia Military Institute where General George Marshall received his military education.

I suppose that Virginian society was narrow and old-fashioned, but after European crises it seemed to me a haven of rest and disengagement. It was the only few days of real peace that any of us were to have for six long years, and even in Virginia Jack and I talked of the inevitability of war. I was an outcast from Soviet Russia with a sentence of death passed on me in my absence, and Jack was on the Nazi Black List and had a narrow escape at the time of Hitler's blood bath of June 30, 1934, when Schleicher, Röhm, and many others, including Jung, Papen's secretary, were murdered. In that last week of June Jack was in Berlin and living at the Kaiserhof where Disraeli stayed during the Congress of Berlin. All the time he was in close touch with Jung and went to see him in the Grunewald on June 28. On the 29th Jack was summoned to Lausanne. General Sir Neil Malcolm's daughter Angela was dying. Jack left at once. On the next day the Gestapo came to the Kaiserhof to arrest him and ransacked his room. It was a close call.

Jack was in the United States when the Second World War started and was at once enlisted by the British ambassador, Lord Lothian, for services with the British Library of Information. Very soon he obtained permission to form the British Press Service which was created by Jack, Aubrey Morgan, and Alan Dudley of the Foreign Office. Eventually the British Library of Information and the British Press Service were amalgamated under one Director-General, Sir Gerald Campbell, with two special assistants in Jack Wheeler-Bennett and Aubrey Morgan, whose knowledge of the United States made both of them invaluable.

With his remarkable knowledge of the actions and reactions of foreign affairs Jack's services were being sought by various departments. When in July, 1941, the Political Warfare Executive was formed and I became eventually its Director General, I was determined to get him as an assistant.

Luckily for me he came over to England on official business just about this time. It was a week of crisis. Changes were being made in the conduct of our war propaganda and, much against my will, I was being taken away from diplomatic work with the Czechoslovak Government in London. When Jack arrived, my appointment to the Political Warfare Executive had not been announced and, although I knew that everything was settled and that changes were being made in the Government, I was bound to secrecy.

Jack had come over with his boss, Sir Gerald Campbell, who was retiring. I got hold of Jack at once, but, in the circumstances, I could not make him an offer. Meanwhile, he was very eager for me to succeed Campbell in the United States. I was not interested, for I was already committed. Moreover, I could not have filled Campbell's shoes. He had been the most popular British official in North America, understood Canadians and Americans, and always made the right speeches at Canadian and American functions.

Incidentally, his career, which was otherwise uneventful, brought him into touch with two remarkable men. As a Vice-Consul he served under Roger Casement and as Consul in Venice in October, 1913, he had to deal with the estate of Frederick Rolfe, better known as Baron Corvo, author of *The Chronicles of the House of Borgia* and *Hadrian the Seventh*. On the subject of the two men Gerald Campbell keeps the silence of diplomacy, but in his brilliant biography of Rolfe, *The Quest for Corvo*, A. J. A. Symons described how Campbell went through Rolfe's papers and to his horror found letters, drawings and notebooks which showed that Rolfe had been a pimp both for rakes and for homosexuals.

It was between two dinners in honour of Gerald Campbell that my new appointment was announced. On July 15 Jack gave a dinner in the Savoy for Campbell and still I could not speak. Two days later the late Victor Cazalet also gave a dinner for Campbell, this time at the Dorchester. Both Anthony Eden and Duff Cooper were present, and, although the changes in the Government had not been announced, it was known that evening that Duff Cooper was going from the Ministry of Information and was being succeeded by Brendan Bracken. I sat next to Harold Nicolson, who was then Parliamentary Under-Secretary in the same Ministry. He had no idea then that he would be going himself. The next day a messenger came from number Ten to the Ministry to ask for his resignation by return.

The Cabinet had wasted considerable time over the changes and over the differences between information and political warfare. But once a decision was taken, Winston Churchill never allowed action to be delayed on it, even if sometimes the method was harsh.

Even then I had to be diplomatic with Jack who took a rather gloomy view of the attitude of the United States. Our diplomatic failures had been considerable, and the chances of the United States entering the war had receded. So long as this situation continued, he thought it was his duty to stay in the United States.

He was right, but I had always realised that the war would be long, and I therefore asked him for first refusal in the event of the United States entering the war. The first step to commit him was to make him head of our Political Warfare Mission in the United States, and eventually he came to me first as personal assistant and finally as Assistant Director-General. He was reliable, a tremendous worker who never spared himself, and his immense knowledge of men and affairs enabled him to write most valuable reports.

I owe him much. P.W.E. was a difficult department and Jack was the one man on whose judgment and loyalty I could rely implicitly. When I was ill and had to go to Scotland for special treatment, he came to see me and gave me marvellously clear pictures of the situation. Later he shared a house with me. It must have tried him highly, for he was tidy and methodical and horrified by the amount of papers that flowed into me. I had to take decisions not only daily, but hourly and had no time to be tidy. In a job like P.W.E. yesterday's memoranda were dead.

How Jack's physique stood the strain and the bombing I do not know. He looked tired, and every day his face became more and more like the colour of yellow blotting-paper. But he worked harder than ever. I knew that he did not sleep well, because about once a week he would retire to bed early and say he was going to take a 'Micky Finn'. This was a powerful narcotic which took its name from the American boxer who knocked most of his opponents out for the count. But when I saw him going to sleep immediately after dinner sitting in an arm-chair and holding a glass of untouched whisky, I realised that he needed a rest. In war-time people need more leave than in peace-time. By 1945 Whitehall had lost most of its spring and efficiency and was only barely ticking over. Jack, however, would not give in until at last he developed a severe attack of jaundice. When he recovered, I made him go on leave, but it needed two doctors to make him obey. He went to Virginia for his re-cuperation and got married. He always teases me that I summoned him back from his honeymoon.

I am afraid that it must be true, but, if it is, he repaid me with a kind action which I shall never forget. The legend is that during the war I was a tough, unobservant boss who thought only of the day's work and took no notice of my staff or of my three secretaries. We were supposed by envious officials to have the best bevy of ' beauties ' of all government departments. They worked long hours, and I plead guilty to indifference, partly because I was busy and partly because, as head of a department of mixed sexes, I felt I had to be both prudent and stern.

One day when there had been tears, Jack, who was then my assistant, came to me and suggested firmly that I might be a little more human in my relations with our secretaries. It would make, he said, a great difference. Full of remorse, I reversed my tactics and the very next evening I went into the secretaries' room which was next door to mine, chatted with them, and then, when conversation flagged, I spotted a very neat little hat and a tiny lady's umbrella on a peg behind the door. I put on the hat, took the umbrella, and did a shuffle dance down the corridor. Jack came in during the performance, looked dumb-founded, and asked if I wanted a doctor.

All was well, however, and, much to my own surprise, this incident led to my marriage which my friends say is the most sensible thing I have done in my life.

After the war I retired and Jack entered into a decade of intense activity. He had conquered his stammer and had regained his health. From 1946 to 1948 he was British Editor-in-Chief of the captured archives of the German Foreign Ministry and remained as Historical Adviser to the Foreign Office until 1958. In between times he was attached to the British Prosecuting Team at the War Criminals Trial at Nuremberg and lectured on International Politics at New College, Oxford.

Irrespective of these activities, he was working steadily and with great thoroughness on historical works which will perpetuate his name. In 1948 *Munich, Prologue to Tragedy* appeared and five years later he published *The Nemesis of Power*, the greatest study of the German Army in politics that has ever been written by any historian.

The latter would not have been such a widely read book had it been written by anybody with a less original mind than Jack's. His ability to find unusual and amusing ways of expressing his thoughts carries his readers with him and makes his books acceptable to many people who normally would not be attracted by works of such erudition.

Perhaps, however, his greatest strength in writing is the way he can identify himself with his characters. The first time I saw him after the publication of *The Nemesis of Power*, he was using a monocle. In answer to my comments on this new acquisition he said : " Occupational disease, my dear Bruce, contracted as a result of having spent so much of my time lately among German Generals."

In 1955 came the invitation to write the life of King George VI. The task took him to many places including Balmoral. The writing of the book occupied him for the best part of three years and was accomplished with the same arduous zeal for accuracy that he brings to all his books. *King George VI* was published on October 31, 1958, the author's fifty-sixth birthday, and was acclaimed in all countries. In the following New Year's Honours List he was made a K.C.V.O. and in the same year a new office was created for him and he became the first Keeper of the Royal Archives.

He is to-day a very different man from the young invalid whom I first met in the 'twenties. Now he is full of vigour and confidence and should have many more years of activity. In appearance and in personality he is unusual. His studies and his travels have given him an interesting mixture of Continental, American and British characteristics which cause him to stand out sharply defined against the background of his more stereotyped fellow countrymen.

In addition to all his hard work he is very much the squire of Garsington and has done great work in running the village football and cricket club. The Garsington Sports Club has more Vice-Presidents than any other club in the world. The hundred or so Vice-Presidents pay a guinea a year for their privilege. Jack is the President and each year he brings a team, which always includes some Oxford Blues, to play cricket against the Sports Club. The Club gives an annual prize for the best catch, and great was the joy of all when in 1958 the President himself received the prize for a remarkable catch in the long-field.

And, writing of clubs, I think that Jack must be a member of more clubs than any other Englishman to-day. They include six of the most select London Clubs, two in the United States, the New Club in Edinburgh, and one in Paris.

I know no one who has had a more exciting life or has met so many interesting people all over the world than Jack Wheeler-Bennett. I hope that sooner rather than later he will write his autobiography.

CHAPTER SIX

A Welshman in the States

' There is much care and valour in this Welshman.'

ONE of the lost characteristics of the English race is decisive-ness. Winston Churchill could take decisions with a minimum of discussion. The label ' Action To-Day ' on his Out-tray meant what it said. Since the war, if not before it, the politicians have lost the art. It may still linger in our best industrial concerns, but its real home is now in the United States and Canada.

The most decisive and forceful official that I knew during the war was a Welshman who married a daughter of Dwight Morrow, the well-known American financier and ambassador, and settled in the United States. His name is Aubrey Morgan.

I had met him before the war during one of his visits to England through his brother, J. T. Morgan, who captained the Cambridge Cricket Eleven in 1930 and made a century in 1929. Aubrey himself was an excellent cricketer who played several times for Glamorgan as a fast medium bowler. What impressed me most was his knowledge of the United States and his forceful way of imparting it to others. He was never at a loss for a word. He never spoke too much. He left on me the impact of a great leader and organiser.

In 1939 I met him again in the Sports Club. Men who knew the United States and were in a position to influence Americans were badly needed. Here was a man who had all the necessary qualifications. Comfortably off in his own right, not only was he through the Morrow connection closely in touch with Morgans' and many of the leading men of the United States, but he could also speak to them in the same decisive language which they themselves spoke but would not take from an ordinary Britisher.

I begged Aubrey to do nothing for twenty-four hours. I telephoned to Vansittart at the Foreign Office and begged him to see Aubrey and to find him a job. Van saw him almost at once and decided that he must go back to the United States. Important work would be found for him.

As a result of this encounter and its quick result, Aubrey now calls me his ' founding father ' because he had come over to England to fight and I had launched him on an official career, a turning-point in his life which never in his wildest dreams had he imagined. He had no great respect for officials. Indeed, this was one of the reasons why I valued his services. The other main reason was his complete and natural courage and self-confidence. He would kow-tow to nobody. Not even a Churchill could bully him into agreeing with something which he thought was wrong or foolish.

Back went Aubrey to the United States where Jack Wheeler-Bennett and he became a most powerful combination not only in running the British Press Service in the United States but also in influencing all the ' high-ups ' from Lord Lothian, the British ambassador, to the powerful finance house of Morgan, and President Roosevelt's closest entourage. Neither in physique nor in method were Aubrey and Jack alike. Jack had immense knowledge of both American and European politics and also of officialdom, but was more cautious than Aubrey to whose zeal for action, contempt for all pomposity, official or unofficial, and capacity for driving clean through any difficulty, he acted as a safety valve. They were firm friends and ragged each other with the greatest good humour. When Jack was given an extra job of looking after foreign nationals in the United States, the Czechoslovak exiles protested to our Embassy in Washington on the ground that he was pro-Habsburg. Later, when Jack was writing his book on *Munich*, Aubrey said to me : " You've never done, and never will do, a better propaganda job than your conversion of Jack from a pro-Habsburg into a pro-Beneš and pro-Eden man ! "

I have no doubt that Jack got more than his own back in guiding Aubrey along the slippery paths of diplomacy in Washington. Aubrey was certainly no respecter of diplomats and was hard on young British attachés who tried to patronise Americans. This is, or was, the besetting sin of the English upper class in the United States. The arrogance not only annoyed the Americans, but went to almost unbelievable lengths. One

Englishman who went to stay with Tom Lamont sent his menus in advance and complained after his arrival because the hot oysters he wanted had not been baked in the shell.

The first time that I saw Aubrey performing as an official was when he was brought home for consultation in 1941. He came to Woburn to address our 'political warriors' on the proper way for Englishmen to approach Americans and on the perils which arose from the assumption that, because they spoke more or less the same language, Englishmen and Americans were alike. This kind of lecture was Aubrey's masterpiece. Many people—Ministers of the Crown, ambassadors, travelling politicians, and editors—have spoken on the same theme, but none of them approached the skill and verve with which Aubrey rammed home every precept with an unforgettable example which invariably took the form of an Anglo-American story quite new to his listeners.

The effect on his audience was prodigious. None of the listeners had the slightest idea that he was being talked at, but went away convinced that wisdom had come to him and that, whatever other Englishmen might do, he would avoid all the pitfalls. In time Aubrey's knowledge of the United States was to take him to the highly important post of Private Secretary and Adviser on American affairs to the British ambassador.

Unlike most officials Aubrey was always ready and often eager to take action without reference to higher authority. In this respect both Jack and he were fortunate in their immediate superior, Sir Gerald Campbell, who gave them considerable latitude in both planning and decision.

Given a light rein, Jack and Aubrey set their wits and energy to reorganise British propaganda in the United States. In the earlier days of the war it had not been exactly successful. There was the sending over of the British 'Heroes' to Montreal and New York. This bright idea was conceived by the armed forces, and the Heroes included airmen, soldiers, and representatives of the Navy and of the Commandos. The Heroes went first to Canada, and when they were due to arrive in New York, Major-General 'Paddy' Beaumont-Nesbitt, Air Commodore Thornton and Admiral Pott went down to Newark to meet the aeroplane. Twentieth Century Fox was financing the visit as a stunt, and a huge crowd had assembled. As the three service attachés arrived, the cameras clicked furiously, and there were loud shouts of ' Here come the Heroes '. The crowd surged forward to embrace them, and an awkward situation was averted in the nick of time by a stentorian roar from Beaumont-Nesbitt : ' We are *not* the Heroes, we are from the British Embassy.'

At last the real Heroes arrived. They had had a very rough night in Montreal, and one of them had nine stitches in his head. The wound had been caused, not by the Germans, but by a broken bottle wielded by a French Canadian. Tired though they were, they were at once mustered, plied with liquor, and taken off to Broadway where Twentieth Century Fox had arranged a ' do ' with Duke Ellington's orchestra. Duke also added to the gaiety by pulling on to the platform Beaumont-Nesbitt who in his nervousness set fire to his tie with his cigarette. Amid loud cheers it was put out with a syphon of soda.

By this time the Heroes were showing signs of wear. So the three service attachés took them away to give them a rest and to prepare them for the big performance at Madison Gardens in the evening. Seventeen thousand people filled the hall, and the Heroes were given a wonderful welcome. Here the only curious incident was the blessing given by the padre before the meeting opened. He recited the Lord's Prayer. It was listened to in silence and was loudly cheered when it ended.

All the British present realised that there were, indeed, wide differences between the British and the Citizens of God's Own Country. Indeed, Aubrey Morgan, who has learnt much about foreign affairs during the past twenty years and, being an athlete, used to express them in terms of national games, says that the Soviet Union's game is chess. All the moves are carefully planned ahead. If after forty-two moves, a pawn is lost, there is a delay while a new series of moves is prepared. The game of the United States is poker, a game in which you risk all on one hand. The American hand to-day holds H-bombs. Why not use them ? The English game is cricket, and the English people, who watch patiently a Test match which lasts five days, are quite happy if the game ends in a draw. Though the Soviet Union now has the bombs, Aubrey's interpretation of foreign affairs in terms of sport is true enough especially as regards Britain where already too many people accept Britain as a third-class nation condemned inevitably to reduction to the size of Holland or Portugal.

In peace-time one of the bugbears of experts abroad is the travelling member of Parliament who flies for a week-end to Peking or Washington and comes back full of knowledge. More often than not he has an *idée fixe* and is invited to visit a country or a capital by a foreigner who has the same *idée fixe*. Inevitably both agree, and this blissful week-end will provide the M.P. for several years with an introduction to at least half a dozen speeches beginning with the words : ' When I was in Helsingfors in 19 . . .'

In war-time the expert comes into his own. If he is an information officer or a propagandist, he takes not only decisions, but also risks. Jack Wheeler-Bennett and Aubrey Morgan were effective in decision. Their biggest risk failed, perhaps fortunately for them. I do not know which of the two hit on the bright idea of trying to subsidise the Willkie Youth Club at the time of the first vote on ' Lease Lend '. This highly interesting situation took place soon after Lord Lothian's death and before the arrival of Lord Halifax as the new ambassador. As it was by no means certain that ' Lease Lend ' would be accepted by Congress, Jack and Aubrey persuaded Nevile Butler, then in charge of the Embassy, to release a large sum for the special purpose of enlisting the sympathy of the supporters of Mr Willkie, Franklin Roosevelt's opponent for the Presidency.

Jack and Aubrey had made all the necessary arrangements and had already arrived in their New York office with the money, when the telephone rang. The voice came from the British Embassy. The two conspirators were to come back to Washington at once. The deal was off. Nevile Butler had very properly telegraphed to Whitehall to seek permission for the transaction. Whitehall, of course, was horrified.

My guess is that Aubrey devised this scheme. On the principle that most things are fair in war, he was justified, for the first vote on ' Lease Lend ' scraped through by a very narrow majority. As a Celt Aubrey would have made ' siccar '.

By the time the war was over Aubrey had learnt a great deal about officialdom and, although still contemptuous of it, he knew how to handle Ministers and ambassadors. What was he to do ? His own inclination was to go back to Oregon and farm. All who had been witnesses of his work were eager to retain his services for his country, but, when war is over, the officials come back into their own, and the temporaries are sent away empty or, at best, with a ministerial letter of thanks.

Aubrey went back to his farming, but in the summer of 1946 he paid a visit to England and Wales, and many people, including myself, urged him to come back to the political world which he now knew so well. At this time I was seeing much of Anthony Eden who was then, as indeed always, eager to reform the Conservative Party and to introduce co-partnership into industry and financial assistance to tenant farmers to enable them to buy their farms and, in general, to give a stake in the country, and therefore in the Party, to the small man.

I knew that this was very close to Aubrey's heart, and in the hope that he would be tempted to take on the job of re-organising Conservative literature and propaganda I took him to Eden's house in Sussex. All went well. Aubrey was tempted. He made it quite plain that he saw no future for Britain except in a reformed Tory Party. He told Eden that his problem was a pull between private interests in the United States and a patriotic duty over here. If there was a job for him to do, of course he would put duty first. He wanted no money, nor was he seeking a job.

Eden, who had already discussed Aubrey with me, asked him if he might tell Lord Woolton and get him to see Aubrey. I cannot remember whether Woolton saw him or not, but nothing came of it. The impression that remains in my mind is that, as Chairman of the Conservative Party and boss of its organisation, Lord Woolton had more power than most people realised. He lost a first-class man.

A younger and greater man found a better use for Aubrey. This was Sir Oliver Franks, one of the most successful British ambassadors in the United States. His own charm and brilliant intellect would have made him popular and respected wherever he went, but he would be the first to say that he owed much to Aubrey Morgan both as his Private Secretary and as his confidential adviser on American matters. He would also be entitled to give himself a pat on the back for being so wise in choosing the right man.

It is now nearly three years since I last saw Aubrey. When Sir Oliver Franks retired from his ambassadorial post in Washington, Aubrey went back to Oregon to live a life exactly the opposite of what he had lived in Washington and New York. As a farmer he is up with the sun and sometimes before it. As an official he had to function more by night than by day.

He comes to England and Wales every second or third year to see his relations and friends, but I think that, excluding war, his official career is ended. He has never had a high opinion of bureaucrats in general or of diplomats in particular. His view is that Washington is the most dangerous place for indiscreet wise-cracks because everyone likes them and therefore tempts the innocent new-comer to have a go. Needless to say, every good or indiscreet wise-crack is circulated round Washington with rocket speed.

In warning British new-comers of the dangers of Washington, Aubrey had plenty of examples to illustrate his precepts. The career of Sir Cecil Spring-Rice, ambassador in Washington during the First World War and author of *I Vow to Thee, My Country*, was ruined by a wise-crack. At a large dinner-party he was placed next to a garrulous American politician who was an ardent admirer of Woodrow Wilson and who drove the ambassador nearly mad by repeating Wilson's numerous good qualities. When he said, " Wilson is the shepherd of his flock ", Spring-Rice lost patience and snapped back, " And I suppose McAdoo is his crook." McAdoo, who had not a very high reputation, was not only Secretary to the Treasury but also Wilson's son-in-law. The story went round until it reached the President who thereafter had no more use for the British ambassador.

About the same time a young British secretary at our Washington Embassy made an even greater gaffe. He, too, was at a smart dinner-party and enjoyed a brief triumph by saying that, when Wilson proposed to the second Mrs Wilson, she was so surprised that she nearly fell out of bed. He, too, was black-listed by the Wilsonians and had to be transferred.

It would be good if there were at each one of our Embassies a permanent Aubrey Morgan with the necessary local knowledge and flair to smooth the way both for ambassadors and their staffs. Such men, however, are rare in this world, and in a long experience of foreign travel I have found only one Aubrey.

CHAPTER SEVEN

Two Best-Selling Authors

' No man but a blockhead ever wrote, except for money.'

IT is a widely held belief that an author writes only one best-seller, and, indeed, the use of the superlative *best* might imply that the belief were true. Doubtless, there are many writers who have one book which has sold more copies than all their other works put together. There are also authors all of whose books have very large sales. I feel sure that, after he had established his reputation, the late Warwick Deeping received ample royalties for nearly all his books. Another author who should have made big money was the gentle Jeffrey Farnol. His *The Broad Highway*, *The Amateur Gentleman* and other books had great success. Alas ! Farnol himself, who began life as a scene-painter in the theatre, made a poor contract with his publishers, and his best work was done before the harm was repaired.

There is one curious fact about best-sellers. The authors who write the largest best-sellers are rarely those who are hailed by the leading critics. There are authors who live completely out of the glare of publicity, but whose every book is a best-seller. There are also authors like the late Edgar Wallace who, possessed of vivid imagination and remarkable energy, earn large sums by the immensity of their output. Once popularity is achieved, a writer of this type can make a fortune in almost any branch of writing. In this chapter I give one portrait of a sheltered, but highly successful, novelist for adults, and another of an imaginative and industrious author who makes big money out of books for juveniles.

I

In my choice of the best-selling novelist for adults I have taken a man whose name rarely comes into the conversation of high-brow critics but is mentioned often, and always with rosy satisfaction, in the counting-house of the firm of Collins.

My novelist is Howard Spring who has, and has had for over twenty years, a faithful following of readers and worshippers on both sides of the Atlantic, not to mention large sales in translation in numerous countries of the world.

I have come into his life more than once in a rather intimate manner. On October 24, 1931, Lord Beaverbrook, who was near the end of a whirlwind tour in favour of Empire Free Trade, returned from Lancashire where he had been speaking in Darwen. At that time the *Manchester Guardian* had a roving reporter who was allowed to write more or less what he liked. Seeing that Beaverbrook was going to speak at Darwen, he decided to have a look at this newspaper proprietor whom he had never seen before. He therefore betook himself to Darwen, inspected the town, and then took his place in the hall in which Beaverbrook was to speak. When the speech was over, the roving reporter had an hour to wait before getting a train back to Manchester. And it was on the cold, wind-swept platform of Darwen station that he wrote his piece on Lord Beaverbrook.

I waited on his Lordship on his return from Lancashire. He was in high delight and wanted to know who remembered a song which ended with a line about making dreams come true. Having heard an English cabaret artiste called Kitty Moran sing it nightly for three weeks in a Prague Nachtlokal a few years before, I remembered both the title, *Meet Me To-night in Dreamland*, and also the words, and earned merit for the last line ' And make all my dreams come true ".

The reason for Lord Beaverbrook's delight was the report of his Darwen speech in the *Manchester Guardian*. It was not unkind, but it was the caption—The Pedlar of Dreams—which enraptured Max. The article, he told me, was by a man called Howard Spring. Did I know him? I didn't, but I knew what was coming. Lord Beaverbrook picked up the receiver. " Get me the editor of the *Evening Standard*, " he said to his telephone clerk. Howard Spring was to be got at once, and at any cost.

From that moment Howard never looked back. As he tells in his short autobiography of his childhood, he had to leave school in Cardiff at the age of twelve. His father, whose trade ' was that of a man who did such jobs as he could get in gardens ', had died, and the young Howard had to find work in order to help his mother to bring up his eight brothers and sisters. He began as a butcher's boy. He had come up the hard way and was determined never to return to it.

Everything went smoothly. As even the Beaverbrook Press could not afford to run a ' Pedlar of Dreams ' story every day, another job had to be found for Howard. Arnold Bennett, whose weekly article on books had been a most successful feature of the *Evening Standard*, had died that year. J. B. Priestley, who had succeeded him, was not so successful, or did not please Lord Beaverbrook. Howard Spring got the job and made a big success of it.

Then came the thought that comes once or many times to every journalist. How am I to be free ? When he was still with the *Manchester Guardian*, Howard had written a short book for children called *Darkie & Co.* and had sold it outright for fifty pounds. Every author makes at least one blunder in selling a book, but in those days fifty pounds was almost a fortune to a miserably paid reporter. His ambition now soared higher and in his spare time he wrote a novel. He called it *Shabby Tiger* and did not know what to do with it. In the *Evening Standard* there was an able man who looked after the publishers' advertisements for the book page and in his spare time spotted talent for Collins. He read *Shabby Tiger*, liked it, and took it to Collins. That was how William Collins found his most successful author. The partnership has lasted to this day.

Howard and I were friends, and he has done me many good turns, including a superlative review of my first book, *Memoirs of a British Agent*. *Shabby Tiger* did well, but did not take Howard out of the *Evening Standard*. He wanted to be sure before trying to make a living from books alone. He would give up journalism when he sold 100,000 copies of a book.

I therefore left the *Evening Standard* before he did. In the early months of 1939 I was in Boston, Massachusetts, on a lecture tour. Among other engagements I lunched with Ted Weeks, the editor of the *Atlantic Monthly* and a most successful lecturer and broadcaster on books. At that time he was full of a book called *My Son, My Son* which had captivated all America. The same evening I was given a dinner at the select Tavern Club and was shown the great book which contains many famous

names. Side by side were the signatures of Jack London and
H. G. Wells. Jack London signed : ' Yours till the revolution '.
Wells, who had been the next guest, had added : ' There ain't
going to be no revolution '.

At my dinner there was also much talk of *My Son, My Son*,
and I was asked if I knew Howard Spring. I was able to say
' yes ' and give some details. The English title was *Oh !
Absalom !* but the American title had to be changed, because
William Faulkner had written a book called *Absalom, Absalom !*

In the original English and American editions *My Son, My Son*
sold over 200,000 copies. It took Howard Spring out of journalism, although he remained with the *Evening Standard* throughout the war and, with H. V. Morton, was the only other British
correspondent who accompanied Winston Churchill in the
battleship *Duke of York* to the Atlantic Charter meeting. The
trip was a great experience for the two correspondents, but it
brought them no other reward, for they were not allowed to
write a word. The United States was not yet in the war, and
President Roosevelt did not want the American Press to have
any other version of the meeting than his own.

After the war Howard Spring came to Cornwall and stayed
for a few years at Mylor. He had married while he was still
with the *Manchester Guardian*. While Jimmy Bone, the famous
London correspondent of the *Guardian*, was on three weeks'
leave, Howard Spring was sent from Manchester to carry on
the equally famous ' London Letter '. He fell in love with Bone's
secretary and married her. Marian Spring is a Londoner and the
daughter of a London merchant who was a well-known amateur
gardener and had a house in Cornwall, a county in which the only
two subjects of conversation are sailing and gardening.

Marian Spring is to-day a famous gardener and, when they
bought the most attractive *White Cottage* in Falmouth, she turned
Howard into a reasonably good gardener. The reason why
everyone in Cornwall gardens is because all you have to do is
to make a hole in the ground and whatever you put into it grows.
Howard is allowed to make the holes : Marian does the
planting.

Finding the Edinburgh winter rather too long and too cold
after so many years abroad in central-heated houses, my wife and

I came to inspect Cornwall as a winter resort. Falmouth was the place we chose. Barely a quarter of a mile from the hotel in which we winter is the *White Cottage*, and I got to know Howard better than ever. The *White Cottage* is a house of a very comfortable size and has a beautifully sheltered garden where superb camellias, magnolias and wonderful rhododendrons and Mexican flame trees flower freely, and there is colour the whole year round. The Springs have one of the tulip trees which are rare in England, and their tree bears tulips. Not being a gardener, I am impressed by the general beauty of the surroundings, but carry away with me in abiding memory the majestic and noble oak-tree which, according to Howard, is the oldest thing in Falmouth.

Howard himself has a goodly-sized and very tidy working room with a massive book-case and a wall of shelves. One long row contains copies of his novels in foreign translations including Chinese and Japanese. In the middle of the room is a handsome desk. He does not use it for writing his books. When he is working, he sits at a table in the corner of the room with his back to the window so that the beauty of the garden shall not disturb his concentration.

He is the best-organised writer that I know. He rises at eight a.m., has a small bowl of porridge for breakfast and is at work at nine a.m. He writes till one p.m. for five days of the week, and does about 1000 words daily. His novels are fairly long, but he can finish them comfortably in a year. Yet he only brings out a novel every two years. " Why should I write a book a year," he says, " when I can live happily on one book every two years ? " One day he devotes to writing his review article for *Country Life* and one day is entirely free from writing. Always, however, his writing day is over by one p.m. In the afternoon he works in the garden or plays with his eight cats. From four p.m. to five-fifteen p.m. he reads the books which he has to review. At six p.m. he has a light high tea. After tea there is more reading. From nine p.m. to ten forty-five p.m. Marian and he do a crossword together or play some game. He is in bed by eleven or soon after. With few exceptions this routine is observed rigidly. He is methodical in all things and as regular as a clock. He subscribes to no press-cutting agency. He never reads the reviews of his books. Apart from his long white hair flowing in the wind, I have never seen him ruffled.

I should say, too, that he is the best business man among authors. He knows the value of money. He was aware of it as a child and learnt it in a harder place than Scotland—the North of England. After several years as a messenger boy on a Cardiff newspaper, he went to the *Yorkshire Observer* in Bradford where he eventually rose to a salary of thirty shillings a week. Then he transferred himself to the *Manchester Guardian*. The atmosphere was wonderful, but the pay was miserable. C. P. Scott, the owner and editor, was what the North calls ' close '. Moreover, he really believed that it was prestige enough for anyone to work for a newspaper like the *Guardian* for next to nothing.

For Howard on one occasion it was literally nothing. He was sent to Dublin to report on the Black and Tan troubles. On his own admission he had a very interesting time. When he came back, he wrote a piece for the *Guardian Miscellany* in which so many subsequent famous writers have made their *debut*. His contribution was printed and he expected a cheque for three guineas. No payment came, but a little later he received a letter from C. P. Scott who had retained the cheque. The letter pointed out that Howard's expenses to Ireland had been paid by the *Guardian* and that the experience he had acquired from the newspaper's generosity had enabled him to write the article which had earned the three guineas. Strictly speaking, therefore, Scott explained that the cheque should be his, but ended his letter with, ' Let us split the difference.' Howard got £1 11s. 6d.

Scott was a great editor, but lacked the human touch. He had no use for anyone who had not been to a university. After the war the *Manchester Guardian* rose again to great heights, and Howard was delighted, because Wadsworth, the editor, had been a poor boy who had come out of a council school.

Marian Spring is a confirmed Tory, but she is very proud of her self-educated husband. I remember one occasion when we were discussing universities, and she burst out suddenly : " Well, we sent one of our sons to Oxford. He took a degree in English, and we think and he thinks it's a good week when he earns a fiver. And here's Howard, who never went to school, let alone a university, paying off half the National Debt in income tax."

If Howard belongs to any Party, he is a Conservative, although I think he is not very interested in modern politicians except Sir Winston Churchill. He certainly has something to conserve. All his novels are in print and, apart from one or two very big financial successes in the United States, he has a large and loyal following in Europe, especially in Italy and Germany. Because his novels appeal to the people, they are translated into languages like Danish and Dutch. His revenue from Danish translations is quite amazingly large. What he has paid regularly in income tax since the war would make the mouth of almost any other British writer water.

Howard Spring is a kind man who in a quiet way has done many a good turn to authors and journalists less fortunate than himself. He is no club-man, and the only literary organisation to which he belongs is the National Book League. In this connection there is a story. Before the National Book League was formed, there was a National Book Council which ran short of money through paying too much for a propaganda film on books. One of the directors appealed to Howard for help, and, as Howard was a family friend of the director and his wife, he drew up a scheme. He would give the N.B.C. five per cent of the profits of his next book. The directors, he suggested, should put up this proposal to famous authors. Five per cent might be too much, but they might come in on a two and a half per cent basis.

The famous authors did little or nothing. Howard's next book was *My Son, My Son* which had vast sales both in the United States and in Britain. The National Book Council became solvent. A group took it over, reorganised it completely and changed its name to The National Book League. It made Howard a life member.

I do not think he goes there very often, for he rarely visits London. He thinks Falmouth the best place that he has ever found. He gives support to the Falmouth Polytechnic, the cultural centre of a sea-port town which prefers rugby football to reading and beer to books. He also does much to maintain the Falmouth Drama Group. In other respects, he is something of a recluse, happy in his own home and content with his one real hobby outside it which is sailing. He is the only poor-boy journalist who has achieved his boyhood dream; to write best-sellers and to have a boat of his own and sail it.

This does not mean, however, that he is blind to his position as a popular author with a world audience. Indeed, he knows and plays his part very well when occasion demands it. No one that I can think of looks more literary. He is thin without an ounce of spare flesh on him. His rather gaunt face almost exaggerates what is a fine and impressive forehead. His eyes, which are rather piercing, compel your attention. His hair, quite white and rather sparse on the top, falls down on to his shoulders so that at the end it turns up like a cavalier's curls. He is not interested in clothes and prefers slacks, a tweed coat, and the oldest hat he can find.

He is an excellent raconteur with a first-class memory of all the stories about publishers, authors and journalists which he has collected during his life-time. When the fans and worshippers come to see the sage of Falmouth—and they come from near and far and are of all nationalities—Howard turns the tap on and the stories flow easily and smoothly. I met two charming and highly educated Americans who spent most winters studying world problems. They had been to Coventry to buy a Jaguar in order to see England in comfort, and their first trip was to Falmouth to call on Howard Spring. They were worshippers.

On such occasions, if his visitors are pleasant and interesting, Howard does his act. He shows them into his study, takes his place by the mantelpiece, pushes the long white hair back with his left hand and points to his books with the outstretched right hand. If he is asked how he works, and nine times out of ten it is the first question, he goes through his daily routine without exasperation or impatience. Then, as a great favour, he opens the drawer of his desk and produces the pen with which he has written all his books. It is the first pen that he ever had. He bought it in Cardiff and it cost twopence. Incidentally, his handwriting is as neat as Arnold Bennett's.

Marian Spring stands by in admiration. She has typed every word that he has written. She regards it as a miracle that now through Howard's success she can have everything she wants.

Where does the money go ? On mink coats ? They do not enter her mind even in dreams. The Springs have not even a car. Marian's face lights up and she says : " It's lovely for me to be able to buy all the bulbs and manure that I want ! "

Howard beams blandly. " I'll write your biography one day. The title will be : *She Married For Manure* and the chapter-headings will be Horn and Hoof, Fish Meal, Dried Blood, Liquinure, Bone Meal, and Seaweed."

There is enough for all the manures in the world and to spare. Howard Spring has never taken an advance from any publisher. He sets aside in advance what is likely to be his income-tax and pays it on the nail. Marian and he fulfil their obligations to the social life around them, but they live in a little world of their own which is all-sufficient for their desires. They have no wish to go on cruises. Who does, when you can sail your own boat ! They have no longing to go to Switzerland or to take one of the villas on the heights of St Moritz which was once described by the *Daily Express* as the ladder of success ; being, in fact, inhabited by boot-kings, cinema stars, and chain-store millionaires. But they are a very kind and simple pair who are, I wager, very much happier than others who go chasing pleasure with money.

There is no safety in wealth or in very much else these days, but I think the Springs will live comfortably to the end. And why should they not ? For the last ten years I have gone around the book-shops of London regularly in order to find out how my own book or books are going. I begin always with the same phrase : Who is selling well this Christmas ? The answer is generally : Sir Winston Churchill or Evelyn Waugh or Nancy Mitford, but always without exception—' and Howard Spring '.

2

My selection for the best-selling author of juvenile books is not Miss Enid Blyton, although she must be one of the most successful writers in this country. My choice falls on the man who provides the reading for boys—and I believe quite a number of girls—from the ages of eight to fourteen or fifteen. His name is Captain W. E. Johns. He has an adventurous record.

Born in Hertford in 1893 and educated at the local Grammar School, he entered the Army in 1913. He served right through the 1914–18 war, at first in the Army in the Middle East and, later, in the Royal Flying Corps to which he transferred in 1916. At the end of the war he remained in the R.F.C. and was employed continuously on flying duties both at home and abroad until 1930. He was then thirty-seven. His time was up, and he had to make a decision.

Realism keeps a man's feet on the ground and more often than not makes him a slave. Flying stimulates and excites the imagination, and Johns had imagination before he began to fly. Life in the air had given him a new world to exploit. He left the Air Force to take up aviation journalism. He launched and edited two periodicals, *Popular Flying* and *Flying*. Then out of imagination came inspiration. During his flights he had often put himself in the position of a young man learning flying. He saw the tremendous adventures of the future and worked them out in his mind from the beginning to the end. There was one asset which he possessed in great abundance. He had a marvellous knack of tying up with remarkable speed an adventure story to the latest scientific invention.

In 1939 he was forty-six and old enough by several years to hesitate before starting a new profession. There are, however, circumstances in every man's life when to be prudent is to lose everything. He abandoned his aviation journalism to lecture to Air Cadets and, as he said himself, ' to develop a British type of adventurous character for advanced juvenile fiction.' During his journalistic career he had written several serious books on the Royal Air Force and its exploits and also short stories with a background of aviation. Now he was to put juvenile fiction before everything.

Biggles, the boy adventurer-hero, was born during the war. I am not quite sure of his birthplace, because the 1939-45 war intervened and Johns was working for the Ministry of Information. But when the war was over I ran into him in the most unlikely of places. In the summer of 1946 I betook myself as usual to Tomintoul, the highest village in the Highlands and the refuge of my Macgregor forebears after they had been harried out of their own country. It lies close to the A'an, the largest tributary of the Spey and, though over-fished, is an excellent and most exciting salmon and sea-trout river. And here in the Richmond Arms Hotel I found Johns and also the indefatigable Mrs Johns who types all his books.

A sturdily built man of medium height, Johns had come to Tomintoul in the spring of 1944 and had devised for himself an ideal life. First, he learnt the finer arts of salmon-fishing from Duncan McNiven, the proprietor of the Richmond Arms and a great fisher and angling mentor. With his usual energy Johns took to salmon fishing as if it were the only object of life. In the summer he did no other work. In the winter he was an Edgar Wallace writing and dictating books with the speed of a Paris-Lyon express.

Biggles, his standard hero, was a combination of all that is best in the three fighting services, the Foreign Office, and the Secret Service. Somewhere in each book and often in each chapter he was in the air. Moreover, thanks to Johns' wonderful speed in concocting and writing a new story in a few days, Biggles, printed, bound in stiff covers and jacketed, would be in Korea within a month or two of the Korean war starting. That was, and is, the Johns technique.

Biggles goes everywhere. The titles cover earth, sky, sea and outer space : *Biggles in Korea* ; *Biggles Air Detective* ; *Biggles as Secret Agent* ; *Biggles Breaks the Silence* ; *Biggles Flies Again* ; *Biggles Hunts Big Game* ; *Biggles Takes Charge*, and, not surprisingly, *No Rest For Biggles* ! They are healthy books. Biggles gets into scrapes, but he does the right thing and gets away somehow. His adventures sell in large numbers.

By the time this book is finished I cannot say for certain how many Biggles books will have been written. But up to January, 1958, Bill Johns had written a hundred and twenty books, not including radio plays and a successful adult Television play in which Douglas Fairbanks took the lead. I should say that Biggles books must account for more than half the total of one hundred and twenty. I do not know how many Biggles books Johns wrote in Tomintoul. What I can relate is that after three years in Tomintoul Johns took a six years' lease of Pitchroy, one of the pleasant shooting and fishing lodges on the lordly Spey. The lodge looks over one of the loveliest salmon stretches

of the river. There is a grouse moor and round the lodge itself
there is pheasant shooting. It is in all respects but one an ideal
and inspiring home for any author. It is like the Collerado-
Mansfeldt Castle at Dobřiž which the Czech Communists have
given as a rest-house to their subservient hack-writers. The
one trouble about Pitchroy is that very few authors in the world
could pay the rent.

Here in these Utopian surroundings Johns divided his time
in the usual way. From February 15 to September 30 he was
on the river at least three or four days in the week. I can only
guess how much time he devoted to shooting, but I imagine
that in the long dark winter nights he was at his desk.

It was a fertile and fruitful period, for between the years
1948 and 1952 Johns published thirty-seven books, of which
sixteen were Biggles books. This gives an average of over seven
books a year for a period of five years.

Captain Johns is a minor genius in enlisting the latest scientific
inventions for his adventure stories. He may not have been
the first English writer to exploit outer space, but he was and is
certainly in the front row. Space-travel books now flow from
his pen every year. The rate is a little slower, not more than
two or three a year, and alas ! Biggles, the airman, does not
appear in the latest of his space books that I have read (*To Outer
Space* ; November, 1957). Nevertheless, Biggles books continue
to appear, and most of them are still in print. Biggles has been
translated into seventeen languages ; and then Bill Johns has
two other heroes, Gimlet and Worrals, who are quite separate
from the Biggles saga.

This multitude of books would seem to indicate a feverishly
active life on the part of the author. But when I turn to *Who's
Who* to discover in what other recreations, apart from fishing
and shooting, Captain Johns indulges, I find the following entry :
' Other Publications : *Fighting Planes and Aces*, 1932 ; *The Air
V.C.'s*, 1934 ; *Milestones of Aviation* ; eighty-five fiction books
with aviation background and many short stories, some drama-
tised and broadcast, in British and U.S. publications ' !

This is still not the end of the story. Two or three years ago
I went into Harrods book department. A notice informed me
that Captain Johns was lecturing in the building at that very

moment. I asked the manager if I could get a seat. " That would be impossible," he said. However, he took me to the door of the lecture-room and for ten minutes I listened to Captain Johns. The room was packed with juveniles and their mothers, not to mention quite a sprinkling of fathers or uncles. Johns was a first-class lecturer.

Such energy and industry deserve their reward. Captain Johns left Pitchroy in 1953 and now lives in England. He is sixty-six. I hope he will catch many more salmon and many more readers. Books which please and inspire boys are worth nearly all the works of angry men, whether they be twenty-five or eighty-five.

CHAPTER EIGHT

Political Warrior

' Thou wouldst be great, art not without ambition.'

IF Richard Howard Stafford Crossman, O.B.E., ever becomes Prime Minister or Foreign Secretary—and he has the ability and perhaps the ambition to be both, he may perhaps, in a moment of remembrance, think kindly of me. For four years of the Second World War he shortened my hours of sleep, strained such reserves of tact as I possess, and in times of crisis earned my admiration.

I first met him in 1940 in the country, at a weekly meeting of propagandists at which, as a member of the Political Intelligence Department of the Foreign Office, I attended. I was there only in the capacity of an observer and by keeping my mouth shut and my eyes open I soon realised that, as regards propaganda to Germany, the two stars were Freddie Voigt and Richard Crossman. Every good propagandist is like a prima donna and must be given a reasonable amount of latitude. I soon realised that Voigt knew far more about Germany, but that Crossman was the better propagandist. As it is virtually impossible to have two prima donnas on the stage at the same time, it is equally impossible to have two experts on the same country in the same organisation. One has to go, and it was Voigt who went with hurt feelings and considerable bitterness.

In this country temporary war departments start with heavy birth pains and rarely, if ever, attain the smooth running of an official establishment like the Treasury or the Foreign Office. During the Second World War the various organisations conducting propaganda or political warfare to enemy and enemy-occupied countries were no exception to this disordered dislocation. The regional directors were in the country forty miles from London. The B.B.C. European Service, which was an all-important political warfare organisation, was in Bush

House in London, the military wing was in Fitzmaurice Place and the Minister responsible was Dr Dalton, then head of the Ministry of Economic Warfare, with Mr Eden in the Foreign Office in Downing Street keeping a keen eye on policy.

Although early in the war I had become British representative with the Czechoslovak Provisional Government and was interested in this work, I was taken away, much against my will, to try to bring some tidiness into the disorganisation of our political warfare.

As both the Foreign Office and the Chiefs of Staff wanted the organisation under one head in London, I made an early visit to the country headquarters to annouce the policy of return to London. I was met with what amounted to a blank refusal. The strongest argument for remaining in the country was put forward by Dick Crossman.

As I could not sack the whole organisation, I played for time. In the long run it paid, but it was a wearing trial. On December 15, 1941, Dick's thirty-fourth birthday, squabbling between London and the country was at its worst, and in my diary I wrote : ' Our organisation is appalling and can never work. I do not know what to do. The machine is so big and cumbersome and inhuman that no one man can be anything more than a tiny cog in a vast piece of rumbling machinery.'

Fortunately I was given more power and, thanks to Ritchie Calder, who started a movement in the country for the return to London, all was well. When the return took place, Dick Crossman led it.

By this time I had learnt much about him from his fellow Wykehamists in the Foreign Office. He had been brilliant both in scholarship and in the Winchester brand of football. At Oxford he had taken a First in Mods. and a First in Greats and had been a Fellow and Tutor at New College at the age of twenty-three. A year before the war he became Assistant Editor of the *New Statesman*.

All the Foreign Office Wykehamists were unanimous about his exceptional ability, but there were different opinions about his ambition and his ruthlessness. However, he got the best ' chit' both for ability and character from Roger Makins, possibly the best Wykehamist, and probably the best official, in the Office.

The Political Warfare Executive was not a well-run organisation, for by its very nature it could not be. I regarded it as my duty to allow to the experts as much latitude as I could, without contravening official policy and provoking ministerial censure. Inevitably the experts on Germany regarded themselves as the key men in the organisation, and Dick Crossman was a German expert.

Even at this stage I am not going to make invidious comparisons or to give a ranking list of our war propagandists, but Crossman had remarkable qualities for this kind of work. He was full of ideas, had great driving force, and in a crisis could work at immense speed. Not even his greatest enemy could say that he lacked self-confidence. On the contrary he was full of it and was inclined to go ahead on his own initiative without reference to me or to anyone else. The main trouble was that Dick believed in giving the Germans a saving clause which might induce the anti-Hitler Germans to take action before the end of the war. Official Anglo-American policy was ' unconditional surrender ', and, whatever view one takes of the policy, it was clearly a handicap to political warfare.

On several occasions Dick fell foul of Ministers, but I always stood up for him because I was quite sure that I could not replace him. When I look back to-day at the various incidents in which he was involved, they seem very trivial. But at the time they were serious, and on at least two occasions I saved his career as an official political warrior.

There were Tory and even Labour Members of Parliament who were critical of him and, doubtless, of me. One favourite form of attack was that Dick had never lived long enough in Germany to acquire instinctive knowledge of German reactions and that he waged political warfare against Goebbels over the heads of the German people.

This kind of back-biting goes on in every country in wartime. Both Parliament and the Press are irritated by not being allowed to inquire into departments which are dealing with secret matters. I suffered plenty of criticism myself, and on September 17, 1941, the *Evening Standard* had a leader entitled ' S-sh, We Are Observed '. It was an attack on the Foreign Office, on diplomacy and on the secrecy which enveloped

P.W.E. Among other choice epithets the leader stated that
' the British Dr Goebbels had *locked* his *heart*.'

This was legitimate warfare on the home front. I was there
to be shot at whether Dick Crossman or anyone else in the
department was the real target. Dick had real charm when he
chose to use it, but I don't think he was in any way grateful
to me at the time. He was then too cocksure and considered
that foreign affairs could be taken in a stride. Because I was fair
to him, he regarded me as a weakling. Not knowing the ways
of departments he would say to others : ' I can always wind
the Director-General round my little finger ' without realising,
and perhaps not caring, that within an hour the remark would
be repeated to me by more than one person.

Much criticism of Dick Crossman was a result partly of
political intrigue and partly of the over-lapping of temporary
departments which were full of enthusiasm and eager to take
on jobs other than their own. Dick sometimes invited trouble
by pushing his own policy in his broadcasts. As several Members
of Parliament knew German and listened in, this form of free-
lancing provoked Parliamentary questions. In war-time Ministers
could persuade Members to withdraw awkward questions on
the ground that publicity would help the enemy, and I remember
vividly when the existence of the Political Warfare Executive,
known familiarly as the ' Pee-Wees ', was first mentioned in
the House of Commons in September, 1941. The Prime Minister
had said as little as possible and had indicated that for reasons
of secrecy questions should not be raised. A Conservative M.P.,
Mr de la Bere, challenged him : " What is the difference between
a secret question and an awkward question ? " At once Winston
Churchill replied : " One is a danger to the country ; the other
is a nuisance to the Government." Good humour was restored,
and there were no serious questions.

Nevertheless, Ministers did not like having to kill questions
about war-time departments and relied on the senior officials
to ensure that policy should be followed and that there should
be no reason for complaints.

When the Americans came into the war and were preparing
for the landings in North Africa, they were eager to set up their
own army psychological warfare units. As the Americans were

new to this adjunct to warfare, we sent to Algiers a small but experienced team headed by Dick Crossman. I was ill at the time, and the appointment was made by my deputy Dallas Brooks.

I was sorry to lose Dick, because, with all his defects as a civil servant, he was the outstanding figure in P.W.E. Nevertheless, the appointment was the right one. Doubtless, he would still play his own hand and take risks on policy, but he would and, indeed, did teach the Americans more than any American or other Englishman could have taught them.

In Algiers he found himself in happier surroundings. He was remote from his political critics in London. His Minister was Mr Harold Macmillan and Mr Macmillan's right-hand man was Roger Makins, a fellow Wykehamist. Bob McClure, the American Brigadier-General in charge of the Psychological Warfare Division, was delighted with Dick and, whenever he came to London, sang Dick's praises to me. Later he took him with S.H.A.E.F. to Germany.

When the war in Europe was over, Dick came to see me and raised immediately the problem of his standing as a Parliamentary candidate for one of the Coventry divisions. I gave him the Treasury circular from which it was clear that he would have to resign on or before the day on which the date of the election was announced.

Although at this period most people were happy that the war against Germany was over, Dick then proceeded to do a typical Crossman act. He had been badly treated. There had been no confidence in him. London—meaning his colleagues—had adopted a dog-in-the-manger attitude. The flow was non-stop, but, as I refused to show annoyance, he calmed down and we began to talk about the election. In the end he went away quite happily, confident that he would win his seat in Coventry.

I did not hear from him again until, bursting with an 18,000 majority at Coventry, he came to see me on August 1, 1945. All the gloom of the past had vanished, and he was full of charm, benevolence, and, of course, energy. He was even good enough to ask me what line he ought to take when he took his seat in the House.

As he had already told me that he was not likely to have any job in connection with the Foreign Office because he was not a ' Bevin boy ', I advised him to lie low for six months or so, study all the rules of the House, and make himself master of one subject before attempting to speak. I suggested that entering Parliament was like going to school again, and new boys should tread warily.

For a few years I saw nothing of him, but I followed his career with interest. As always, he was full of energy, but not of restraint or caution. In the *New Statesman* there appeared articles criticising the Foreign Office for disbanding the whole organisation of our foreign propaganda. If the articles did not come from Dick's pen, the information came from his brain. There was much wisdom in the articles, but Ernie Bevin was Foreign Secretary and the right hand of Mr Attlee.

Dick had not exaggerated when he told me that he was not a ' Bevin boy '. Soon after the Labour Government took power, I had a long talk with Hector McNeil whom I had known from his journalistic days. I asked him why the Labour bosses were so foolish as not to give a post to Dick Crossman who had more brains than all the Parliamentary Under-Secretaries put together. Hector shook his head. " That young man goes too fast for Attlee and Bevin. As long as these two are at the top, I cannot see Crossman getting office."

Dick, however, did not seem to mind. In order to improve his knowledge of foreign affairs, he travelled as fast as his thoughts. He studied the Palestine problem on the spot. He cast an eye over Czechoslovakia and sought information from Zdeněk Fierlinger, a former Socialist who double-crossed Beneš and his own Party and, by jumping at the right moment on to the Communist band-wagon, not only saved his skin, but also landed himself into the most comfortable job in the Government.

More recently Dick went even further afield and flew to China for a week to study the communes and, on his return, was able, I think, to breakfast in Peking in the morning and sleep in his own bed in London on the same night.

His enterprise is to be commended. In these days it is more important than ever for Members of Parliament to see something of our changing world ; but two cautions are necessary. Members of Parliament can rarely spend a long time in one country. They must not assume that because they have spent a week in

Nyasaland or Burma, that they have an expert knowledge of these countries. Above all, they must not go out with an *idée fixe* that Herr X is a stout Conservative or Monsieur Y is a sound Socialist and will give all the facts and the proper picture that they require.

When the Conservatives came back to power in October, 1951, there was considerable demand, especially among retired generals and officials, for more and better efforts to counter the rampant propaganda of the Soviet Communists. Early in February, 1952, I was invited by the Royal United Service Institute to take the chair at a lecture on political warfare by Richard Crossman, O.B.E., M.P.

Having lectured at the Institute myself, I felt that the audience of senior officers would be severely critical of Dick Crossman, who had believed in ' good Germans ' and had been against ' unconditional surrender '. Moreover, some of the generals like the late ' Q ' Martel, who was sure to be present, had very definite ideas of their own about political warfare.

I therefore decided to accept and to get into touch with Dick. On February 20, I gave him luncheon, before the lecture, at the Carlton Grill. It was a lovely sunny day with the first breath of spring in the wind. Optimism was high and rose still higher with an excellent bottle of Liebfraumilch. Dick was full of confidence. The best part of his work during the war had been done with the armed forces. He was not afraid of generals.

The lecture was a brilliant success. It surprised even me. At one moment he almost persuaded me that P.W.E. was the most peaceful and the best-run organisation in the war and that I myself was Dick's greatest friend. His account of the aims and possibilities of political warfare was exactly what the soldiers wanted to know and what they believed was right, but had not been able to define it with the same precision as an expert like Dick who already knew all the snags.

At the end of the lecture there was more applause than cross-questioning. So pleased were the officers that they invited Dick to give another lecture.

I went away well satisfied with life and wondering more than ever why Patrick Gordon-Walker, who as a member of the B.B.C. European Services worked under P.W.E. in the war, had been made a Labour Minister, while Dick Crossman was left on the side-lines. The answer, I think, is that Patrick Gordon-Walker is a conformist. He has the team spirit. Dick Crossman is an individualist and a kind of political lone wolf. He is now between fifty and fifty-five, an age which can still be called young for Ministers and, in 1945 I would have backed him heavily to win ministerial rank.

To-day I am not so sure. Like many men with brilliant minds, Dick Crossman tends to be impatient and, as Irving Kristol wrote of him in the April, 1956, number of *Encounter*, " one hesitates to agree with him, because one is never certain that he agrees with himself." He is never likely to go to the Foreign Office. If Labour had won the 1959 election, he would almost certainly have been Minister of Pensions.

It may therefore be that his greatest contribution to the Labour Party will be his skill as a propagandist. In this political art he has no rival. He has the skill of saying much in very little space. He hits hard, and each punch finds its mark. His language is direct and simple enough for anyone but a complete moron to understand. Here is an example of his method :

' Consider, for instance, the mental contortions of the loyal, docile Tory since Colonel Nasser grabbed the Suez Canal :

(1) He applauds the decision to attack Suez.

(2) He applauds the decision to stop halfway.

(3) He applauds the decision to replace Sir Anthony Eden with Mr Macmillan rather than with Mr Butler, believing that Mr Butler ratted on the Eden policy inside the Cabinet.

(4) He applauds Mr Macmillan when he decides to abandon the Eden policy and do a deal with Colonel Nasser.'

Not for nothing did Dick Crossman spend the five years from 1939 to 1945 in political warfare. They changed him from a don into a first-class propagandist and journalist. If he can restrain the more visible characteristics of his ambition, he may yet go very high.

CHAPTER NINE

Empire Jack

'After me cometh a Builder. Tell him, I too have known.'

ALTHOUGH I have spent the best years of my life in Europe, I have an intrinsic interest in the British Empire. My maternal grandfather, one of a family of sixteen, emigrated to New Zealand when my mother was born. He prospered sufficiently to enable him to come home to save the family distillery and farm. I still have relatives in New Zealand, and since the Second World War my nephew Rab, better known as a 'rugger' international than as a scholar, has become head-master of Wanganui in the South Island. My paternal grandfather, who inherited money, was an Empire dreamer and travelled round it in leisurely fashion. He took his wife with him, and an aunt of mine was born in Cape Town and my father in Montreal. Apart from these parental heritages, I was for several years very close to Lord Beaverbrook and from 1929 to 1932 took an exciting and strenuous part in his Empire Crusade.

Long before this, however, I had met the original Empire Jack, and of all places in Moscow. His original name was John Griffiths. His father was of Welsh descent. His mother was an Avery of London, and John, ever afterwards to be called Jack, was born in Somerset. He was a fine, tall, strapping youth who developed into a good-looking and powerful man with dark hair and moustache and a magnetic personality.

As a youth he was restless and unsettled. Adventure was in his blood from the day of his birth. By the time he was seventeen, Kipling was coming into popularity, and Jack Griffiths could not be held back any longer. On his own initiative he signed on as a seaman in a wind-jammer bound for Australia. In a very real sense he went as a hand before the mast.

Australia was a lucky choice for his venture, because, soon after his arrival, he found a billet with an engineering firm. It was no desk job. He was sent far and wide over the country to take part in the practical work. He learnt it as if he had been born for this special task. Engineering and tunnelling were to make him and, in the end, to destroy him.

From Australia he went to South Africa and was soon involved in his first war. In 1896 the Matabeles rose against the white man, and Jack Griffiths, then only twenty-five, raised and commanded a body of scouts. Three years earlier Major Wilson of Fochabers with some twenty British soldiers had been surprised by a horde of Matabeles. They fought bravely till their ammunition was finished. The last to fall was Wilson who, as a Matabele warrior afterwards described him, " fought on, a grim smile on his face and the fire of a devil in his eyes. He took guns and bullets from his fallen brothers, and fought on to the end. After his cartridges were finished and he could find no more, he stood —silent and alone—waiting for us to come in and make the final thrust."

Jack Griffiths never forgot ' Wilson's Last Stand '. He told the story to me in Moscow. He, too, could fight with a grim smile and the fire of a devil in his eyes. To the very last day of his life he clung to one belief : a nation which has lost its willingness to sacrifice has lost its will-power to survive.

Before he left South Africa the Boer War broke out in 1899. Jack Griffiths volunteered at once and served as a squadron-leader in the South African Field Force. Later, he became adjutant to Lord Roberts and captain of his body-guard. He took part in some of the worst battles like the Modder River, was present at Cronje's surrender at Paardeberg, and had three mentions in despatches.

When the war was over, Griffiths settled down to make a fortune as an engineering contractor. He travelled all over the world, building railways, bridges and dams in Portuguese West Africa, in Canada, and in South America. His travels had increased his almost fanatical enthusiasm for the Empire. Now a rich man, he had become senior partner in the firm of Norton, Griffiths, Bruce Marriott & Co. and in 1910 he entered the House of Commons as M.P. for Wednesbury, a constituency

which he represented till 1918, when in the December election
of that year he switched to Wandsworth Central.

It was in the House that he received the sobriquet of ' Empire
Jack '. Very properly he regarded it as a great compliment and
never did he lose an opportunity of proposing and supporting
projects for strengthening the ties of Empire. One of his ideas
was the founding of a special town in Canada for British emigrants. Unfortunately his most active period as a politician
coincided first with a Liberal administration and, later, with the
First World War.

Nevertheless, the war was to bring to Jack Griffiths fame and
high honours. There was a good deal of Winston Churchill in
him, and, if he did not precede Churchill's habit of having a
special tray of documents marked ' Action To-Day ', it was
because Empire Jack had no use for trays and always acted at
once. Indeed, government offices and especially the War Office
nearly drove him demented.

As soon as the war started in August, 1914, Jack Griffiths
put an advertisement in the *Evening Standard* requesting old
colonial soldiers who wished to serve their country to come
to his office at No. 3 Central Buildings, Westminster. Hundreds
came at once. After what Empire Jack would have called official
obstruction, Lord Kitchener allowed him to raise the second
regiment of King Edward's Horse. It bore no relationship to the
first regiment. Indeed, it was the only new irregular regiment
allowed, a fact which speaks much for Empire Jack's persistence
and obstinacy. He organised and equipped the regiment at his
own expense.

This contribution to the war was just a beginning. In point
of fact, while the men of his regiment were training, Empire
Jack became very restless. He could never remain inactive, and
soon he had a new and brilliant idea. When he realised that
trench warfare was likely to develop into a permanency throughout the war, he quickly made up his mind that mining would
be one of the most useful weapons. After studying the nature
of the soil in which trenches were being built, he was quite
certain that he was right.

His firm, which had been carrying on in a small way, was
building part of the Manchester Ship Canal in very much the

same kind of clay soil. The engineers were using a method called clay-kicking or workers on the cross. The men were strapped on to pieces of wood. Then, lying on their backs, they dug the clay with their feet. This enabled them to make very small tunnels with great speed.

Once Jack Griffiths had a fixed idea in his head, he did not leave it there. ' Action To-Day ' operated at once. In the excellent notice of Empire Jack in the *Dictionary of National Biography*, there appears this sequence of sentences : ' In December, 1914, he (Norton-Griffiths) suggested to the War Office that coal-miners and other under-ground miners should be specially en-listed for military mining purposes. In February, 1915, he was authorised to enlist a party of these workers for service in France. . . .' One might assume from this statement that the War Office acted with commendable speed. Indeed, many officials, both civil and military, might say that the action was speedy.

This was not Empire Jack's view. He had the greatest difficulty in persuading the War Office even to listen to his proposals, and an ocular demonstration of the method seemed to create more amusement than conviction. Eventually the scheme was listed as ' Moles ' and was put into a pigeon-hole.

Action came quickly when early in February, 1915, the Germans mined and blew up a trench under the 16th Lancers. On February 13 the War Office called for Empire Jack. He rushed up to Manchester, selected, enlisted and equipped his men. On February 17 they were in the trenches, never having carried a rifle or done a drill in their lives. It was Empire Jack at his typical best. And there were even better things to come.

Once in action he was not the kind of man to be denied, not because he blustered and bullied, but because he had charm in even greater abundance than strength of character. The com-bination made him irresistible. He acquired authority to take any man with mining experience out of any regiment he liked. He trained and disciplined his motley collection of mining men and put great heart into them, partly because he himself worked harder than they did, but mainly because he so obviously enjoyed the task and believed so fervently in its value to the war.

Results were not long in coming. His job took him to every front, and he never spared himself. The first success, however, came in France when he mined the sinister Hill Sixty. His effort certainly surprised the Germans.

Elated by this minor triumph, Griffiths turned his mind to greater things. Very early on he realised that one of the great nuisances to the Franco-British armies was the Messines Ridge. It was a formidable obstacle, but by now he had a force of some 25,000 experts, formed in twenty-five Imperial and seven Overseas Companies. He had great faith both in them and in himself, and he was quietly confident that he could blow the whole Ridge into the air. He worked out his own scheme and had it approved by General Harvey. Once again, however, the highest authority—this time G.H.Q.—would not look at what they considered the fantastic idea of a crack-pot. Griffiths might be a great civil engineer, but war was war, and civilians did not understand war.

Griffiths, however, could be as obstinate as any general, and after endless persuasion it was G.H.Q. which gave way and finally approved the project in January, 1916. The crack-pot's scheme was, in fact, a marvellous and almost miraculous conception. The miners worked literally like moles. Tunnels were made miles long to avoid detection, and for the final explosion Griffiths used ammonal in quantities never previously conceived, let alone employed.

The explosion took place on June 7, 1917, and, as Griffiths had predicted, it was a complete success. A valuable vantage point was denied to the enemy, and in the Allied trenches there was much rejoicing. Alas ! the man who by his foresight and determination had planned the project was not there to see the Ridge go up in the air. For once, however, the War Office did the handsome thing. They invited him to go over to France and see the results of his work at Messines, and he was a proud man when he saw what his vision had accomplished. He had already received three mentions in despatches. Now he was given a D.S.O. and was promoted to the temporary rank of Lieutenant-Colonel. Hitherto he had been working as a Major attached to the Engineer-in-Chief. To-day the promotion seems niggardly, but in the First World War the professional soldiers were very jealous of rank and believed genuinely that the top ranks should be held by regular officers.

With his mining companies now working smoothly, Jack Griffiths was in great demand by the Ministry of Munitions which was in need of an expert who knew what was wanted at the Front and how to get it quickly at home. Griffiths accepted the job, but before he had taken it up he was summoned to the War Office by General Macdonagh who was then Director of Military Intelligence. The date was autumn, 1916, and the subject was Rumania, which from the beginning of the war had given a headache to the ministers and diplomats of the Allies. There were two schools of thought : one which believed that it was better to leave Rumania as a neutral state in the hope that Germany would not occupy the country and the other which wanted ardently to bring Rumania into the war in order to strengthen the left wing of the long Russian line.

I have told in *Memoirs of a British Agent* how a copy of Marshal Pau's report on Rumania came into my hands in Moscow. It gave a devastating picture of conditions in Rumania. The Marshal thought nothing of the Rumanian army and less of Allied diplomacy in Bucharest. On the strength of this report I became a strong supporter of the neutral school, and on October 15, 1915, I wrote : ' We are trying to bring Rumania into the war. Time will show the result, but I fear the Russian military failure has impressed the Balkans more than anything else.'

By the autumn of 1916, however, it was clear that, mainly as the result of Allied mistakes, Rumania would soon be occupied by the Germans. This was the subject matter of General Macdonagh's secret talk with Griffiths. Rumania was rich in oil and corn ; Germany was short of both. It was of the utmost importance that the oil and corn must be denied to Germany. There was only one way to do this successfully. The oil and corn must be destroyed. Would Griffiths take on the job ?

" What regiments do I take ? " asked Empire Jack.

" You go alone," replied Macdonagh, " but you may take your batman."

Just because he gave orders to others and expected them to be obeyed, he, too, never hesitated to obey the order of a superior officer. Otherwise, he would have asked for a higher rank than that of a temporary Lieutenant-Colonel for a job which not only was of supreme importance but also was to bring him into close contact with the highest Rumanian authorities from Queen Marie downwards.

Every British subject going to Rumania had to travel via Norway, Sweden and Finland and then via St Petersburg and Moscow. Such few travellers as there were had important missions and, because of the difficulties of transport from Moscow to Rumania, most of them stayed a night or more in Moscow. In this manner I met Empire Jack both on his way to and from Rumania. Sir George Buchanan had requested me to do everything possible for this British officer who arrived in mufti, and, although I did not know the nature of his mission until his return journey, I gave him dinner and did all I could to make him comfortable. My first impression was of his immense strength, and I reflected what a wonderful ' rugger ' forward England or Wales had lost in this powerful man who had left home so young and who, like myself, had been a wanderer in many lands.

When he came back, I was in St Petersburg, and it was with the greatest difficulty that any of us could drag his story out of him. The Rumanians, a very polite race, had been helpful at first, but when they realised that he had come to *destroy* utterly both their oil and their corn they adopted delaying tactics which in the circumstances were perhaps not unnatural. They shilly-shallied for a few days, but they were up against the wrong man. Griffiths went straight to Queen Marie, got her backing, and more or less did the job single-handed. He took five engineers from the Anglo-Rumanian Oil Company, gave them commissions, and fitted them out in any kind of uniform he could find for their safety if they were caught by the Germans. With some valuable help from Prince Bibesco the six of them tackled the oil-wells. Apparently they had more difficulty in getting them to burn than the ordinary mortal would imagine. However, all went well, and Empire Jack, handling a huge sledge-hammer as if it were a feather-duster, smashed all the drilling machinery he could find and shoved the broken parts down the drills to the wells. Soon the whole district was as black as night, and the belching smoke held back the Germans who were approaching rapidly. Working day and night, the six stalwarts finished the job in ten days.

After this was well and truly done, Griffiths turned his attention to the supplies of wheat and maize. Here again he had the support of Queen Marie and General Avarescu. This time the job was easier, and more in line with his war work. He tackled the stores of corn as if it were the Messines Ridge and blew them up into the four winds.

When his oil and corn mission was accomplished, the Rumanians, who had never seen even a German get down to work so quickly, begged Griffiths to re-organise their transport which was in a state of permanent chaos. Griffiths wisely refused. He was now eager to get home. Returning the same way by which he had come, he spent a day or two in St Petersburg. His great exploit was now public property, and, although he loathed the demolition of materials which provided food and heat to innocent people and detested the nickname of ' The Angel of Destruction ', which was afterwards given to him, he was hailed everywhere as a hero. The Tsar sent for him, complimented him on a job well done, and decorated him with the Order of St Vladimir with Crossed Swords. The date was early in March, 1917, and was the last day that the Tsar spent in St Petersburg before the outbreak of what is still called by Russians the February Revolution, although by our calendar it began on March 12. Empire Jack was therefore the last officer of any army to be decorated by the Emperor Nicholas the Second.

On his arrival in England Griffiths was given a magnificent welcome. The War Cabinet and Mr Balfour, then Secretary of State for Foreign Affairs, had already congratulated him on his triumphant feats, and he received the K.C.B. and the Grand Star of Rumania, and was appointed Officer of the Legion of Honour. In 1917 he had assumed by deed-poll the additional name of Norton. When his K.C.B. was awarded, he was still in Rumania, and General Macdonagh, who had conceived the idea and chosen the man, sent him this signal : ' Lieutenant-Colonel Sir John Norton-Griffiths, K.C.B. Very many congratulations on your wife's honour.'

When the war was over, Norton-Griffiths went back to his engineering firm and to his constituency. It was from his political work and from his never-flagging interest and belief in the Commonwealth that he acquired the title of Empire Jack. Before he switched to Wandsworth Central in the khaki election of December, 1918, he had been for ten years member for Wednesbury. It was a tough apprenticeship, but he thrived on it. He always fought his elections with an enormous map of the Empire behind him. He made many supporters, but in a rough constituency like Wednesbury he had his own way of dealing with hecklers. If a heckler became really offensive, off came Empire Jack's coat, up went his fists, and very rarely did this strong man need to use them. The meetings were sometimes rough, but he won even the admiration, if not the votes, of his opponents. It was they who christened him Hell Fire Jack, and both he and they were proud of it.

In 1922 he was created a baronet. Its conferment was a reward for his political services, and two years later he resigned from Parliament. His expenditure on raising regiments and on Empire schemes and, not least, in his open-handed generosity in founding and helping to finance organisations like the Comrades of the Great War, had cut rather heavily into his pre-war fortune, and the time had come for him to attend more closely to his businesss.

In February, 1929, the Egyptian Government decided to raise the height of the Assuan Dam by twenty-three feet and invited firms to submit tenders. Norton-Griffiths' firm got the contract, and Norton-Griffiths himself went out to the Nile to superintend the work. He was then in his fifty-ninth year, and still a man of fine physique. In all parts of the world he had been remarkably successful in handling men. The Egyptians, however, eluded him, and he was not the first or the last person to find them shifty and that they rarely lived up to their promises. In particular, Norton-Griffiths found it hard to get on with the resident Egyptian engineering inspectors who, he thought, were unnecessarily obstructive and who he suspected were delaying the work on all sorts of pretentions in order to make their own jobs last longer.

Almost from the start of operations there was bad feeling,

and on September 21, 1930, the British firm stopped work on the ground that obstruction by incompetent Egyptian engineers and officials was delaying the task to such an extent that it could not be continued.

The Egyptian Government hit back as hard as it could. It complained that the work had not been carried out with sufficient speed, because the British firm had not sufficient money and hinted that financial stringency was the real cause of the stoppage.

Events now moved rapidly to the final tragedy. Norton-Griffiths was not the man to let the Egyptian roughnecks dictate to him and, in a written communication, he declared that the stoppage had nothing to do with finance. He also stated that obstruction by the Egyptians had rendered it difficult for his firm to spend further money on the scheme.

Six days after the original stoppage, on September 27, 1930, John Norton-Griffiths was found dead in a boat close to the Casino Hotel at San Stefano, a sea-side resort of Alexandria. A revolver lay by his side. He had shot himself, presumably in a moment of despair. He was a man who could not stand failure, and by their delaying tactics the Egyptians had driven him to the final act.

It was a sad end to a splendid life which had been lived to the full both in war and in peace. He had rendered great services to his country during three wars, and I cannot help feeling that, if there had been no wars, he would have been so successful as an engineer that he could well have placed the Empire on a sounder and stronger foundation than it was in his time or is to-day. But as long as the English peoples of the world continue to speak the same language, they will remember this great-hearted man who first conceived the splendid vision of a united British Commonwealth, and who earned for himself for all time the unforgettable title of ' Empire Jack '.

BOOK II

THE FOREIGN SCENE

' What experience and history teach is this—
that people and governments have never learnt
anything from history.'

CHAPTER ONE

The Last Days of Clemenceau

' Show them plainly that you are not crushed by your
afflictions. Those who face calamity without flinching and
who offer the most energetic resistance, these, be they states
or individuals, are the truest heroes.'

Pericles

IN his novel, *Les Taxis de la Marne*, Jean Dutourd wrote the
following prescription for the recovery of his country :

' In order to re-make the political map of Europe, we need
a phlegmatic cardinal believing neither in man nor in science
and fully convinced that in a thousand years human nature will
be exactly the same as it was in the reign of Clovis.'

In the post-war decline of Western Europe, Britain has had
one great advantage over France. In each of the two world
wars she produced a great leader : in the first war David Lloyd
George and in the second Winston Churchill. In the Second
World War France lacked both military and political leaders of
genius. In the First World War it produced Georges Clemenceau.
When I look back on those sun-lit days of November, 1918,
when all France and, indeed, the whole alliance of Europe and
the United States poured out their gratitude to the gnarled and
obstinate old man who by sheer insistence saved his country
and ours, I think that to-day France needs, not a cardinal, but
another Clemenceau, to lead them out of the political morass
in which they have been too long embedded.

Père la Victoire they called him, and I have often thought of
writing a parallel biographical sketch of Clemenceau and
Churchill. Some characteristics were common : the same resolu-
tion, the same defiance in defeat, and, curiously enough, the
same easy capacity for emotional tears. Both were men of quick
decision. Churchill had his special tray marked ' Action To-Day '
and, doubtless, appreciated Clemenceau's ' of all the faults
a man can commit only one is infamous—inaction '. Like

Churchill, Clemenceau allowed no one to talk to him for more than ten minutes. There were, too, the common gifts of tongue and pen and the magnetism of leadership which attracts devoted followers almost in spite of themselves. Clemenceau, a much more rancorous and uncharitable man than Churchill, had in 1885 attacked very violently Jules Ferry for the allegedly unjustifiable evacuation of a town in Cochin-China by the French troops. Although Ferry was not responsible, Clemenceau would not end the feud and so vehemently accused his opponent that a maniac emptied his revolver into Ferry's chest. Although Ferry was not killed, a bullet near the heart ended his career and shortened his life.

When Clemenceau took office on November 13, 1917, he invited Abel Ferry, Jules Ferry's only son, to join his Ministry. Abel Ferry refused, but agreed to be the great man's Commissioner at the Front. Although Abel Ferry was killed two months before the Armistice, he served Clemenceau with the highest loyalty and increasing admiration.

There was in both Churchill and Clemenceau the same complete indifference to danger and the same itch to go to the front and see what was really happening. Churchill was more interested in discussing strategic problems with generals. Clemenceau's preference was for the men. He talked with them not only to encourage them but also to extract information from them. What they said, he felt, was more important to the political situation than all the military reports put together, and it was typical of him that in his final book, *Grandeurs et Misères d'une Victoire* he should have dedicated his last chapter to the ' Unknown Soldier '.

There were, however, great differences between the two men. In spite of his American mother, to whom, doubtless, he owes his remarkable energy and strong constitution, Winston Churchill was an Englishman through and through with a line of notable ancestors behind him. Clemenceau was not a Frenchman. He was a Vendéen who believed the family tradition that the Clemenceaus were descended from a band of Mongols left behind in a Vendée village after one of the Mongol invasions of Europe. His enemies liked to attribute to his Mongol descent the yellow parchment texture of his skin, his features, and his

cruelty. To be a true Vendéen meant to Clemenceau to be suspicious of all Frenchmen, to be radical in regard to privileges
of all kinds, and, above all, to be anti-clerical. Throughout his
life he carried his disbelief in the existence of God to absurd
lengths. After qualifying as a doctor, he spent several years in
the United States where in 1868–69 he taught French and riding
in a seminary for young ladies in Greenwich, Connecticut. One
of his pupils fell in love with him and he with her. She wanted a
religious marriage. " Choose between God and me," said
Clemenceau, as he was about to leave for Europe. She chose
Clemenceau, and they were married in New York. It was not a
very happy marriage. Clemenceau despised most men, but
especially those who were dominated by women. No wife, I
think, would have been wholly happy with him. The marriage,
however, bore two daughters and a son.

Again, at the greatest moment of his life, when a temporarily
grateful nation unanimously wanted him to be President, his
atheism ruined his chances. He refused to attend the victory
Te Deum at Notre Dame and forbade his Ministers to do so.
With the presidency virtually a free gift, he deliberately went
out of his way to affront and insult the Catholics, and in the
election he was beaten by the mediocre Deschanel. Patriotic
Frenchmen shed tears. Barrès described his defeat as the triumph
of Parliamentary intrigue over the will of the people, and Lloyd
George said : " This time it is not the English who have burnt
Joan of Arc."

Here again Churchill and Clemenceau, the artificers of victory,
seem to have shared the same fate of ingratitude at the hands of
their people. Churchill, however, did not expect defeat and was
disappointed by it. He mistook the plaudits of the multitude for
favours to come, whereas they were only a tribute to what he
had achieved. During the war Labour propaganda had spread
far and wide the slogan : ' Churchill is the man for the war
but not for the peace.'

Clemenceau seemed almost to despise the honour of the
presidency and to throw it away on purpose. He pleaded old
age and he was then in his eightieth year. But obstinacy was his
undoing and he could never master it. As far back as 1893, he
wrote to a lady who had shown sympathy for the deaths of

Maximilian and his wife in Mexico : ' You think I am ferocious ;
what is far worse is that I am intractable.' It is not certain, but
Churchill would probably have come to the top even if there
had been no war. It is quite certain that, had there been no war,
Clemenceau would have been forgotten or remembered merely
as a tiresome politician who wrecked Ministries and created
nothing.

Churchill made no disguise of his disappointment. By his
friends Clemenceau was said to have taken his rejection with
apparent indifference. Nevertheless, the wounds remained, and
he put the salt of bitterness in them in order that they should
be remembered. In October, 1933, Admiral Lacage, a reliable
witness and a great admirer, wrote these words :

' The year before his death (in 1928) Clemenceau said to me :
" I am disgusted by my country and by my compatriots." There
was no bitterness in this statement pronounced in a tone of
detached, lofty judgment which was without appeal. I protested :
" How can you say such a thing, Mr Prime Minister, when you
are the living incarnation of the country ? " Clemenceau replied :
" I saw the French during the war. They are no longer the same.
Those who at the height of the torment were so ardent, so
generous, so brave, and always ready for total sacrifice, are now
cowards led by cowards. And all this has happened with a
rapidity which has stupefied me and alarmed me." '

Old men's words ? Who knows ? They were prophetic of
France in the Second World War. Sooner or later they come
true to all nations.

It was not the first time that he had given way to despair.
Although he was a French citizen and loved *all* France much
more than he affected, France very nearly lost him. In the early
'nineties he was almost down and out. He had lost his seat in
the Palais-Bourbon. His journalism was at a low ebb. He wrote
to his old friend, Charles Edmond : ' I am misunderstood in
my home life, betrayed by my friends, deserted by my Party,
ignored by my electors, suspected by my country. *La Justice*
has closed its doors. Creditors besiege my house. I am en-
cumbered with debts and have nothing more, nothing, nothing.'

He was determined to go to the United States and become a
naturalised American. He ran into M. Sarraut, the owner of

La Dépêche, who offered him more journalistic work. The mood passed and, again like Churchill and yet so different, he took up his pen to make a living until he could ride the storms of politics once more.

Clemenceau was in his seventy-ninth year when he withdrew from politics and, indeed, from the social world. He kept on his flat in the Rue Franklin in Paris. He went to India and to the United States, for since his early manhood he had never forgotten the joy of his first journey abroad. In India *le Tigre* shot two tigers and missed two. In the United States he lectured, was cheered, and received huge sums, all of which he handed over to the victims of the war.

His political work, however, was over, and he refused every offer but one to return to it. Graciously he accepted the post of mayor of Mouilleron, the Vendéen commune in which he was born. There remained the pen, and, again like Churchill, he spent the autumn of his life in writing books, including an excellent biography of his great painter friend, Claude Monet.

With the first warmth of spring he would withdraw to his beloved Vendée where he knew almost every inhabitant by his or her Christian name. In my youthful years in France I hero-worshipped two heroes whom I never got to know personally. They were Pierre Loti and Georges Clemenceau. In Paris I was introduced to Loti, and it was his books which drove me to the East. In 1906 I was staying at Denain for the week-end with a soccer-playing French friend, the son of a big coal-owner. It was in the middle of the great strike after the Courrières disaster where many miners died after an underground explosion. Surrounded by French cavalry, we were kept indoors while the strikers yelled threats and hurled stones. It was an unpleasant situation. Then the Minister of the Interior arrived. He paid no attention to the stones. He silenced the threats. The angry rioters listened, and in twenty minutes the strike was over. The Minister of the Interior was Clemenceau.

When he retired to the Vendée for the best part of each year, I at least was favoured to follow in his steps. Millicent, Duchess of Sutherland, a great admirer, used to go sometimes in the spring and early summer to Les Sables d'Olonnes, a popular summer resort for Parisian *petite bourgeoisie*, but out of season a most attractive little fishing village. Its great attraction was that Clemenceau's little country cottage was within easy walking distance from the town.

I went often to it, although by the time I came to Les Sables d'Olonnes Clemenceau was dead. Here was a gulf between the austerity of a Clemenceau and the luxury of a Churchill. The little house at the tiny village of St Vincent-sur-Jard was nothing but a simple fisherman's cottage. Its official name was Bel-Ezbat, but the locals and Clemenceau himself called it La Bicocque. Its walls were almost lapped at full tide by the Atlantic and, not long before my first visit, the tiny garden had been badly damaged by the sea.

The little cottage was kept by Brabant, who had been Clemenceau's chauffeur for twenty-four years, and his wife. Both were admirers, and I plagued them almost daily with questions. In the cottage itself I did not know what surprised me more : the austerity of the bedroom or the ghastliness of the reception room or drawing-room. The latter was a jumble of bad taste. There was a carpet from Rabat given by Lyautey, a pair of china dogs presented by the Koreans, and an extraordinary mixture of bad French furniture. He had names for the Korean dogs : *Richesse* for one which looked like a Rothschild, and *Sagesse* for the other which resembled Pasteur, one of his heroes.

On the other hand, the kitchen, which also served as a dining-room, was a period piece with a fine old table and dresser, old pots and a Louis XIV watering-can. Incongruous only was the cast of his hand covered with the glove which he wore to hide his eczema. The glove, of course, was also part of the cast.

The bedroom, however, was the room which revealed the real Clemenceau and seemed to retain something of his personality. It was simpler and more puritanical than a schoolboy's cubicle. It was of course much larger, but the bed was of hard wood and had no spring mattress. It was abnormally high, and I asked Brabant how the old gentleman managed to climb into it. " Ah," said the chauffeur, " there's a story to that bed. Monsieur le Président watched the whole construction. When it was finished, he lay down in it and rose at once in a rage. The carpenter trembled because he had made it low, thinking that, if he made it high, old men like Clemenceau could not climb into it. But Clemenceau's anger did not come from the insult to his age. He was furious because he could not see the sea. The bed, therefore, had to be jacked up till he could see the whole seascape." And what a view it is with the Atlantic studded by the Ile de Ré, where the convicts used to be kept before being embarked for Devil's Island, and alive with every imaginable colour of sail, with brown, orange, green and cobalt blue predominating, as the sardine fishing fleet takes to sea from the port of Sables d'Olonnes.

A tiger-skin, a trophy from his Indian voyage after the war, covered his bed. On the skin lay his death-mask. There were other trophies of his rifle on the walls. But everything else in the room was simplicity itself. The hand wash-basin was tiny and still held his last piece of soap, his small sponge, and his hair-wash. By the window, not far from his bed, was his desk. At once I was all interest. It was on this desk that he had written part at least of *Grandeurs et Misères d'une Victoire*. I examined it carefully. It was the cheapest, simplest desk that I had ever seen. It consisted of a plain board which could be pulled out on a hinge from below the window and was kept up by two iron rods. During my visits it was kept out. On it were Clemenceau's ink-pot, the quill pens which he always used, and his sand-box which he preferred to blotting-paper. Handy to his right was a small book-case with Michelet's *History of France*, Camille Jullian's *History of Gaul;* and the works of Voltaire. Lying open on the desk was an English book entitled *The Man Who Didn't Win The War*. The sub-title was 'An Exposure of Lloyd Georgism by Centurion. Published by the National Review.'

In spite of the superb view from that window, I must assume that the old Tiger nursed to the end his great hates, among which Lloyd George, Poincaré, Briand and Foch came high, although Foch was much more unfair to Clemenceau than Clemenceau ever was to him. After all, he could claim with some right that he had made Foch.

And yet for all his bitterness and obstinacy there was just one tiny piece of that hard-frozen heart that sometimes thawed. He hated all churches and especially the Catholic Church : yet the best of all the true Clemenceau stories concerned a Catholic. The window of his study in his ground-floor flat in the Rue

Franklin in Paris was obscured from the sun by a tree which grew in the garden of a Jesuit priest, Father Trégard, who lived close by. Clemenceau asked him to lop off some of the branches. The priest cut the whole tree down, and Clemenceau thanked him in the following letter :

' Mon père, I must thank you for the service you have done for me. I am very grateful. You will not be offended by my calling you " Mon père ", since after all you are the father of my days.' Not to be outdone, the priest replied : ' My son, what would one not do for Père la Victoire who saved France. . . . Do not be surprised at the title which I have given you in calling you " My son ", for I have just revealed Heaven to you.'

Clemenceau was moved by this kindness and, when the priest was dying, Clemenceau went to see him.

But for Clemenceau himself there was no Christian funeral and by his express wish only a few Vendéen villagers and his nearest relatives attended the burial.

I must have been one of the earliest British subjects to see the grave. Clemenceau died on November 24, 1929, and almost exactly four months later to the day I was staying with Millicent Sutherland, at her monastery house at Juigné-sur-Loire near Angers. She was a fervent admirer of Clemenceau and, with spring already in the air, she was eager to visit the great man's grave.

The southern sun shone on our little adventure. As we passed from Anjou into La Vendée the landscape changed. The soft plains and stately poplars had given way to hedges, stone dykes, undulating hills, and swift-running streams. Yellow gorse ran riot over grassy banks. Winter aconite stood out like yellow studs in a carpet of green. Peach blossom decked the farmhouses. But the dominating colour was emerald. We were in the most conservative, the most stubborn, and the most Irish part of France.

At dinner the night before at Juigné, the Curé had said : " Clemenceau was a Vendéen. When you have said that you have explained everything." A few weeks before his death a Benedictine monk had written to him : ' Monsieur le Président, if I were to throw myself on your door-step and kneel there until you consented to soften your heart, what would you do ? ' The Tiger had replied : ' My Father, I would give you a straw mattress.'

As we drove farther into La Vendée, the scenery became more savage. There were fewer habitations, fewer peasants—only Druid's mistletoe and magpies in such profusion as would have left superstitious people breathless with joy at seeing so many together.

After four hours of fast driving we came to the brink of earthly desolation. At last we found a peasant digging near the road. ' The grave of M. Clemenceau ? ' He waved a dumb hand towards the Bay of Biscay and the West. We had arrived.

Leaving the car by the roadside, we made our way along a narrow path towards a hill overhanging the banks of a tiny trout-stream. On the hill-side there was a wild, over-grown grove, and here, amid the pines and chestnuts, lies the Tiger.

He is buried behind his father. Two low iron railings separate the two graves. Otherwise, there is nothing ; no stone, no dates, no names. The place is untended. The grass grows wild. There are no wreaths. The small plaque of Pallas Athene resting on her sword was given to the Tiger after the war by a grateful Greece. It was placed by Clemenceau himself over his father's grave. True to his belief or, rather, to his unbelief, he would have no memento, no symbol of any kind over his own tomb. He was an atheist. He insisted on being buried as an atheist.

" A dog's grave," said the chauffeur. " Yes," said Lady Millicent, " and, apart from his family, no Frenchmen but Tardieu and Mandel were allowed to be present at the funeral. Even the handful of reporters who travelled down on the day were kept at a distance. And, even if they had been given free entry, they could not have got very near to the grave for the mud and the rain."

As she walked away with the chauffeur, I stayed behind for a last look. In the almost oppressive silence I could hear clearly the murmur of the little stream far below me. It seemed to echo the Tiger's last words : ' Love thy neighbours as thyself. What nonsense. What a ridiculous submission ! A future life— madness ! Poincaré, poltroon ! He stole my place. Foch ! I could have broken him. Where would he have been without me ?

Who made the single command over the Franco-British armies ? The Chamber of Deputies. Bah !—the cowards. When the Tiger had done his work, they drew his teeth in order that they might start again their nefarious profiteering.'

That is the Clemenceau who will be forgotten. But there is the other Clemenceau—the Père la Victoire, the Tiger who held Germany at bay, the terror of the *défaitistes*, the profiteers and the selfish pacifists who said the others first, but we last ; the Clemenceau, whose iron will and Vendéen obstinacy saved his country from shame and ruin.

That Clemenceau will, I trust, never be forgotten. For whatever may happen to France—and she has sore need of a Clemenceau to-day—Frenchmen and Western Europeans of future generations will remember that in the critical years of nations courage, determination, and even obstinacy are worth all the ideologies of the garrulous and the wisdom of the philosophers.

It is now thirty years since I visited the simple grave of this simple man. I hope that his admirers and his family have left him, as he wished to lie, among the wild flowers which more than marble or granite will keep his memory green so that in the end future generations will repeat what his own Vendéen countrymen say to-day : ' For the Tiger La Vendée is a better resting place than the clammy vaults of the Panthéon. After all, he was one of us.'

CHAPTER TWO

Two French Travellers on Russia

'The Russians are fickle, jealous, deceitful, and gross, and respect only what they fear.'

Jacques-Henri Bernardin de Saint-Pierre, 1737–1814

I

FROM her earliest beginning Russia has been and still is a forbidding country, a land in which suspicion of the foreigner precedes a generous hospitality. To an Empire emerging from the dark ages the Western nations brought enlightenment in various forms. As early as the middle of the sixteenth century the English merchant adventurers brought the commerce of the West. An embassy followed the trade, but a hundred years later the English ambassador's wife was not allowed by the Tsar to meet the wives of other Englishmen in Moscow. The Scots provided mercenaries, great generals like Patrick Gordon and Marshal Keith, numerous Court physicians, and in Admiral Samuel Greig the creator of the Russian Navy. France sent culture and two literary visitors, one in the eighteenth century and the other in the nineteenth century, both of whom have left remarkable accounts and reflections of their travels.

The first was Jacques-Henri Bernardin de Saint-Pierre, the subsequent author of *Paul et Virginie*. An improvident idealist brought up on *Robinson Crusoe* and on other books of travel, he decided to go to Russia in order to found a Republic and to give it laws. Borrowing some money from friends, he set out in 1762 soon after Catherine the Great had ascended the throne. He was then just twenty-five. By the time he reached St Petersburg he had spent more than was wise. Nevertheless, he had letters of introduction, was hospitably entertained, and was sent off to Moscow with a recommendation to the brother of his hostess in St Petersburg.

On his arrival in Moscow he discovers that the brother is

away. The *izvozchik* drives him to an inn and, after paying the sleigh, he has no money left. He receives a note with the strange words : ' If you do not wish to lose your friend, beware of mentioning his name.' He discovers that his friend and host has been exiled to Astrakhan. However, he is passed on to Count Orlov and, as he had a knack of getting help at the most difficult moments, he was able to see all that he wanted from a favourable position.

Those who think that the French are stingy must make reservations for French officials abroad. As travellers were very rare in those days, perhaps the French felt a special obligation to be generous. Be this as it may, Bernardin de Saint-Pierre's compatriots, especially the ambassadors and officials, were extraordinarily generous to him, replenishing his purse very handsomely and passing him on to his friends.

His book, *Voyage en Russie*, is a bulky volume in which history is enlivened by anecdotes and his own observations, which are rarely flattering either to the country or to the people. The volume starts with two lines of verse by Crebillon :

> ' La nature marâtre, en ces affreux climats,
> Ne produit pour trésors que du fer, des soldats.'

Unkind nature in these terrible climates produces nothing but iron and soldiers.

There are stories, probably second-hand, of wolves which go in packs and often follow the traveller, but what lends value to the book is the author's vivid and often acid pen-pictures of the races and people whom he met.

Here is a paragraph on the Cossacks : ' They inhabit the Ukraine and are fine-looking men. They ride tireless horses which feed on the bark of trees and moss which they eat without stopping.

' The Cossacks are fond of booty, pillage what they want, and smash and burn the rest. They respect neither churches nor tombs and have a barbarous game of dragging out corpses and setting them up in horrible positions in people's houses. They do not spare the living and thousands have been seen satisfying their lust on a single woman.'

Such a paragraph would not have sounded extravagant in 1905–6 or during the worst of the civil war in 1918–20.

All his peasants wore beards, as, indeed, they did up to the October Revolution of 1917. They were, too, serfs to be bought and sold by landowners. They had no sense of shame. Men, women and girls bathed publicly and quite naked. They ate salted cucumber as they do to-day, but then it was regarded as very healthy and almost as a medicine. They refused to eat pigeon because ' they thought that the bird was like the Holy Ghost '.

The author has much to say of the Russian officer and soldier. The standing army was then 500,000 men, half of whom were in garrison towns and the other half always in camp and ready to move. The soldiers do not go to war to acquire riches or glory. They march in silence like victims who go to death and expect to be killed. They think that eternal silence is the portion of those who die for their prince. They receive high praise for their power of resistance ; ' no armies can stand better the fatigues of war '. Frederick the Great said of them at Zorndorf that they were easier to kill than to conquer.

Soldiers were rewarded for good conduct with medals with blue ribbon ; for bad conduct they were caned.

Officers were still under the influence of Peter the Great, whose picture Bernardin de Saint-Pierre says was everywhere, although he had been dead for thirty-seven years. Peter's punishments for officers were still in force : reduction to rank of private or exile to Siberia with no opportunity of saying goodbye to wife and children. Peter had done much to abolish the duel which, before his reign, had been popular among officers. The aggressor was punished by a fine of a month's pay and reduction to the ranks.

Our author says the Russians of his time had a natural aversion from the sea and were poor sailors. The cavalry was not good, but the Russian artillery was the best in the North of Europe.

In general Bernardin de Saint-Pierre, who moved in good circles, had a low opinion of the Russians. He writes : ' The Russians are fickle, jealous, deceitful, and gross, and respect only what they fear. One must never become familiar with them ; otherwise, they despise you immediately.'

'They get drunk frequently. . . . They are subject to fits of melancholia which often have a terrifying effect on the foreigner. Some of them become insane ; others commit suicide.'

Only the Russian women receive the Frenchman's praise : 'The Russian women,' he writes, 'are very beautiful. One of their poets was right when he said : " Nature has placed its precious stones and riches in the East ; its most delicious fruits in the South ; and its industry and its arts in the West. But it has done more for the North, for it has given us the most beautiful women in the world." '

Even with regard to the women Bernardin had reservations : 'They are in general more dark than blonde, are a little inclined to *embonpoint*, but are of a dazzling freshness. All, including the women of the people, use rouge which spoils them. They have such a passion for this colour that, in order to say a girl is beautiful, one tells her she is ' red '. (The Russian adjective *krasny* can mean according to the context either ' red ' or ' beautiful '.) I have seen some very pretty women who blackened both their nails and their teeth.'

Although many of his observations are accurate even to-day, his opinion of Moscow and St Petersburg differs widely from that generally held by both Russians and by foreigners during the reign of the last Tsar. Contrary to the general view, he considered Moscow more beautiful than St Petersburg, then barely fifty years old. Referring to Moscow, he wrote : ' Nothing is so magnificent as the aspect of this city with its nearly twelve hundred belfries, some of which are gilded, and their tops end with a crescent surmounted by a Cross.'

He is less enthusiastic about St Petersburg which, he declares, has no advantage except its situation. ' If one enters the city by the Neva from the sea, its aspect is of dazzling magnificence but, as one draws nearer, this splendour vanishes. . . . One recognises that in this city the planning has been too quickly carried out.' He gives only 50,000 inhabitants to Moscow and 150,000 to St Petersburg.

Interesting and accurate are the author's comments on the restrictions imposed on foreigners. Both on entry and on leaving the country the visitor had to go through a maze of official bureaus. There were export visas for the foreign traders as well as export visas for the individual foreigner who, before leaving, had to advertise his departure three times at intervals of eight days. This measure was enforced to prevent foreigners from leaving the country without having paid their creditors. All correspondence was opened by the secret police. Diplomatic correspondence was not exempt from this practice, and the despatches of Allied diplomats were scrutinised even more strictly than those of neutral or hostile diplomats, for, as Bernardin de Saint-Pierre writes, ' the Russians are even more suspicious of their allies than of their enemies '.

With very slight changes these controls and inspections remain the same to-day.

And here is another of the author's observations which will give a laugh to the least informed student of Russia :

' As soon as some useful novelty is produced by their neighbours, they (the Russians) adopt it *and sometimes usurp the honour of its invention.*'

Having arrived in Russia in July, 1762, Bernardin de Saint-Pierre did not return to his native Le Havre until November, 1766. Much of this time was spent in Poland and in straying from country to country, following his quixotic sense of adventure, writing copious notes for his book, and perhaps following the star of Venus, for he had an easy disposition to fall in love. His early life had been stormy. Trained as an engineer, he had quarrelled with his family and had served in the French army, from which he had been dismissed for insubordination.

He must have had good manners and personal charm, for he succeeded everywhere in getting to know the best and most generous people in all the countries that he visited. As his publisher wrote, ' he arrived unknown, poor, and without support ; nevertheless, he was soon beloved.' In one sense it was obviously a good time to travel, but, to judge from his book, he brought back little pleasure from his journeys. All Europe seemed to present to him a series of depressing pictures. The ghastly contrast between wealth and poverty aroused his anger and he wrote savagely of the unfortunate Polish peasants who slept with their cattle, had no linen, no chairs, no tables, nor any other necessary pieces of furniture, and who worked all the year round for barbarous masters who had the right of life and death over them.

In Russia he had seen nothing but nobles and slaves. Prussia seemed to offer him only a multitude of little ambitions crawling before a superior ambition. Holland was merely a vast *entrepôt* of merchandise, divided into shops, warehouses and offices where one found clerks, Jews, and merchants.

' Every piece of legislation seemed to be based on some vice or passion. In Russia only rank was worshipped, in Holland industry, in Malta courage, in Poland shame, in Austria the number of quarterings, and everywhere gold.'

It is perhaps just as well that he did not visit England.

Soon after his return to France he made a voyage to Mauritius, then called Ile de France, and his book on the island gave him his first literary success. He was fifty-two when *Paul et Virginie* was published. It gave him fame, a sinecure as Superintendent of the Jardin des Plantes in Paris, and a happy old age with two successful marriages. His *Voyage en Russie* has been more or less forgotten, has never been translated into English, and has, I think, not been re-published in France since the edition of 1834.

2

' In spite of the intentions inspired into the Russians by Peter the Great, Siberia begins at the Vistula.'

Marquis de Custine, 1790–1857

My second French traveller to Russia was Astolphe Louis Léonor, Marquis de Custine, who was born on March 18, 1780. From the first he was handicapped by the early loss of his father and by the amorous idiosyncracies of his mother. His grand-father, Philippe, Comte de Custine, was a famous general who took part in the American War of Independence, went over to the Revolution, and for a time commanded the army of the North against the Royalists. With the advent of the Jacobins to power, he was sent to the guillotine on August 28, 1793. He was booed by the mob as he passed on his way and is remembered by his last words : " Are these the people who celebrated my victories ? " His son, the father of Astolphe, perished in the same way only a few months later. Astolphe was then only three.

His mother was a Sabran, an ancient family more aristocratic than the Custines and had connections with the English Royal family, a daughter of a Sabran mother having married Henry III of England. Astolphe's mother, however, was almost a nymphomaniac and had numerous lovers, including Chateaubriand.

The young Astolphe suffered from two phobias : a fear of the Terror, which he never could forget, and a strong dislike of his mother's lovers. He was endowed with high intelligence and literary tastes and, as his mother and her relations were rich, he was able to indulge his desire to travel. Unfortunately, he had a tendency towards homosexuality, for in a country where morals were at their lowest, homosexuality was the only sexual vice that cost a reputation.

In 1822 he went to England with an English companion, Edward Sainte-Barbe. Like most foreigners of that period, he found little to his taste. London was the most boring town that he knew. Society was much more frivolous and vacuous than in France. The English lacked imagination and any liking for the arts. There was no rhythm, no poetry, in their life. The industry was impressive, but it was hard to see any difference between a Newcastle miner and a Roman slave. " I am the born enemy of this nation so solidly greedy and governed so hypocritically in the name of humanity and of liberty. I prefer the vices of others to the virtues of England."

Soon his own virtues were to be criticised. He had married unwillingly in 1821. Not long after his return from England his young wife died of tuberculosis in July, 1823. Sixteen months later on his way from Saint-Denis to Epinay he was beaten up by the sergeants of a cavalry regiment. This fracas appeared in the newspapers, and the unfortunate marquis was unable either to ignore the incident or to take proceedings, for the sergeants themselves went directly to the magistrate to explain what they had done and why they had punished him.

For the marquis it was disgrace, and curiously enough it seemed to dispel his fears and his passion for introspection. Shunned by society, he travelled and developed the literary talent which he had exercised from his early youth. After his mother's death in 1826, he was not only free but very comfortably off.

G.C.—9

It was on June 5, 1839, that he set out from Ems on the voyage which was to make him famous. He travelled by steamer and entered St Petersburg on July 10. He crossed the Russian frontier into free air on September 26. He was actually on Russian soil for less than three months, but no other foreign visitor has put his time to such good use. He had useful recommendations. He was presented to the Emperor Nicholas I and the Empress. He met many of the leading people. An experienced observer who could make comparisons with other countries that he had visited, he spent his days in studying the country and its people. At night he was indefatigable in preparing the material for his book. It was written daily in the form of letters, many of which are as long as the chapters of a goodly sized novel.

Custine was surprised and disappointed by Russia, a country in which he saw little beauty and no virtues. Valiant for truth, he wrote without reservation what he saw and what he felt. There was praise for St Petersburg as one of the marvels of the world. Moscow was unique because as a city it retained the picturesqueness of the country. But of the government and the ruling class there was not a good word to be said: ' In Russia the government dominates all and gives life to nothing. In this immense Empire the people, if not tranquil, are silent. Death hovers over all heads and strikes them capriciously ; there man has two coffins : the cradle and the tomb. Mothers must lament even more the birth of their children than their death. . . . It must be said that the Russians of all classes have great dexterity in lying, a natural gift for falseness, the success of which revolts as much as it frightens any sincerity. . . . In Russia fear replaces, that is to say paralyses, thought. . . . I believe that of all countries of the world Russia is the one where man has the least amount of real happiness. . . . For all its immensity, this Empire is only a prison of which the Emperor has the key, and in this state which can live only by conquest, there is nothing to approach the unhappiness of its subjects in time of full peace unless it be the unhappiness of the Prince. The life of the jailer has always seemed to me to be very like that of the prisoner. . . . The more I see of Russia, the more I commend the Emperor for not allowing Russians to travel abroad and for making it difficult for foreigners to enter his country. The political régime in Russia could not withstand twenty years of free communication with Western Europe.'

Most of these sentiments were written just after he had been seeing a good deal of the Emperor who, in fact, had spoken very frankly to him.

His most remarkable predictions are to be found in his *Résumé de Voyage*. It is here that he makes a prophecy which applies equally to Russian Tsarists and to Russian Communists :

' Russia sees in Europe a victim which will be delivered to her sooner or later by our dissensions. . . . Bear in mind, I beg you, that if ever the Russians succeed in dominating the West they will not govern it from their own country, after the manner of the ancient Mongols ; on the contrary they will come out of their glacial plains with the utmost urgency and will leave their own country *en masse* as soon as the road to other countries is open to them.'

His book appeared in 1843 and became a European best-seller. The four volumes in French were soon sold out. English and German translations appeared at the same time as the original. Pirated editions flowed copiously from Brussels. The second French edition appeared in 1844, the third in 1846, and a fourth in 1856.

In Russia the upper class from the Emperor downwards was furious. The marquis was accused of abusing hospitality. The Emperor appealed to Balzac to denounce the alleged slanders of Custine, and by doing nothing Balzac suffered, for the Emperor then refused to consent to his marriage to Madame Hanska. Custine, however, refused to withdraw a line. He had no obligations to Russia. He had come as a traveller to study and to see the country. The Russian aristocrats said that in three months he had seen badly. Custine's reply was short : ' *Il est vrai, j'ai mal vu, mais j'ai bien deviné.*'

Like all best-sellers, the book had its day or decade and, apart from clandestine editions in Russian, for it was in Russia that the book had its most violent influence, it lay forgotten from 1850 to 1930. Towards the latter part of these eighty years there was a rapprochement between Russia and the West, and Frenchmen like Eugène Marie Melchior de Vogüe and the Englishman Maurice Baring wrote kindly and intelligently about the Russians. Nevertheless, although the book was more or less forgotten, every writer and speaker on Russia quoted unwittingly characteristic comments which had passed into all languages and which were the creations of Custine.

Then came the Custine revival, possibly the most curious incident that has ever happened to any book. In 1930 an official Russian translation was published in Moscow under the auspices of the former political prisoners and exiles of the Tsar. The preface, approved of course by the Communist censors, described the book as ' the most intelligent work on Russia ever written by a foreigner '.

Less than fifteen years later the Soviet Union not only was in the war as an ally of France and Britain, but also was developing imperialistic ambitions in spite of Stalin's adherence to the Atlantic Charter which forbade all territorial annexations. Foreign historians and far-seeing Ministers began to feel anxious about the future, and it occurred to some Slav scholars that what the Marquis de Custine had written about the Tsarist régime applied with even greater force to the Communist régime.

Before the end of the war an abridged edition in one volume of *The Letters From Russia* appeared in France and was followed again by a number of translations in various European languages. The book became the bible of the diplomats, especially of the American diplomats. To give only one example, General Bedell Smith, the brilliant Chief of Staff of General Eisenhower who became American ambassador in Moscow, wrote a very competent book on the Soviet Union. Nearly every chapter had as a sub-heading a line or two of Custine's words of wisdom.

When the second glory came to his book, the Marquis had been nearly ninety years dead. On September 25, 1857, he had been struck down suddenly by a cerebral haemorrhage in his Château de Saint-Gratien. He was then sixty-seven. He had been through the revolutionary year of 1848. It made him uncomfortable, but it did not alter his judgment. One of his last literary efforts was a word of advice addressed in his diary to Napoleon the Third : ' You will make a reasonable revolution in the name, and to the advantage, of the nationalists. Organise Poland, liberate Italy, awaken Hungary, and in an instant you are master of the world. Austria will perish or at least will sink to the rank of a second-class Power. What matter; after all she has deserved it.'

Prescience was Custine's genius. He succeeded as a writer and observer because he was able to recognise the permanent characteristics of a nation or a people. He is at his best in the last paragraph of the abridged edition :

' I have spoken without personal hate, but also without fear and without restriction. I have defied even the danger of boredom, for one must have lived in this solitude without repose, this prison without leisure which is called Russia, in order to realise all the liberty which is enjoyed by the other countries of Europe, no matter what form of Government they have adopted. . . .

' When your son is discontented in France, take my advice. Say to him : " Go to Russia." It is a useful journey for every foreigner. Whoever has had a good look at this country will be content to live anywhere else. It is always good to know that there exists a society in which no happiness is possible because, by a law of nature, man cannot be happy without liberty.'

The advice holds good to this day.

Lenin as Sportsman

'I love all waste and solitary places.'

INCLUDING the three years of his deportation to Eastern Siberia, nineteen of the thirty-four adult years of Lenin's life were spent outside Russia proper. Gorki relates in his *Days with Lenin* how Lenin, listening to stories about Russia and the country, would sigh enviously and say, "I know very little of Russia—Simbirsk, Kazan, Petersburg, exile in Siberia, and that is nearly all." Although his father was an Inspector of Schools and his mother, who had German blood in her veins, had a modest property near Simbirsk, Lenin had to earn his own living in the difficult circumstances of a deportee and later of an exile. To keep himself fit he lived as much of an open-air life as he could. Of all the prominent Russian revolutionaries he was the keenest sportsman. From boyhood he had been fond of shooting and skating. Always a great walker, he became a keen mountaineer, a lively cyclist, and an impatient fisherman.

Exile in Central Siberia gave him opportunites of sport such as he had never imagined even in his dreams. The life of a political deportee in Tsarist times may have been unpleasant and irksome, but it was paradise compared with the icy coalmines to which Stalin sent his opponents to die of starvation and cold. Shushenskoe, the little village to which Lenin was exiled for three years, was no tourist-resort, but he had a certain freedom of movement, could correspond with his family, and was allowed to have books and journals and, through devious ways, was even able to obtain at least some of the political newspapers and treatises which he wanted most. Shushenskoe, which he called Shoo-Shoo, had several advantages in his eyes. It was near a tributary of the Yenisei, and there he could bathe. His horizon was bounded on one side by the Sayan mountains. There was a forest which added to the scenery, and in his first letter home he asks for a waterproof because he is not yet sure whether he will be allowed to go to the nearest ' town-village ' of Minoussinsk to buy one.

This first letter, which is dated May 18, 1897, and is addressed to his mother, shows what was the real attraction of Shushenskoe in his eyes. He writes, ' Shooting here, it seems, is very good. Yesterday I went about eight miles from here and was after duck and snipe. There is plenty of game, but without a dog and, above all, for a poor shot like myself, it is fairly difficult to make a good bag. There are even wild goats here and in the mountains and in the " taiga " * (about twenty to twenty-five miles from here) you find squirrels, sables, bear and deer.'

To compare again exile under the Tsars with Stalin's conception of it, Krupskaia, Lenin's faithful life-companion, was condemned to deportation a year later. Lenin suggested to her that she should try to have herself sent to Shushenskoe. She succeeded in doing this, and from that moment until Lenin's death they were never separated. Incidentally, Lenin married her in Siberia. Although both were atheists, the ceremony was performed by a local priest, no other marriage but a religious one being then legal in Russia.

With her arrival Lenin settled down to hard work, writing articles on Marxism, carrying on polemics with his Socialist deviationists, and translating the works of the Webbs. He was a good son and an excellent correspondent to his mother and his sisters, and his letters rarely fail to give some practical example of his belief that open air and physical exercise are essential to the brain-worker.

At Shushenskoe he had pleasant quarters—' half a house with yard and kitchen-garden attached '. Later, Krupskaia and he had a girl-help. Food was cheap and plentiful, and, according to Krupskaia, there was plenty of milk for both Lenin and Jenny, his Gordon setter, which he soon acquired. Summer must have been pleasant in country which was not unlike the Scottish Highlands, but on a grander scale. Krupskaia could grow beetroot, cucumber and pumpkins in her garden, while in July, 1897, Lenin writes again to his mother : ' As regards health, I do not think I am worse off than you are at Spitz. I bathe twice a day in the Yenisei, I walk, and I shoot.'

* Marshy pine forest.

In September he is still shooting. The partridge and *coq de bruyère* are new to him, but he finds life pleasant and writes, ' I must get used to it.' There are also plenty of hares, and he has a curious companion, a Polish worker called Prominski, who helps him to train his dog, goes hare-shooting with him, and sings revolutionary songs with zest taught to him by Lenin. Prominski was a hat-maker by trade and had a great idea of killing as many hares as possible and then using their skins to make fur-coats for children. His one dream was to get back to Poland. He died of typhus on the way home.

On November 19, 1897, Lenin still writes cheerfully, ' I live as before, quietly and without worries. Winter is already here and for some time now we have been snuggling behind the double windows and heating our stoves. Moreover, the big frosts have still to come and up to now we have had autumn days when one can walk comfortably in the forest with a gun. Even in mid-winter I shall certainly not abandon this recreation. Shooting hares is just as interesting in winter as in summer, and for me I have the extra advantage of being in the country.'

This love of the country and the open air keeps Lenin good-humoured. As many Russians and several foreigners have pointed out, every Russian who has spent a month in prison for a political offence considers it a sacred duty to write a book about the sufferings of his soul. This was never Lenin's way. Throughout the whole of his long correspondence from Siberia there is hardly a single complaint.

At Christmas time (although an atheist) he writes cheerfully to his mother and sister who have sent him two small sums of money : ' We lead an excellent life and we walk a great deal. After a certain day (about ten days ago) when the frost was thirty-six degrees Réaumur below zero and was followed by several snow-storms, the days have been mild and we have done a lot of shooting with more zeal than success.' One can hardly imagine one of Stalin's victims writing such a letter even if he had been allowed pen and paper.

Lenin's wants are few. All that he seeks from his mother are a suit of very strong cloth, ' because I tear my clothes terribly when I'm out shooting ', and a pair of doe-skin gloves without finger-holes to keep off the mosquitoes in summer. 'I have a net over my head,' he writes, ' but my hands suffer badly.'

By February, 1898, however, the real frosts have come, and he has to give up shooting. He is now anxious about his young brother Mitia, who after two and a half months in prison is in bad health and is flabby. Lenin writes strongly to his mother : ' Is he following a régime in prison ? Probably not. There a régime is necessary. Does he do gymnastics ? Almost certainly not. This also is necessary. I speak from experience. I did gymnastics every day before going to sleep and benefited greatly. . . . I can recommend him a gymnastic exercise. Let him make fifty reverences to the ground—that was the task I set myself. But he must do them fifty times running without bending his knees, and touching the floor with the ends of his fingers.'

In May of 1898 Nadejda Krupskaia arrived with her mother. It was dusk when they reached Lenin's log-cottage. He was out shooting, and it was pitch-dark when he came back. The two sat up talking for most of the night, and both wrote back the next day to Lenin's mother. Lenin writes, ' Nadejda does not look well. She will have to pay some attention to her health here.' Krupskaia writes, ' In my opinion, he has gained in health enormously and looks quite wonderful compared with what he looked like in Petersburg. . . . He is quite mad about shooting. Moreover, all the men here are keen shots, and it looks as if I shall have to finish by going out with them to spot the duck and other creatures.'

In June Krupskaia writes again to Lenin's mother : ' The famous game-dog goes with us on our walks, runs incessantly like a lunatic after the birds and annoys Volodia (Lenin). V. does not go shooting just now, for the birds are still sitting on their nests. . . . Instead of going shooting, V. tried fishing. Once he went off for the whole night to catch burbot on the other side of the Yenisei. But, as he didn't even get a bite, we've heard no more about burbot.'

Burbot (lota) is the only species of its kind. It is a fresh-water fish and resembles a ling. It grows to two feet, is known in England, but not in Scotland, and in Asia is common in the rivers and lakes of Siberia.

In point of fact, Lenin was no fisherman, even if the

opportunities were scarce. When he went to Capri to stay with Gorki, he was eager to go sea-fishing with the local Italian fisherman and laughed with joy when he caught a fish. He never cast a fly.

In this letter about fishing, Krupskaia writes with enthusiasm about the summer at Shushenskoe and adds, ' In general, our actual life makes us compare it with a real holiday.'

Apart from the separation from his political friends and also enemies, Shushenskoe was an important and healthy interlude in Lenin's career. He had spent his twenty-seventh birthday on the long journey to his place of exile and was then in the prime of life. Shushenskoe gave him time to think and concentrate his final thoughts on the type of revolution which he felt was practical. It also gave him the open-air recreation which later he was to have so little, and which he needed for his health. In the long hours of darkness there was chess, the chessmen being fashioned by himself out of birch-wood. For the rest of the year there was shooting—and, yes, even fishing.

In September of 1898 he goes grouse and partridge shooting with several companions. He takes Krupskaia and her mother with him. Krupskaia has a higher opinion of the birds than of the shooters. Here is her comment in her letter to Lenin's sister, ' We have been after grouse and partridge. They are noble birds, and to get at them one doesn't have to go into the swamps as after duck. But, if we often looked for them, we did not find them. True, we had some lovely walks. Once, however, we saw a covey of twenty partridges. We and all the colony of Shoo-Shoo were on a cart. Suddenly up got the partridges like a cloud. Imagine the emotion of our shooters. Volodia (Lenin) gave a sort of groan. He was able to get his gun up, but the partridge did not even fly away. It just walked off! In general the shooting is very poor. They never get anything except when Oscar hit the eyes of Jenny (Lenin's dog) ! We thought that the poor animal would become blind, but happily she is all right again.'

By the end of November Lenin had found a new sport. He had been allowed to go on a shopping expedition to Krasnoyarsk and had brought back skates. He took the leading part in making a skating rink on the river, and Krupskaia wrote : ' Volodia skates perfectly. He even puts his hands in the pockets of his jacket like a true sportsman.' He had skated as a boy on the Volga at Simbirsk.

By the beginning of 1899, however, his thoughts are back on shooting and he writes to his brother to get him a new gun— a twelve-bore from Francotte of Liège. He charges his brother to be sure to try the gun before buying it. There is no hurry about sending it. He can wait till the end of March. Meanwhile, he had been learning some new figures in skating and had had a fall and bruised his arm so badly that he could not write for several days.

On April 11, 1899, he acknowledges the receipt of the gun from his brother and writes, ' Dear little mother, I received Mitia's (Dimitri's) parcel on Tuesday. Very many thanks. I am satisfied with the gun.' Can one imagine any political exile during Stalin's régime ever being allowed to write a letter, let alone having a gun sent to him ? One has only to read Lenin's letters to see how foolish is the belief in human progress in so far as it refers to the nature of man. Up to 1914 world opinion was far stronger against the Tsarist régime for sending political exiles to Siberia than it ever was during Stalin's régime. Admittedly, the world did not know the truth about Stalin's activities. George Kennan, a cousin, several times removed, of the present Professor George Kennan, the American expert on Slav affairs, was allowed to visit Siberia by the Tsarist régime and was able to expose the truth. Even Krupskaia writes, ' We are not really allowed to go to the town, but these are liberal times.' There was nothing liberal about Stalin.

With the advent of the summer of 1899 which is to be his last in Siberia, Lenin doubles his enthusiasm for ' la chasse ' because, he writes almost sadly, ' it will soon be the end for me.' Krupskaia notes a success, ' Volodia shot some woodcock with which we regaled ourselves.' It was apparently not a very good summer, for there were strong winds. Lenin was working hard at his translation of the Webbs' works. ' *Volodia travaille maintenant le Webb*,' writes Krupskaia on November 17. ' We shall soon be able to skate ' and adds wistfully ' we have now three months and thirteen days till we leave.' With this letter the shooting entries cease.

After his departure from Siberia in March, 1900, Lenin was to see no more willow grouse and woodcock, and no more snipe and duck. From July, 1900, to November, 1905, he was in exile out of the Russian Empire, in Munich, in Geneva, and in Paris. He was too busy to engage in sport. He was still a Social-Democrat, but he was now on the way to split the Party into Bolsheviks and Mensheviks. He worked long hours on his political work, but the natural desire of the open-air man was for exercise. Towards the end of 1900 he writes that he is planning to get some skating on the artificial ice-rink in Munich. Already, too, he delights in the excellent swimming baths. Town-life, however, offered few opportunities for sport. The cost of living was high for poor exiles, and he had to write to make money.

From 1901 to 1905 he was much preoccupied with Russian affairs. On April 14, 1902, he paid his first visit to London. He does not seem to have indulged in any sport there. Like President Masaryk, he was fond of riding on top of buses. He liked the city and said later that, if he had a choice of living in one city, it would lie between London and Geneva. It was in London at the end of 1903 that the Congress, which split the Party, was held. With the outbreak of the unsuccessful revolution of 1905–6 he was off to Russia like a homing pigeon. With the failure of the revolution, a warrant for his arrest was issued in November, 1907. With two tipsy Finns to guide him, he determined to cross the ice on the Gulf of Finland by night in order to board the steamer which was to take him out of the Tsar's clutches at a neighbouring island. On this occasion he came very near to death. At one place the ice began to move away under his feet, and he barely succeeded in getting back on to a firmer stretch. Nevertheless, in spite of the police being after him, he spent the best part of June and July, 1902, at Stirsuden, a little resort in Finland where Krupskaia and he bathed every day and cycled on incredibly bad roads. Unlike most foreigners, Lenin had no fear of cold water. His cure for insomnia was a cold bath. It was nearly always successful.

From November, 1907, until his return to Russia in a sealed compartment of a German train in April, 1917, he was in continuous exile, spent mainly in Geneva, Paris, and Cracow.

He liked Switzerland best, because he could get easily to his beloved mountains, but he did not like the fogs of Geneva in winter. By the late autumn of 1909 he was in Paris and had a flat at 24 Rue Beaunier. The flat was on the outskirts of the south side of Paris and was not far from the Parc Montsouris. It is ' as calm as if we were in the country,' he writes, ' and the flat is far enough away from the Bibliothèque Nationale ', where he went almost daily to work.

To keep himself fit and perhaps to save money he cycled to and from his work. Later, Krupskaia and he moved out to Longjumeau, fifteen miles from the Paris of those days. Paris was full of exiles of the 1905–6 Revolution. Some were in dire poverty. One, insane with starvation, committed suicide. His corpse was found in the Seine with heavy stones tied to his neck and feet. He was not the only suicide among the exiles. To keep the revolutionary spirit alive, Lenin and Krupskaia set up a revolutionary school at Longjumeau. He still rode his bicycle, especially in summer. Krupskaia and he thought nothing of cycling fifteen miles each way to spend an afternoon with the Lafargues, Mrs Lafargue being the daughter of Karl Marx.

He was now forty and, although the traffic in Paris was not so dense then as it is to-day, he was a sturdy and slick cyclist. His slickness saved him. Coming back to Paris from Juvissy early in 1910, he was run down by a motor-car. His bicycle was smashed to bits, but he himself vaulted off the cycle so quickly that he escaped serious injury. The standers-by had noted the number of the car and several had offered to give evidence if there was a law-case. Lenin was determined to sue for damages. Most probably he could not afford to buy another bicycle. He writes to his sister : ' I have discovered the owner of the car. He is a viscount—the devil take him—and I am now at law with him.' Ten days later he wrote with satisfaction : ' the case about the bicycle has ended in my favour.' In April he informed his sisters that he had started cycling again and was exploring the environs of Paris.

A more remarkable example of his physical fitness was his mountaineering exploit in the autumn of 1911. He had gone from Paris to Switzerland for a meeting of the International Socialist Bureau in Zurich. He writes to his mother from Lucerne under date of November 10, 1911 : ' Yesterday I climbed

Pilatus,' and to show that he is not without pride he adds : ' 6,685 feet.'

In the autumn of 1912 Lenin and his wife went to Cracow, partly on account of Krupskaia's health and, partly, in order that Lenin might be in closer touch with Russia and with those Russians who could cross and re-cross the frontier. With the advent of winter Lenin thinks again of skating, and in February he is telling the family in Russia : ' I have bought new skates and skate enthusiastically. I think of Simbirsk and of Siberia. I have never skated abroad.'

Until the First World War breaks out, there are no more entries in his or Krupskaia's correspondence concerning sport or even exercise. In August, 1914, the Austrian police kept him under arrest for several days until his Socialist friends secured his release. He went to Switzerland and spent the war there. In the little Republic nearly all the extreme revolutionaries had found a refuge. Soon Lenin became the leader of the most extreme group. Here he held the two historic conferences of Zimmerwald and Kienthal, the main decision of which was ' to turn the imperial war into a civil war '.

He never spared himself when he was working, and the Zimmerwald Conference had taken toll of his physical and mental strength. The Conference lasted from the 5th to the 8th of September, 1915, and one may be sure that the delegates had little sleep. It was, however, typical of the open-air man that, the day after the Conference ended, he joined Krupskaia at their summer hide-out in Soerenberg and climbed the Rothorn which is over 4,000 feet. ' We climbed,' Krupskaia writes in her memoirs, ' with a glorious appetite, but when we reached the summit Ilyich (Lenin) lay down on the ground, in an uncomfortable position almost on the snow, and fell asleep. Clouds gathered, then broke ; the view of the Alps from the Rothorn was splendid, and Ilyich slept like the dead. He never stirred for over an hour.'

He owed his physique to nature, but his constant good health to Krupskaia who every summer took him away from the city to the mountains. At Soerenberg he rose early and finished his work by noon when he had the main meal of the day. Then, when the weather was fine, Krupskaia and he went to the

mountains for the rest of the day. 'Ilyich,' Krupskaia writes,
' loved the mountains. He liked to get to the crags of the Rothorn
towards evening when the view above was marvellous and,
below, the fog was turning rosy.'

For the last time husband and wife went to the mountains—
on this occasion, to the Chudivise rest-home not far from
Zurich, but very high up and not far below the snow-peaks.
The home was very cheap, the charge was two and a half francs
a day for each person. On the other hand, the food consisted
solely of milk, with bread, butter and cheese. The two Russians
rebelled against this milk-diet, but managed to supplement it
with raspberries and blackberries which grew in great profusion.
They had also to do their own chores. Krupskaia did the room,
and Lenin thoroughly enjoyed doing Krupskaia's and his own
shoes because it gave him an occasion to convert the other
amateur boot-blacks who foregathered in the court-yard every
morning. They were, as Krupskaia writes, ' detached from all
affairs and roamed the mountains for days on end.' There is,
however, no mention of conquering new heights.

This summer of 1916 was really the end of Lenin's sporting and
open-air life. In her memoirs Krupskaia says that in his later
years, when he was in Moscow as head of the Bolshevik Government, he went out shooting several times. His ardour, however,
had ebbed, and his wife recounts how a fox-hunt was organised
for him. The shoot, arranged like a bear-shoot, was so directed
that the fox would run straight towards Lenin. He put his gun
to his shoulder, but no sound came. The fox stood for a moment
and looked at him. Then it turned and made off into the wood.

" Why didn't you shoot ? " everyone asked at once.

" Well," said Lenin rather sheepishly, " he was so beautiful."

In many respects Lenin was quite different from the other
Bolshevik leaders. He had a stronger and more obstinate
character, and, as the result of exile, he had a much wider knowledge of the world. Unlike Stalin and unlike Trotsky he had an
excellent command of his temper and had no personal vengeance
in his heart, although he would not have hesitated to ' liquidate
a hundred thousand men and women ' if he thought this necessary for the triumph of Communism. Apart from the civil war
which was utterly cruel on both sides, the biggest terror during

his six years of dictatorship was when he was lying unconscious after being fired at point-blank and hit twice by the Jewish girl, Kaplan. When he recovered consciousness, he at once gave the order to stop the terror. Had he been born a mid-Victorian Englishman, he would probably have been a hospitable land-owner obstinately mad on shooting and salmon fishing.

CHAPTER FOUR

Three Americans

' Experience joined to common-sense
To mortals is a providence.'

I

IN his two celebrated books, *Russia Leaves the War* and *The Decision to Intervene*, George Kennan devotes considerable space to Raymond Robins and to his assistant, Alex Gumberg. During the first four months of 1918 Robins and Gumberg were in close, though unofficial, contact with the Bolshevik Government which at that time was not recognised by either the United States or Britain, although the American ambassador remained in Russia during this period.

I was in a happier position, for the British Embassy had been withdrawn and I had been sent out by the War Cabinet to maintain relations with the Bolshevik Government. Although the relations with an unrecognised government are inevitably unofficial, I had an official position vis-à-vis my own Government and I communicated direct with the Foreign Secretary and the War Cabinet, whereas Robins communicated direct to President Wilson over the head of the American ambassador.

Until May, Robins and I were the advocates of recognition of the Bolshevik Government and opponents of intervention by the Allies. Robins, who had to wrestle both with Francis, the American ambassador, in far-off Vologda, and with the American Consul-General in Moscow, gave up the struggle in May and went back to the United States to persuade President Wilson to accept his view and not to intervene against the Bolshevik Government with armed force.

Robins was unable to stop the intervention, and in Moscow I came to a bad end, because the British Government did not give the British in Moscow sufficient time to leave the country before Allied troops landed at Archangel.

In both his books, but especially in *The Decision to Intervene*,

George Kennan criticizes Robins for high-handedness, arrogance and tactlessness. The criticism is not entirely unjust, Raymond Robins was a great orator, an emotionalist who could dramatise even the slightest incident affecting himself, and a Christian, whose faith had been strengthened by a miracle in his own life. As a young man he went to Alaska to seek gold. After some failures he found a rich stretch, marked out a claim, and set out for Dawson City. On his way he ran into a blinding blizzard. He had no compass and no idea of his bearings. There was only one chance in a thousand of his reaching the town.

While he was staring death in the face, there was a break in the mass of grey cloud, and in the gap there appeared a white cross. Without hesitation he went straight in the direction of the cross and reached Dawson City safely.

This escape from death affected Robins until he died. Now rich, he went to Chicago where a Professor Taylor ran a kind of Toynbee Hall. Eager to do good with his money, Robins worked with Taylor in the slums of Chicago.

Robins was convinced that he was guided by God. He believed in great men, and worship of Rhodes led to worship of Lenin. He believed in his own mission with an iron determination which amounted to arrogance towards anyone who disagreed with him. In Russia his weakness was his ignorance of the country, the people, and the language. Above all, he had no knowledge of how foreign affairs are conducted.

Had he been more tactful, he might have succeeded in persuading President Wilson not to intervene in the affairs of another nation, because he had in Alex Gumberg an assistant who at that time knew more about the Bolsheviks and how to handle them than anyone else on the side of the Allies.

Both in Russia in 1918 and again during my visits to the United States in 1934 and 1939 I saw a good deal of Alex Gumberg. Indeed, when you live cheek by jowl with a man for four months in a vast city in which both of you are suspect to the authorities and you yourself mistrust everyone else, you get to know a man better than someone who lives next door to you for a life-time.

Raymond Robins was a great actor who had always to be in the centre of the stage. When the play was over, he retired to his bedroom with his Bible. Alex Gumberg and I were spectators who liked to study every aspect of the curious world in which we found ourselves. He was born in Russia, the son of a poor Odessa Jew who emigrated to the United States when Alex was a boy. When I first met him, he was about thirty and was clean-shaven with a rather sallow countenance and dark eyes which lit up his whole face when he smiled. In a sense he was a cynic, but he was a merry cynic, and I never saw him lose his temper or his judgment. Bi-lingual in Russian and American, he understood the Bolshevik mentality far better than any Anglo-Saxon. In 1918 the Bolshevik Party had numerous Jewish members, many of them like Trotsky, Zinoviev and Radek in high places. Alex himself had a brother who, under the name of Zorin, was a minor Commissar.

Inevitably all the American and British security organisations were full of suspicions and, of course, put them on paper and forwarded them to their superiors. The general tenor of their reports was that Alex Gumberg, a most suspicious character, ran Robins and that Robins had mesmerised Lockhart.

This interpretation is entirely false. From January, 1912, I had been in Russia right up to September, 1917, with only one short leave of one month in the six years. Soon after the Bolshevik Revolution took place in November, 1917, I was sent for by Lord Milner. I told him that in my opinion it was crazy for us not to have some kind of representation with the Bolshevik Government. At the end of December I was sent out to St Petersburg to do my best to establish good relations with the Bolsheviks and to keep them in the war. Inevitably I met Robins. But when the Germans threatened to march on St Petersburg, Robins withdrew to Vologda with the intention of joining the American diplomatic train which was to take them via Siberia to Vladivostok in the event of the Germans occupying Russia.

Afraid lest Robins should leave, I begged Arthur Ransome, then correspondent of the *Manchester Guardian*, to go to Vologda and to hold on to his coat-tails. In this he succeeded, and I am mainly responsible for Robins's return to Moscow.

As for Alex Gumberg we all benefited from his knowledge, but he made no attempt to make policy. He was a philosopher and not a thruster. He could have been a Commissar himsel if he had wanted to be one. But he was entirely dedicated to the United States, and in a wide experience I have never come across a less excitable American.

True, he was against armed intervention by the Allies. So were most of us who lived with those events. Even I, when I knew that intervention was inevitable and 'hedged' because I was an official and did not wish to lose my job, told the Government at home that, in the event of intervention, the amount of support we should get from the anti-Bolshevik Russians would be in exact proportion to the number of troops we sent ourselves. As we landed in Archangel with just over a thousand men, disaster was inevitable. Intervention galvanised the Soviet Government, and to-day the Soviet leaders still boast regularly and exaggeratedly of their victories over the Americans, the British, the French and the Japanese.

All the anti-interventionists suffered more or less for their views, but the chief victim was Alex Gumberg, to whom to the end of his life the British security authorities denied a visa.

In the winter of 1934 I made my first lecture tour in the United States where my first book, *Memoirs of a British Agent*, had a big success. Within two days of my arrival I was lunching with Raymond Robins and Alex Gumberg. Raymond was friendly, but critical. He had not liked my book. He twitted me with having 'ratted' over intervention after he left Moscow and said that he had been reluctantly unable to invite me to the dinner given in the Waldorf-Astoria to Litvinov, when at last the United States recognised the Soviet Union. This was Raymond's greatest triumph, and he made the speech of the year. All who had suffered in any way for supporting the Soviet Union were toasted, Robins extending his arm and chanting : "Prisoners of starvation, stand up ! Heroes of recognition, stand up ! " In turn the prisoners and then the heroes arose and were cheered for minutes on end.

It was the last time that I ever saw him. In 1931 he visited the Soviet Union more as a tourist than as a political visitor. He was well received, but his day was over as a power in the United States. He withdrew to Florida where, while pruning a tree, he fell and damaged his spine. Till his death in 1942 he lived in a chair. He was perhaps the most dramatic speaker that I have heard in any country.

Alex Gumberg had changed not at all, and on Russia I found myself in close agreement with him. He could not have been kinder than he was. He gave parties for me, guided me through all the traps of lecturing, and took me into high finance. He was now in it himself and was a member of the Atlas Corporation which at that time was one of the very few big New York companies that had prospered after the slump of 1929. He also took me as his guest to the New York Bankers' Club to a luncheon at which Troyanovsky, the new Soviet ambassador, was to speak. There was a record attendance of nearly six hundred which seemed to me to prove that American big business men (and perhaps English business men) will deal with the devil if his money bags are full.

Troyanovsky was a poor speaker, but he was a rare type of Bolshevik. He had been a Tsarist officer, but had joined the Bolshevik Party clandestinely many years before the October Revolution. He was the first person to denounce Malinovsky as a traitor to the Party, but was disbelieved by Lenin and had to resign. He was different from most Bolsheviks in those days in that he played both tennis and bridge.

In the winter of 1939 I went back to the United States for another lecture tour to fill in time ; for, after Munich in September, 1938, I was certain war was coming. On this occasion my tour lasted three months. It was a difficult time because nearly all Americans thought that we should have fought Hitler instead of surrendering at Munich, although the Americans themselves had no intention of taking any part in the war.

Once again Alex Gumberg came to my rescue both by introducing me to influential people and in giving me good advice. The counsel was necessary, because, although I was anti-Munich, I was not prepared to attack the British Government in a foreign country, and, apart from the permanent anti-English bloc composed mainly of Germans and Irish, the Americans were very anti-Hitler and even more anti-Chamberlain. Alex's advice was to start a good-humoured offensive against the Americans and to twit them with talking big and doing nothing.

Almost uncanny in his accurate vision of world politics, he

was quite sure that there would be war before the end of the
year, and on January 21, 1939, he declared that Hitler would
achieve the miracle of ensuring for Franklin Roosevelt a third
term as President.

As regards influential people, he could not have been more
helpful. He gave cocktail parties to which came philosophers,
politicians and journalists. He took me to the Stork Club where
I ran into Raymond Massey, whom I knew before, and listened
to Walter Winchell's life story. It was, I think, on this occasion
that Raymond told us the story of his duel.

In 1918 Raymond was with the British troops in Siberia.
Life was boring. Raymond had a bottle of Haig. Meeting some
Czech soldiers, he saw an officer with a patch over his eye and
a rather bald head. " Shampoo or drink, sir ? " said Raymond.
Then he poured half the bottle over the officer's head.

Big trouble followed. The Czech officer challenged Raymond
to a duel and asked where and to whom he should send his
seconds. Raymond, a little non-plussed, got an American officer
and a British major as his seconds. The next morning the Czech
seconds arrived and demanded a parley with Raymond's seconds.
Much to Raymond's relief the Czech said the duel must not take
place. The officer with the patch on one eye was General Syrovy,
the Czech Commander-in-Chief.

In 1939 Alex was depressed by the purges in Russia. He told
me that long before the First World War the Bolsheviks had
approached him. They needed men like him. Later they offered
him important posts. Alex always refused. His roots were in the
United States. He showed me a letter about his brother, who
had been arrested in 1931. Alex had used all the influence that
he could bring to bear on the Soviet Government, but his
efforts were vain. He did not know then whether his brother
was alive or dead. The brother had been a friend of Zinoviev
and Serebriakov.

In that all-important year of 1939 Alex was still on the British
black list for a visa. Almost more than anything he wanted this
stigma removed, and I promised to do what I could to help
him on my return to London. Before I could make any progress,
I received a telegram from Aubrey Morgan stating that Alex
Gumberg had died suddenly in New York from a heart attack.

He was a wonderful example of the poor European boy making good in the United States. He knew everybody in Washington and in New York, but he had not the power to persuade the Soviet ambassadors to the United States not only to get his brother released, but even to give news of him.

Quite apart from Raymond Robins, who owed much to Gumberg's knowledge, Allan Wardwell, a well-known New York lawyer and a man of superlative integrity, paid at different times compliments to Alex Gumberg's intelligence and loyalty, and said that Morgans thought highly of him. George Kennan was more careful. In his *The Decision to Intervene* he wrote : ' It would be wrong, incidentally, to allow Gumberg to appear as a sinister or anti-American character. He was neither. . . . He was a well-informed man, with unique contacts in the higher Soviet circles. Robins, and for that matter the other Americans as well, had a great deal to learn from him that they could learn from no other source. Corrected by competent and responsible critical appraisal. . . . Gumberg's contribution could have been of prime value in enabling America's officialdom to find its way through the crucial mazes of the first year of Soviet power. Lacking this corrective, it became at times a source of weakness and confusion.'

Kennan's judgment is right. It is easy enough to understand why the British authorities refused Alex Gumberg a visa in the early years of the Bolshevik régime. Anyone who opposed intervention was suspect, and by leading the opposition among the Allies in Russia to the intervention I ruined my career.

I did not see Robins in 1939. He was still paralysed and still in Florida. Wardwell, who had been to see him, said that his mind was all in the past and that he could talk only of Alaska and of Russia as the two worth-while episodes of his life. He died in 1942 and, like John Reed, a hard-drinking American journalist, who seized the one great opportunity in his life, has become a legend in American history. Both these Americans owe much to Alex Gumberg.

2

Another American with whom I came into touch over Russia was George Kennan. His career, much more brilliant than mine,

ran somewhat on the same lines in that we both began in the
Consular Service, spent most of our foreign service in Slav
countries, and finished as Under-Secretaries in the State Department and the Foreign Office. In our service abroad we covered
quite different periods, Kennan being years younger than myself.
In a letter he sent me at the beginning of 1958 he wrote : ' I
have just finished reading your memoir about Jan Masaryk and
am writing to tell you how moved and impressed I was by it.
There is no one who knew Eastern and Central Europe in the
'twenties and 'thirties who has managed to reproduce as you
have the political and human atmosphere of that part of the
world.

' I followed closely in your footsteps almost everywhere,
coming to the Baltic States in 1928, to Russia in 1933 (for a series
of assignments running up to 1952), to Vienna—for nearly a
year—in 1935, and finally, on the day of Munich, to Prague where
I served for a year, watching the old Czechoslovakia die, closing
up diplomatic missions, and becoming in the end a combination
of diplomatic observer and super-custodian of the deserted
British, French and American Palaces. With all your scenes I
am familiar ; for the characters I was everywhere just too late.'

George Kennan came late into my life and I did not meet him
until three years after his recall in October, 1952, at the request
of the Soviet Government, from Moscow where he had been
ambassador. The reason for his recall was his alleged remark
to a group of journalists in Berlin, when he was on leave, that
the life of a diplomat in Moscow was not unlike his own life
as an interned diplomat under the Nazis during the last war.
The statement was true, but in a diplomatic career the truth is
dangerous, and on this occasion both Kennan and his country
suffered.

Kennan himself went back to the State Department and after
a short spell transferred himself to the Institute for Advanced
Study at Princeton University, where he is now a Professor.
In October 1955 we had a two hours' talk in one of the alcoves
of the Carlton Grill, now alas ! destroyed, in which over many
years I entertained many foreign politicians, revolutionaries and
diplomatists.

In the train to London I had read an article by Kennan on

the Foreign Service of the United States, which he said had been wrecked by the inability of a continental country to run a diplomatic service properly and by the constant appointment of political hacks as ambassadors in spite of the career system introduced by the Rogers Act.

It was good strong meat, and I expected to meet a rather fierce and typically cock-sure American. When we met, he was the opposite of all that I had imagined. Tall, well-built without any adipose weight, he was blue-eyed, and clean-shaven.

I was most eager to meet him, because in my youth almost the first book I had read on Russia was by a George Kennan, a forebear of the present George, who made four trips to Russia and wrote *Siberia and the Exile System*. Although the number of ' exiles ' was tiny compared with the political prisoners in Stalin's time, Kennan's book drew tears from many stony hearts. I can still remember one story of a poor chemist named Schiller who ran a drug-store in Poltava and wanted to change to Kharkov. He sent in the necessary petition. For weeks he received no answer. Then one day the Minister of the Interior came to Poltava. Schiller brought his petition to the Minister's house. The sentry refused to deliver it. Schiller therefore wrapped a stone in the petition and threw it through the Minister's window. He was arrested, branded as a political prisoner, and sent to Siberia.

Most of my first talk with George Kennan Junior was about his first volume of Soviet-American relations in 1917–18 which was published in 1956 under the title of *Russia Leaves the War*. In the autumn of 1955 he had only a draft copy and he was eager to discuss the main issues of 1918 : namely, the Allied intervention and the efforts of Robins and myself to prevent it. I told him my formula in 1918. The support which the Allies would get from the White Russians would be in direct proportion to the number of troops we sent. During the war we had not enough troops to send. After the war the troops would not go. Kennan, who rightly regarded the intervention as a grave blunder, was interesting on Robins who he thought was honest, but emotional and not only ambitious but inordinately vain. He also told me that Robins's efforts to obtain President Wilson's active support for his policy were doomed from the beginning, because Robins had begun life as a Democrat and had then switched over to Teddie Roosevelt in his last campaign for the Presidency. This, Kennan said, was to Wilson tantamount to high treason and could never be forgiven. I registered silently in my mind that this was an even stronger proof of Wilson's narrow-mindedness than his failure to take with him any Republican to the Peace Conference in Paris.

I found myself in a large measure of agreement with George Kennan on almost every aspect of the Soviet situation. In particular, I was interested in his remarks on Soviet histories and Soviet encyclopedias which he said were written solely for propaganda and would have to be re-written after any change in the régime. On this subject he was eloquent and convincing in his answer to the question I had raised about English professors writing history based on Soviet histories and encyclopedias.

George Kennan was eager for me to read what he had written about me in his book, but had only two typescripts with him. One was with our Foreign Office and the other was at Oxford. If I could stay two days more, I could read the script. I told him that I could not stay longer and that I had no qualms. After all, he could write what he liked. He assured me that after our talk I could feel satisfied. Indeed, when I received a copy of the book I was treated much more handsomely than I deserved.

In the autumn of 1957 he came to England to spend a sabbatical year at Oxford and to deliver the Reith lectures. His theme was disengagement in Europe, and his lectures attracted a large public. Disengagement is, I think, a better policy than a race in nuclear weapons, more especially since the Soviet satellites have realised from the failure of the Hungarian rising that the West will do nothing physical to liberate them.

Disengagement also has dangers, mainly because many people assume that through disengagement better relations between East and West will result and there will be an end to the cold war. I feel certain that George Kennan has no delusions on this subject. He knows very well what the Russians mean by ending the cold war. The West must stop broadcasting to the East, even if only to contradict inaccuracies arising from the Soviet monopoly of all media of information. On the other hand, the Soviet Union must be allowed to continue to spread its gospel

of Communism in all parts of the world. If ever this propaganda
stops, the Soviet Union will have ceased to be a Communist
state.

When Kennan had finished his Reith lectures, he invited me
to take part in one of his weekly seminars on Soviet diplomatic
history. It was to be held in February, but on account of Kennan's
illness it was postponed until April 30, 1958.

The postponement was very much to my advantage, for I
had the pleasure of seeing Oxford in brilliant weather. The
seminar, held in All Souls, went off very well, and Kennan
was excellent in opening and closing the discussion. The students
asked numerous questions, but two American Rhodes Scholars,
especially young Ullman who was at Nuffield College, were a
long way ahead of the British in knowledge of Soviet affairs.
Both, of course, were older than the British undergraduates.

Both before and after the seminar I had two long talks with
George Kennan who gave me two pieces of information that
were new to me. Like Jack Wheeler-Bennett, George Kennan
takes immense trouble to check his facts. I was therefore surprised
when he told me that he could now prove that in his earlier days
as a Communist in Baku, Stalin was in the pay of the police. It is
certain that he was first nominated to the Party by Malinovsky,
the agent-provocateur and police nark, in whose honesty Lenin
continued to believe in spite of numerous proofs laid before
him. On his first arrest Stalin was not sent to Siberia and escaped
easily. Later, when he stopped his dealings with Malinovsky,
he was given a long sentence, was sent to Siberia, and remained
there until 1917 when he was liberated by the February
Revolution. As regards Stalin's death, Kennan's opinion was
that he was at the time a very sick man, but his lackeys ' helped
him to die '.

The second piece of information was about Kennan himself
and the demand of the Russians for his recall as ambassador
in Moscow in October, 1952. He told me that the Soviet Communists had been gunning for him for a long time. This did not
surprise me. The Soviet bosses mistrust ambassadors who speak
Russian. Kennan himself had been on Stalin's black list ever since
V.E. day in Moscow in May, 1945. A huge crowd had assembled
before the American Embassy. The Americans were in high

spirits, but were certainly not drunk with liquor. They opened wide the windows, put out first a Soviet flag and then the Stars and Stripes, and stood beside the two emblems. The crowd went wild with delirious cheers. An American sergeant, greatly daring, climbed out of the window and stood on a narrow and highly dangerous parapet. The crowd cheered louder than ever, and the noise attracted more and more people.

So loud and so long was the shouting that the Kremlin or the M.V.D. sent agitators to address the crowd and to order them to go away. The Russian crowd, however, had lost all fear and was not to be moved. It remained all evening to cheer the Americans at the window and especially the American sergeant on the parapet. He was the hero of the day and ended it by a daring jump into the crowd. He was carried away in triumph by the cheering Russians and did not return until the next afternoon.

George Kennan did not ask him where he had been. He also told me that Stalin never forgave him for this spontaneous act of American buoyancy.

During the war Averell Harriman told me that the West should always send to Moscow ambassadors who speak Russian. In this respect the Americans have had a great advantage over us, for in George Kennan and 'Chips' Bohlen they have had two ambassadors who speak fluent Russian.

This world will hear more of George Kennan. He is a thinker and in regard to Slav affairs he has a great following not only in his own country, but also in Europe.

3

A third American whom I admired and with whom I had to wrestle amicably during the Second World War was General 'Wild Bill' Donovan.

I saw a good deal of him during the war, but I had met him in London long before. 'Wild Bill' had a knack of being on the spot wherever trouble was to break out, and in 1935 I received a telephone call from him. He had read my book on Russia. Would I dine with him at the Ritz?

I had no idea who he was and should almost certainly have refused his invitation, but for the fact that he added: 'I have

just come back from Ethiopia.' Had he said merely Abyssinia
I might still have refused his invitation. As it was, I was at the
Ritz five minutes before my time.

He went straight to the point. There would be war in Abyssinia.
(He still called it Ethiopia.) The Italians would win with the
greatest of ease. What were we going to do about it ? I could not
tell him. War I agreed was likely. There were, I said, people in
Britain who remembered Adawa and thought that the Italians
might have another disaster.

He shook his head. " The Italians have modern weapons and
aeroplanes. The Ethiopians have neither."

This dapper, clean-shaven American interested me. He spoke
quietly. He knew things and raised difficult issues. To ward
him off I plied him with questions about himself, and that night
he told me a small part of his remarkable life-history.

He had begun his career as a poor Catholic choir-boy in
Buffalo and, as a choir-boy, was fortunate enough not only to
have his singing voice trained, but also to be given lessons in
elocution. From early youth he was keen on amateur theatricals
and was regarded as a budding actor.

His real ambition, however, was to be an attorney, and his
main preoccupation was how to find the money to pay his
college fees. A touring company came to Buffalo. One of the actors
fell ill, and at once Bill Donovan volunteered for the job. He was
given a part and he barn-stormed with the company through the
United States until he had amassed enough money to see him
through college.

He became an attorney, and the golden road of American
success was open to him. He had a gently compelling voice
with a faint echo of an Irish brogue. Better still, he had a splendid
fighting record in the First World War and commanded the
' Fighting 69th Regiment ' in which served such legendary
warriors as Father Duffy and Sergeant Yorke. He was called
' Wild Bill ' for his toughness and his hard training methods,
and he himself gained the Congressional Medal for gallantry
on the French front. At that time he was just thirty-six.

His triumphs as a soldier helped him in the courts, and he
made big money, his most profitable cases being Hollywood
divorces.

I spent a pleasant evening with this energetic American and never expected to see him again.

I was quite mistaken. In December, 1941, the various secret and open intelligence and information services of the United States began to make all the mistakes, intrigues and muddles which we had made. Colonel Donovan was head of the American Office of Strategic Services, which covered both secret service and also subversive operations of much the same nature as our own S.O.E.

He was also bidding for the control of political warfare which the Americans called psychological warfare and, some months before the American Office of War Information was created, had developed quite a number of plans for this purpose.

The first renewal of my acquaintanceship with ' Wild Bill ' was on February 5, 1942, when his London representative called on me in London, and, showing me a telegram, told me that Colonel Donovan wanted a first-class British Political Warfare representative in Washington and had asked for me. After consulting Mr Eden, I refused the invitation as politely as I could.

Although President Roosevelt created the Office of War Information in June, 1942, he did not make clear what were exactly the responsibilities of O.W.I. and O.S.S. The wrangles and intrigues therefore continued and were complicated by the fact that the British S.O.E. were backing Donovan's O.S.S. in the hope that if Donovan was successful in getting control of psychological warfare, S.O.E. would knock out P.W.E. in Britain and get control of British political warfare.

During this trying and, indeed, disgraceful period I saw Colonel Donovan on a number of occasions. I had been told that he would be very difficult. Doubtless like myself, he had aged considerably since our meeting before the Italo-Abyssinian war and so far from being violent and obstinate I found him most reasonable. I knew that both the Foreign Office and the British Chiefs of Staff were quite determined that S.O.E. was to have nothing to do with political warfare. I put all my cards on the table and told Donovan the truth. I asked him to dinner the next evening in the Iolanthe room in the Savoy.

It should have been a success, for my guests included Anthony Eden, John Winant, Brendan Bracken, Alec Cadogan and

Ivone Kirkpatrick, but, as usual when Americans were present, Brendan talked not only to them but at them. However, Bill Donovan seemed pleased, and eventually all our complicated tangles were straightened.

Whenever he came to London we met. In my organisation we changed his name from 'Wild Bill' to 'Big Bill' to distinguish him from Sir William Stephenson, a Canadian who became 'Little Bill' and who worked in New York and rendered most valuable services to the British cause. In my heart I think that 'Big Bill' realised that political warfare was not his subject. He was a man of action interested in war and in subversive operations against the enemy. At the opening of every Anglo-American offensive he managed to get a front seat either in an aeroplane or a motor-car.

This honour pleased him as much as his promotion to General, and he deserved both. There was no braver man in any army. I have no doubt that he was a tough enemy as well as a sterling friend. One of his chief dislikes was Edgar Hoover of the American Federal Bureau of Investigation. 'Wild Bill' spent large sums of money on 'boosting' O.S.S. which he wanted to perpetuate as the secret intelligence organisation of the United States. He was defeated, partly by the army, but mainly by Hoover, whom he regarded as his greatest enemy.

Bill Donovan's courage was proof against all menaces and disasters. One night during the war in Washington he was run into by a drunken F.B.I. chauffeur who was driving on the wrong side of the street.

Donovan's legs were badly damaged. He had a luncheon the next day with Bruening, the former German Chancellor, in New York. It seemed impossible for him to get there, but 'Wild Bill' got to the station. During the journey to New York he had his legs put into splints and arrived punctually for luncheon at the St Regis Hotel. During the meal he spoke well, listened well and was very courteous. He took two stiff brandies and soda— a rare thing for him, for he was almost a teetotaller. Otherwise there was no sign that he was in the greatest pain.

This story is true in every detail. The host was John Wheeler-Bennett.

Bill Donovan, who died on February 8, 1959, was a

non-smoker and a good Catholic. He had a profound zest for life and, when I knew him, needed only four hours' sleep. He had political ambitions, and stood once for Governor of New York, but was heavily defeated. Like most Americans he was ruthless in politics and undoubtedly ' had a dagger '. People said that he was a bad enemy. He was certainly a staunch friend and for all his Irish background he was most loyal to Britain during the war and very proud of the honorary K.B.E. which was accorded to him after it was over.

CHAPTER FIVE

Two Czech Martyrs

> ' It is better to honour your country by your death than to
> dishonour it by living.'
>
> P. J. Šafarik

THE leading Nazis and Communists shared, and share to-day, certain characteristics. Both followed Lenin's maxim, ' anything is ethical and moral which promotes the building of a Communist (or Nazi) society and everything that hinders this is unethical and immoral.' Both Lenin and Hitler believed that ' a small minority can govern tens of millions provided that it has three things : an army, a police force, and a myth ', the myth being the official doctrine. Hitler modelled his Gestapo on the original Soviet Cheka. Common to both Nazis and Communists were ruthless cruelty, sadistic torture, and merciless extinction of all opponents, whose only hope of survival was to face the dangerous hazards of escape abroad. Many perished in the attempt, but hundreds of thousands succeeded in swelling the populations of what we call the Western world. To-day there are over seven hundred thousand French citizens born of Russian exile stock.

It has been my lot to have spent the best years of my life in Russia and Czechoslovakia. In both Russia and Czechoslovakia I was closely connected with the democratic régimes of Prince Lvov and Alexander Kerensky in Russia, and of Thomas Masaryk and Eduard Beneš in Czechoslovakia.

Other countries like Poland, Rumania, Bulgaria and Yugoslavia have suffered similar catastrophes. Nearly every English-speaking person has met at least some of the exiles. Few, apart from the exiles, know the fate of the democrats who remained at home to defend democracy against dictatorship. Indeed, among the exiles abroad there is a kind of classification of the degrees of resistance in the different countries. Most people give highest praise to the Poles for sustained and indomitable courage against both German and Russian oppressors. There is a tendency in the West to criticise the Czechs for sitting on the fence and even for lack of guts. It may be true that in Czechoslovakia, by far the most prosperous of the Soviet satellites, there has been little active resistance against the Communists. But passive resistance has been strong and remains strong to-day. During the last war, when the German ' Protectorate ' in Czechoslovakia was at its peak of repression, opposition to the Nazis was continuous, and the flower of the Czech nation perished.

In this chapter I give pen-portraits of three Czechs, two of whom suffered torture and death at the hands of the Nazis and the Communists. The other, who is still living, has been many years in prison.

I

When I went first to Czechoslovakia in the first days of 1920, I was already received as a friend, because I had done my best in Russia to persuade Trotsky to allow the Czechoslovak Legionaries to leave the country. Among the first leading Czechs whom I met was Dr Přemysl Šamal, President Masaryk's Chancellor. Strongly built with broad shoulders, he wore a short black beard and was of medium stature. He had a charming smile and a warm, kindly look in his eyes. Almost everyone who did not know his record would have assumed from his attractive manners and gentle speech that he was easy-going and far removed from the world of violence and danger. But all Prague was in the know. During the First World War he was head of the famous Maffia, which not only arranged the escape of Beneš abroad, but also did much to sap the foundations of the Austro-Hungarian Monarchy.

When I arrived in Prague, he was fifty-three, twenty years older than I was, but we got on famously, for he was fond of shooting and often took part in the shooting parties arranged by the Czechoslovak Government for the diplomatic corps. I remember one occasion when he brought down two cock-pheasants with as good a right and left as anyone could wish to see. They flew rather nearer to me than to him, but we were on the battlefield of Austerlitz and I was thinking more of history than of shooting.

Šamal worshipped Thomas Masaryk and lived in Carmelite Street close to the famous Hradčany Palace of Prague. He was the most modest of men and was beloved by Czechoslovaks and foreigners alike. The last time I saw him was when I came to Prague in March, 1938, just after seeing Hitler and his troops enter Vienna. All my Czechoslovak friends knew that their turn would come next. In September came Munich and in March, 1939, the Nazis occupied Prague. Immediately the Czechoslovak patriots began to organise an underground resistance movement like the Maffia in the First World War. After Munich many leading Czechoslovaks, including President Beneš, had gone abroad, but many others believed that the nation needed leadership and stayed at home. Among them was Šamal. Much to his surprise, the younger patriots begged him to become again the leader of the underground resistance. He was unwilling to accept. He was now over seventy. Moreover, his activities in the First World War were well known to the German. The Nazis, he said rightly, were quite different from the Austrians. He thought a younger and more active man should be chosen, but when the younger men still insisted and offered him a younger and gallant assistant in Ladislav Rašin he accepted.

In the First World War Czech intelligence was of great assistance to the Allies. During the ' phoney ' period of the Second World War a wireless telegraph link was established between Dr Beneš in England and the underground movement at home, and until final victory valuable information was received from the Czechoslovak patriots.

But as Šamal had pointed out, the Nazis were both cleverer and more brutal than the Austrians, and even before the end of 1939 Rašin was arrested in his flat just as he was about to escape. Other members of the underground were arrested early in 1940, but the movement, based on small cells, each of which was linked only with the immediate cell above it, was not broken. It is true that many members of the original group had to flee the country, but fresh volunteers carried on the movement until the end of the war. The losses were heavy, and the chain of secrecy was passed on literally by one dying hand to another.

In March, 1940, Přemysl Šamal, who had been in hiding out-side Prague, returned to the capital and was arrested in his flat. With pride and great courage he not only admitted his activities, but, taking all the guilt on his own shoulders, he told the Nazi inquisitors that he had forced the others to work with him.

During his interrogation in the Gestapo Headquarters in Prague he refused to answer the questions of the Gestapo bullies. He was, he said, an old man who no longer cared what happened to him. He was then seventy-three years old. Such was the strength of his moral personality that he might have influenced normal people. The Nazi inquisitors, however, were angry and imprisoned him in one of the worst cells in the now ill-famed Pankrac Prison in Prague. His fellow-prisoners cleaned his cell for him and offered him part of their wretched food. He refused every comfort and continued to urge all to endure and have faith in the victory which, he said, he would not live to see.

In the summer of 1940 the interrogations in Prague were completed, and Šamal and other members of the underground were transferred to the Alt-Moabit prison in Berlin where they were to be tried before the People's Court. In the autumn of 1940 one wing of the Moabit prison was destroyed by a British bomb. Šamal's cell was damaged, but he himself was unhurt. From that time onwards he was always escorted to a shelter during an air-raid. The Nazis wanted him alive, for they wished to make an example of him as the leader and instigator of what they called Czech treason.

That he would be sentenced to death and executed was certain. But before the trial opened, Providence intervened, and gentle and painless death cheated the Nazi hangman of his prey.

The Nazis took a fierce vengeance on this fine old man who cared so much more for the fate of others than for his own. They executed the rest of the group. In the summer of 1942 they murdered his son and sent his children to Germany and his wife to the concentration camps of Auschwitz and Ravensbruck.

In May, 1947, Dr Šamal's remains were brought back to Prague and were buried in the Vyšerhrad Cemetery where lie many famous Czechs including my friend, Karel Čapek. Jaromir Smutny, Beneš's Chancellor, who has helped me greatly with this portrait, tells me that Jan Masaryk spoke at the grave and said that Šamal had been a second father to him and that his heroic patriotism was of a quality that no longer exists.

That Jan Masaryk looked on Šamal as a second father is not mere rhetoric. I remember how during the war in his Christmas broadcast of 1942 from London he talked of Prague and told his huge audience what he would do if he could be with them. He would go, he said, 'along Klarov and Carmelite Street. There the late lamented Šamal lived before they took him off to torture. I must bare my head in front of this house. We Protestants did not bare our heads in front of churches and statues. Now we must lay bare our hearts in front of the houses where our saints lived.'

A week after the burial of Šamal's remains I was staying with Jan in Prague. On May 17 we had been to see Beneš at Lany and when we came back to Jan's flat in the Czernin Palace there was a parcel on the table in his bed-room. It contained Šamal's Bible, nearly every page of which was annotated by Thomas Masaryk. Doubtless, he had given it to Šamal. Madame Šamal had been so moved by Jan's oration at the grave that she had sent the Bible to him in gratitude. Jan sat turning over the pages for nearly an hour.

Přemysl Šamal was not only an exemplary patriot. He was also a believer. May his soul rest in peace.

According to the best information approximately four hundred thousand Czechoslovak citizens perished during the Nazi occupation. Of these approximately one hundred and fifty thousand were Jews, nearly four-fifths of the pre-occupation Jewish population in Czechoslovakia. The other Czechoslovaks who perished included the pick of the intelligentsia.

In the next two pen-portraits I shall try to show how much Czechoslovaks suffered at the hands of their own compatriots.

2

For the best part of the first two years of the last war I was the Foreign Office representative with the Czechoslovaks in Britain and with their Provisional Government in London.

Until June 21, 1941, the Soviet Government was in alliance
with Hitler and accused France and Britain of starting an im-
perialist war against Germany. The Czech Communist leaders,
who spent a safe war in Moscow, followed the policy of their
masters and denounced the action of Beneš and his followers
in opposing the Nazis.

Inevitably the British War Cabinet wondered how long this
curious Nazi-Bolshevik alliance would last, and there was much
speculation whether the Soviet Union would be dragged into
the war and, if so, whether its armed forces could stand up to
a Nazi onslaught.

I have pointed out that President Beneš had wonderfully good
information from German-occupied Czechoslovakia. He had
also a remarkable soldier in Moscow who was on excellent terms
with the leading Soviet officers. This was Colonel Pika, head
of the Czechoslovak Military Mission in the Soviet Union and,
after Russia's entry into the war, the Czechoslovak Military
Attaché. Heliodor Pika, who as a young man had served with
the Czechoslovak Legionaries in Russia in the First World War,
was remarkable in that he had the charm and good manners of
a first-class diplomat. He had also the art of winning the confidence of the foreigners with whom he came into contact. A
good linguist with an excellent knowledge of Russia and of
Russian, he was the ideal Military Attaché.

After serving in Rumania at the beginning of the last war,
he went to Moscow at the request of the Russians as head of a
Czechoslovak Military Mission. As Russia was not yet in the war,
the Mission was a secret one.

For many months I spent much of my time in translating
Colonel Pika's reports in Czech and sending the English versions
to the Foreign Office and the Joint Intelligence Committee.
Pika was no Communist, but he believed in the Russian Army
and from the beginning was confident that not only would the
Soviet Union be forced into the war, but also that its armies
would resist to the last and give a good account of themselves.
Of the various so-called British authorities on Russia, there was
only one man who gave any credence to Pika's reports. This
was the late Brigadier Scaife, who had been Military Attaché
in Moscow in the 'thirties.

In due course Colonel Pika's reports were proved to be true. He was promoted to the rank of General and continued to remain on the best terms with the Russian senior officers. Indeed, the Soviet Army could have had no better propagandist than this Czechoslovak anti-Communist officer.

Pika was also the first man to warn President Beneš that Fierlinger, the Czechoslovak ambassador in Moscow, was playing a double game. Again his report was true, but it earned him the jealousy and hatred of his ambassador. Admittedly the situation was a difficult one, for Pika had the right to report direct to President Beneš without showing his telegrams to Fierlinger, who disliked Pika very much, partly because he was jealous of Pika's popularity with the Russian officers and partly because the two men differed widely in their political views. Fierlinger was already intriguing with the Communists. Pika was a non-Party man, but in his reports he commented on the activities of the Czechoslovak Communists in Moscow.

After the war Pika returned to Czechoslovakia and was honoured by the Czechoslovak patriots. By the Communists, however, he was already a marked enemy. After the Communist *coup d'état* of February, 1948, the Communist leaders discovered the whole dossier of Pika's reports in the archives of the Ministry of Defence, and Pika was arrested and was condemned to death by hanging by a so-called Court-Martial. The accusation against him was that he had carried on espionage for the West against the Soviet Union from 1940 to 1945 and against Czechoslovakia from 1945 to 1948.

I received the news from the B.B.C. at 6 p.m. on January 28, 1949, and was shattered. That evening I wrote in my diary : ' This is murder and revenge and also the desire to be rid of an undesirable witness. What callous rascality ! Pika was Beneš's man of confidence, was in touch with the Russians before they came into the war and was *persona grata* to the Soviet officers. The Soviet authorities gave him a special transmitter. They never made one complaint against him. In 1941 the Soviet Union and Britain gave full recognition to the Czechoslovak London Government which appointed Pika Military Attaché in Moscow. How could he have been spying against the Soviet Union from 1940 to 1945 ? The truth is that, from the beginning, Gottwald,

Nejedly and Co., the Czechoslovak Communist leaders in Moscow, were traitors to the Czecholovak Government which the Soviet Union recognised.' The same is true of Fierlinger, and there is little doubt that Fierlinger himself contributed false evidence against the unfortunate Pika. What is more remarkable in this macabre conspiracy is the fact that General Pika had taken no part whatsoever in various intrigues and minor plots engineered by other Czechoslovak senior officers. It is difficult to discover any motive for his condemnation other than revenge and hatred. Sadder still was the indifference of the Western world to the fate of a man who had served it well.

The British Government may have made some protest in Prague, but the step, if taken, could not have been effective, because only six weeks before the Communist *coup d'état* we had changed our ambassador to Czechoslovakia.

For nearly five months General Pika was allowed to linger in prison with the death sentence hanging over him. The Communists wanted more information from him, and in his prison in Pilsen he was subjected to mental and, I do not doubt, physical torture.

His ' zero ' week began badly. On Sunday, June 19, 1949, Archbishop Beran, who had spent the war in a German concentration camp and who was then being kept under house arrest by the Czechoslovak Communists, was allowed to preach in St Vitus's Cathedral. His sermon was stopped by Communist hecklers sent to the cathedral for this purpose. He was, however, able to tell his congregation that he might not be able to speak to them again and that, if he disappeared from their sight, they should never believe any report that he had capitulated to the Communists. He would, he added, always stand by human rights and for the laws of the Church.

Two days later, on June 21, General Pika, still on the right side of fifty-five, was executed in Pilsen. The Communists allowed a priest to visit him before the end, and in this manner it is known that he died as one would have expected him to die— without a tremor or even a curse on his murderers.

He had done his duty to his President and to the legal Government of his country. His only mistake was to keep telegrams which he should have destroyed, for he must have realised that from 1945 onwards the Communists were seeking to inculpate every general who had served Beneš. His only guilt was to have held different views from those of the Communists, and for this audacity he was put to death.

In the House of Lords the noble-minded Vansittart raised the question of Pika's execution and in reply Lord Henderson, the Labour spokesman, said that the Government could not intervene, but made a sharp attack on Communist methods. At the Caxton Hall there was a protest meeting attended mainly by Czechoslovak exiles.

3

The identity of my third Czech resister must remain secret, for he or she is probably still in great danger. Nevertheless, the letter which I received from this individual came to me from a political prisoner who had served seven years and was still in prison. Of all the letters that I have received from behind the Iron Curtain this is the noblest and the most poignant. I can vouch for its authenticity. I have not altered the letter in any way. Here it is :

' For a long time already I have tried to find a way to you. I feel the necessity now to use this opportunity to thank you for what you have done for all of us and for our nation during the last hard years.* This feeling of gratitude lies deep in my heart and I am sure that history may one day value your work.

' I realise that sometimes it is very hard to explain different aspects of the political situation and that the long years, full of promises, but with no positive results, are sometimes hard to be understood here.

' I should like to stress that, especially in the last months, the development shows the rightness of our course—a course that we have not deserted. The Indian Vice-President, Mr Raahekrishvan, has shown a beautiful and genuine picture of our philosophy and point of view. I wish that his speeches could be made known to the nation in the full text.

* Since June, 1947, Sir Robert Bruce Lockhart has broadcast weekly to Czechoslovakia.—Publisher's note.

'I see in these speeches the principal ideals practised by President Masaryk in his life and philosophy. I see that the example of the late President remains always as a firm pillar in the tempest and I should like to say that his example, his social justice, his Christianity, his humaneness, and even his socialism are the right and true symbols of a popular policy for our nation in the future. We do not need to use lies, force or camouflage. The only way that we can see is this one of a fair example and fair play for everybody.

'There are rumours that the political prisoners are aiming to return to old mistakes, to capitalism (as it is called), that they envisage hatred and punishment of all Communists, and so on. I cannot speak for anybody but myself, but, during these last seven years of prison, I have spoken with thousands of my friends and know their point of view. I can assure you that the prisoners are very sorry about the present difficulties of our Republic and are looking forward to help in this direction. Christian love, forgiveness, and the will for a fair and just co-operation with all people of good will are our principal aims. And this way of love, personal liberty, co-operation and eventual help are the only ways that can lead our nation to a better future. I am sure that this is also the goal of all fellow-workers, of all students, writers, and all men of good will, whom I admire very much for their heroic struggle in these days.

'I should like to stress one more thing : Jan Masaryk, your good friend, told me once that for him democracy means to be able to stand on show on the Wenceslas Square and protest openly against the policy of the Government. And this was the biggest moment in his life. He did the same thing as Socrates, as Jesus Christ, as Jan Hus, and by his heroic death he entered into our national history as well as into the history of the world. He denied to serve a régime he did not like and he showed his point of view in the only accessible way at that time. By his tragic death on March 10, 1948, he showed the nation and the world that he had not chosen freedom for himself, but had sacrificed his life for a better future for his beloved people of Czechs and Slovaks.

'And that is all. I am sure that through me you may accept the thanks of all of us and the firm persuasion that ours is a good cause and that, together with Thomas and Jan Masaryk, we may soon enter into the family of free nations.'

Czechoslovakia has suffered tragically from the policies of France, her ally, and of Britain, her friend. She was sacrificed in the vain hope of preserving peace for ourselves. To-day there are Municheers who accuse the Czechs of being spineless in resisting Communism. Irrespective of the folly of premature rising, I hope that these examples of Czech heroism will correct some unfortunate impressions.

CHAPTER SIX

Missionaries of Sport

' For what do we live, but to make sport for our neighbours.

IN 1861 Dostoyevsky, writing in the St Petersburg *Vremya*, asserted that of all countries in the world Russia was the least known and the least understood by its Western neighbours. Doubtless, there are many living British and Russian writers who would say with perhaps less exaggeration that the Soviet Empire of to-day is more of a *terra incognita* than Dostoyevsky's Russia.

Nevertheless, in the seventeenth, eighteenth, and nineteenth centuries the British knew Russia very well and played a considerable part in the modernising of the country. In the seventeenth century and the eighteenth century the Scots provided famous generals like Patrick Gordon, George Ogilvy, Marshal Keith, and Robert Bruce who superintended the building of St Petersburg. More remarkable is the fact that the Russian Navy was created by Admiral Sir Samuel Greig of Inverkeithing. Scots, too, supplied the Russian court with physicians.

In the nineteenth century the English played an all-important part in the Russian industrial revolution and created the Russian textile industry. The managers and technicians of the cotton mills were mainly Lancashire lads, and inevitably they introduced football not only into Russia, but also into the Russian factories.

Curiously enough, the first football game started by the British in Russia was rugby. The bold initiator was a Mr Hopper, a member of a family which was of Scottish extraction and was well known in Russia. A descendant of his, a Miss Hopper, was my most excellent private secretary during the exciting year of 1918. Mr Hopper's efforts to launch rugby football were soon cut short. In 1886 the game was stopped by the police who considered it a brutal game conducive to manifestations and rioting.

In 1887 Clement Charnock inflated a soccer ball in the presence of an interested crowd of workers and peasants. He punted the ball high in the air. When it came down with a thud and bounced high again, the workers ran away.

Clem Charnock belonged to a Lancashire family—I might almost say clan—which came from Chorley. The family was of yeoman stock, but with the industrial revolution switched over to cotton spinning.

Over a hundred years ago three Charnock brothers, William, James and Clement, went to Russia to start the Russian textile industry. In 1860 William became the manager of the John Houston spinning mill at Serpukhov near Moscow. It was the first mill built in Central Russia and the second in the whole Russian Empire, the first mill having been the Krenholm mill which was built at Narva in 1858.

James Charnock opened the Vicoul Morozov mill at Oriechovo-Zuyevo and Clement Charnock senior managed mills near Moscow. William and Clement had sons, most of whom were born in Russia and who, after being educated in Lancashire, followed the example of their fathers and in due course became managers of big Russian cotton mills.

When I came to Russia in January, 1912, there were five Charnocks of the second generation. Clem, Harry, Ted, and Billy were the sons of William Charnock and Jim, their cousin, was the son of Clement Charnock senior. At that time four of the five were in top jobs, Clement junior, who introduced soccer, having retired. Harry was head of the Vicoul Morozov mills, which were far bigger than any Lancashire mill, for both spinning and weaving were done in the same place. Jim Charnock was his assistant, and Billy the chief technical consultant. Ted was manager of the big mill at Serpukhov near Moscow.

All five Charnocks were rabid football enthusiasts, and in 1912 Jim, Ted and Billy were active players. In the early days of soccer in Russia the game had been played, first, by the British among themselves and, a little later, by mixed teams of British and Russians, the latter being mainly students, cadets, and clerks in business houses.

In 1894, however, Harry Charnock, head manager of the vast Vicoul Morozov mills, introduced soccer to the workers. It was an immense step forward in the social life of the Russian worker and, if it had been adopted rapidly for all mills, history might have been changed. But, at first, there was little or no progress except in mills and factories which were either British, like Coates, or Russian-owned, but British-managed.

In 1904 the first inter-city match between Moscow and St Petersburg took place. In 1909 the first Russian sporting weekly appeared. It was not as well produced as anything of the kind in Britain, and football and racing filled more pages than lawn-tennis, gymnastics and wrestling put together. Its name was *Russki Sport*. In 1910 the Moscow League was formed, and this was the real beginning of organised football in Russia. Skill was still lacking, and in 1911 a strong team of English Wanderers played three matches in Russia and won by double figures in all three.

What was most interesting in this development of the Moscow League championship was the advance of the Morozovsti, the factory team organised by the Charnocks. Without a doubt it was, from 1910 to 1914, the best team in Russia, and during the whole life of the original Moscow League, which of course died in 1914, it won the championship every year.

As I come of a family of rugger fanatics, with three generations of internationals, I was brought up to play this game from the age of four, but I am eternally grateful to Fettes where, as an antidote to too much rugger and as a valuable aid to the carrying game, we had house-games twice a week in which rugger was barred and hockey and soccer played instead. I preferred soccer, especially as I had had some training from a page-boy at home who afterwards became a professional. When I went abroad, I played soccer in the North of France and both rugger and soccer in Malaya, and in my state the soccer with two Fosters and two other Englishmen who had played in League football was much better than the rugger.

On my arrival in Moscow in January, 1912, I was snapped up on the first night by Clem Charnock to play for the Morozovtsi. The first taste of vodka and the idea of playing for a team of Russian workers made me accept without an afterthought, and, although the local British took a cold view of my acceptance, I had for once done a wise action in accepting Clem Charnock's proposal. The British team lost nothing, and the Morozovtsi gained little, because I was no soccer star. Indeed, as Ted Charnock, a very fine player, who is still alive, wrote of me in an article on Russian football : ' He was a most dashing go-ahead player, full of energy on the field. Being by up-bringing a rugger-player he depended more on speed.'

The headquarters of the Morozovtsi were at Oriechovo-Zuyevo about sixty-two miles east of Moscow. The ground, not far from the factory town, was dead-level and had a good covering of grass. There was an excellent pavilion with an enclosure with seats in front of it. Many amateur clubs in Britain would be glad to have such a pavilion, because it had dressing-rooms, baths, a dining-room, a large hall for social gatherings and a cinema theatre ; this, too, in the reactionary Russia of the Tsars. At a league match the average attendance was about twelve thousand people, and the women must have contributed thirty per cent of the total.

In 1912, the year in which I played, the team was generally composed of six British and five Russians. As far as I remember, all the British players, apart from myself, belonged to the textile industry. The three Charnocks were the back-bone of the side. Jim Charnock was centre-half and the captain of the side. Although he had begun his career as a rugby player in the Northern Union, he was a good tactician and a great captain who never gave up and who allowed no dirty play of any kind. His influence on the Russian players was of immense value. Ted played left half-back, and Billy, the centre-forward, who had played for Bishop Auckland and had been sought by Manchester City, was the best player in Russia. Among the Russians there were two really first-class players : Mishin, a full-back, and Akimov, the right half-back, who, in his place at least, was the best Russian player. He and I were great friends. His enthusiasm for the game amounted almost to fanaticism, but on the field he had complete control of himself, and his passing, always along the ground, was up to the best standard of the old Scottish type. Between the two wars he came to London on a trade mission. As he may still be alive, I cannot recount all his conversation, but he had certainly not lost his admiration for the British or for Harry Charnock.

Incidentally, I was not the first outsider to play for the

Morozovtsi. In 1911 a Captain Wavell, a Wykehamist, who had been learning Russian for his examination as an interpreter, played for the club and was described as ' in play rather cautious with plenty of dash when the occasion demanded it.' This sounds as if he were a good strategist. He became afterwards Field Marshal Earl Wavell.

In 1912 the Morozovtsi did not lose a single League match. As the best team in the Moscow region, it was often chosen to play against visiting foreign teams. On these occasions skill and endurance were on the side of the visitors, especially in the second half when the British in the Morozovsti were long in years and short of wind. In 1912 I played in three matches against foreigners. We beat a Norwegian team, had a very even struggle with a rough German team, and were beaten 4–1 by a Finnish team which in 1910 had put up a very good resistance to the all-conquering English Wanderers. Against the Finns we were 1–1 at half-time, and I scored one of my rare goals, but in the second half the ancient Britons, faint yet pursuing, could not keep up the pace.

In the League competition the success of the Morozovtsi was remarkable, because the Moscow clubs had the advantage of a professional trainer in Gaskell, who had played for Bolton Wanderers. It was the Charnock spirit which made the difference between the Morozovtsi and the other teams, and Russia should be grateful to this family, not only for what it did for the textile industry, but also for instilling in the Russian mind the ethics of sportsmanship, the standard of which has fallen sadly in Britain itself during the last fifty years.

Another asset of the Morozovtsi in those early years was the junior team which in due course filled the vacant places in the League team.

What was best of all was the complete absence of dirty and rough play. During the three years before the war I saw only two instances of bad sportsmanship. On both occasions foreigners were the culprits.

As football was impossible during the Russian winter, the season corresponded more or less with our cricket season, but, depending on the weather, it started later and continued later. To most British people it seemed curious to play in hot summer and more curious still to look up and see the ladies with parasols in the enclosure.

The Morozovtsi always turned out in beautifully clean kit, provided by the firm, and were played on to the field by the factory band. There was no roar from the crowd—and no booing, though in Moscow I saw the Czechs, who had played a very dirty game, being pelted by the crowd with chunks of turf. At Oriechovo-Zuyevo discipline was perfect and goals and good play were applauded by clapping. This says much for the training of the workers, for the refereeing was far from good, partly because referees operated from the touch-line and rarely moved from the centre of the ground.

There was of course a League Association in Moscow, the members of which had rarely, if ever, played football and were mainly men who had made money and sought distinction of a kind by supporting the new sport. The President was a Mr Fulda, a jeweller of Jewish descent. He did his job well. At the end of the season the League champions received gold medals on the back of which was engraved the names both of the champions and also the name, R. Fulda, of the President. I still have mine. It is probably one of the very few that are left. After the Revolution the Bolsheviks called in all gold ornaments of every kind.

Although to-day there are in the Soviet Union large lotteries amounting to as much as 640,000,000 roubles with half this amount destined for prizes, there was in Tsarist times no betting on football and nothing in the form of football pools. To-day, the owner of a winning lottery ticket has the choice of either a motor-car, a house with a plot of land, a motor-cycle, a piano, a television set, a camera, a vacuum-cleaner and a clock or the cash equivalent of any object to which his ticket entitles him !

Anything in the nature of gambling on sport would have shocked the Charnocks, and in those early days the Morozovtsi were famous all over Russia not only for their skill but, above all, for their sportsmanship. Ted Charnock, who after the First World War became a member of the British Embassy and stayed in Russia until 1927, tells a true story of how Mr Preston, the British Consul-General, and he went to see the post-revolutionary Morozovtsi play in Moscow. Both being fluent Russian speakers, they went on the popular side and stood among the crowd. During the game a foul was given against the Morozovtsi. While the free kick was being taken, an old man, in front of the Englishmen, explained excitedly : " Did you see that ? " Then turning to the crowd, he said loudly : " You should have seen the old Morozovtsi. They were gentlemen."

From what I saw of the famous Russian Dynamos who came to Britain soon after the end of the war I should say that they had inherited something not only of the sportsmanship but also of the style of the Morozovtsi. The Morozovtsi style was based on the old Newcastle and Scottish scientific game of ball control before the English League scrapped it for speed. What the Morozovtsi learnt, the Dynamos copied. Incidentally, the Dynamo football team is or was attached to the M.V.D., formerly the notorious Ogpu. Although the players did not belong to the Ogpu, they received many privileges including not only special rations and exemption from military service, but also a long period of training before their visit to Britain.

It has been said that in Russia I played football against Nikita Sergeyevitch Khrushchev. In 1912 I was twenty-five. As the Soviet dictator was born on April 17, 1894 he was six and a half years younger than me. It is therefore possible on the count of age that he could have played against the Morozovtsi. Without doubt he was an active boy who was fond of adventure and had his first beating from the police when he was caught fishing in the private water of the local landowner in his native Ukrainian village between Kharkov and Kursk. But he could not have played football in Moscow in 1911, for in that year he went to Kharkov and earned his living as a worker in the agricultural machinery factory of Helferich-Sade.

Nikita Krushchev himself has said that he played centre-forward for the Yuzovska team which, he claims, were champions of the Don basin—and runners-up of the factory championship of *all* Russia. Here there must be some mistake, and it is more probable that M. Khrushchev said ' South Russia ', and the sycophantic Soviet journalists altered this to ' All Russia '. In the years before the First World War the standard of soccer in South Russia was a long way below that of the Moscow and St Petersburg districts.

Yuzovska was a British creation and the town was named after a Welshman called Hughes. Up to the Revolution there was a big British steel factory there.

This, however, is by the way. The real work of the Charnock brothers will give them a permanent place in the history of Russian sociology. Their introduction of football was only one of the many measures which they took to create a better life for the Russian workers and to woo them from vodka drinking which on Sunday, the only free day of the week, ended in almost unbelievable scenes of drunkenness. Vodka was a state monopoly and was sold in two categories. The bottle with the blue label cost a shilling ; the one with the red label, which many people, including myself, liked better, cost only sixpence.

Football was not the only remedy for unlimited vodka. Harry Charnock was a man of vision and was able to persuade the Morozov family to put up special workers' flats complete with heat, light, hot and cold water and furniture. There were laundries and the flats were free. Quite apart from football, ice-hockey, and tennis, there were numerous cultural enterprises, including classes in carpentry and in music and painting. There were factory choirs as well as the factory band. Above all, there was a factory theatre in which amateur talent was encouraged by visits from leading actors from Moscow. Indeed, it would be no exaggeration to say that there were few, if any, factories in Britain which could equal, let alone surpass, the best English-managed factories in Russia.

It is a great mistake to assume that in Tsarist Russia nothing was done for the workers. From 1906 to 1914 there was remarkable progress in industry, and, doubtless, but for the war many other Russian factories would have been forced to follow the pattern set by the British-managed concerns. In 1913 it was the Tsarist Government that first appointed a Minister of Sport. His name was General Voyekov.

The First World War, for which the Russian and Austro-Hungarian Governments were largely responsible, brought disaster to both. Millions of Russians were killed and perhaps even more died of typhus.

The Charnock brothers lost everything. Harry Charnock might have been almost a millionaire. In 1916 an American syndicate wanted to buy up the Vicoul Morozov mills. In their usual way the Russian owners, who came of peasant stock, haggled and delayed. While they were still wrangling over an extra 100,000 roubles when millions were at stake, the February Revolution broke out, and the Americans were off the deal with the speed of a space rocket.

The Morozovtsi footballers, who made first-class soldiers, were extinguished almost to a man. Nevertheless, their name, linked to that of the Charnocks, will be remembered as long as football is played in the Soviet Union. Even in the ' twenties ', when hatred of Britain was at its worst, Ted Charnock was given a special ' pass ' by the Supreme Council for the work done by the Charnock family for physical culture in the *old* Russia. It admitted him to various events all over the country and, in some instances, to places to which no foreign ambassador could go. It may well be that in the widest aspect of Anglo-Russian relations sport may open doors that are closed to diplomacy.

CHAPTER SEVEN

Postscript on Germany

' For myself I accept the view that the peoples of Germany stand
out as a nation peculiar, pure and unique of its kind.'

Tacitus

IT is now over fifty years since, as a young man not quite
eighteen, I made my first visit to Germany. It was the first
country, apart from my native Scotland, that I ever saw, for I
went by steamer direct from Leith to Hamburg and then by rail
to Berlin.

I owe much to the Germans. At Fettes rugby football drove
everything else out of my head. The Germans taught me to work.
But in the account book of their profit and loss to the world,
they are still heavily in the red. They bear the largest responsibility for the First World War and the entire guilt for the Second.
It is they who, by their mania for militarism, have destroyed
Europe. They carry a heavy burden on their shoulders, but
they do not admit their culpability.

Nevertheless, I have liked many Germans and I have a real
affection for their beautiful country which in the south is a
glorified Scotland. Ever since that first year of 1905–6 I have
gone back regularly and, apart from the war years, have come
back always interested, often inspired, and sometimes fearful
of the worst.

I used the past tense with regard to my liking for Germans,
not because I dislike the post-Nazi Germany, but because my
best German friends are dead. Some, like Albrecht Bernstorff,
who defied the Nazis, suffered imprisonment, and were executed
in mad rage by the Gestapo a few days before the surrender of
Germany. Many others, representatives of all that was best in
Germany, suffered the same fate. Yet to-day there are many
respectable and well-educated Germans who blame Hitler not
for starting the war or for his other excesses, but because he lost

a war which, but for his megalomania and incompetence as a military leader, Germany could hardly have helped winning.

Since the last war I have gone back to Bavaria roughly once every three years. My first post-war visit was in the spring of 1947 when I travelled by train from the Hook of Holland through West Germany on my way to Czechoslovakia and stopped at Munich on my way back. I was shocked by the destruction. Cologne, Nuremberg and, especially, Munich had been heavily bombed. The much smaller, beautiful town of Würzburg had been almost totally destroyed. Many stations were still in ruins. Broken engines and twisted carriages and trucks lay beside the track. When I awoke in my sleeper in the early morning in Bavaria, the sun shone brightly on the tangled mass of burnt-out aeroplanes on a deserted airfield.

I remembered the one axiom that has been labelled as my own ; namely, that in modern warfare defeat is a greater spur to a nation than victory. On this occasion my instinct was that I had erred. This was not like 1918. This time Germany could never rise again.

Since 1947 I have written a weekly commentary for broad-casting to Czechoslovakia, and this assignment has given me several opportunities of visiting Radio Free Europe. This American organisation has its headquarters in Munich which has long been my ' home-town ' in Germany. As I had always done in more prosperous days, I went on my first post-war visit to the best hotel. In one sense it was a mistake, not because the service was bad, but because, having won the war, we received very little for our depreciated pound.

Nevertheless, by feeding in the popular Ratskeller and other cheaper restaurants I not only saved my precious marks, but also saw how the *Kleinbürger* or *petite bourgeoisie* of Munich lived. Those who had marks certainly fed well and cheaply, and the famous Munich beer was first-class, although it did not seem to me as good as in the years of my youth when a smokable cigar could be bought for ten pfennig, a glass of light beer for the same price, a large dark Munich beer, in a glass with a metal top to it, for twenty pfennig, and single and double volumes of the *Reclam* classics—a kind of German paper-back type of Dent's *Everyman*—for ten and twenty pfennigs respectively. In my hotel and in the restaurants to which the hospitable Americans invited us we saw numerous examples of the German new rich.

In 1952 there were still many signs of the war and in several central streets of Munich like the Theatinerstrasse there were temporary buildings for the shops. I have already told in another book how I went out to my favourite trout stream about ten miles from Munich and was welcomed by the kind peasant family whom I had known in better days. They fed me with fresh eggs and coffee and cream and, when I said that I had not tasted a fresh egg for ten years, the wife's eyes opened wide with astonishment. " Lieber Gott," she said, " you won the war and have nothing ; we lost the war and have everything."

In 1952 everyone seemed to be toiling. Working hours were far longer than ours at home. The people in the shops were polite and kindly as Germans are, except when they feel that they are on top of the world. There were big differences between wealth and poverty, and, while fortunes were being made by big industrialists and merchants, the workers were underpaid.

My feeling was that, so long as the workers did not revolt against low wages and copy our methods of ' ca' canny ', Germany had a good chance of speedy recovery. Munich in 1947 was a shambles. In 1952 there had been great progress. In the summer of 1955 there was a huge increase in the number of motor-cars. The people were much better dressed. Everyone looked happy and seemed to have a song in his or her heart. American capital, fear of Russia, and German hard work and efficiency had wrought a miracle. Curiously enough, a British Trade delegation was visiting Germany at the same time as myself. On its return to England it issued a statement that the Germans worked no harder than our British workers ! I wondered how they arrived at this conclusion. It must have been another miracle !

During my 1955 visit I was much impressed by the attitude of one of the Poles working for Radio Free Europe. He had played a big part in the siege of Warsaw and as a special emissary of the Polish secret army had made a remarkable and most dangerous journey from Warsaw to England during this period. He loathed the Germans, but, as we lunched together in July, 1955, he put forward the theory that prosperity might cure the Germans of their war-lust. He supported his theory with examples of Munich Germans who had been kind to him because, he asserted, they themselves were happy.

I was interested, but not entirely convinced. I had heard more than one of our own British Left-wing intellectuals, who desire revolutionary change merely for the sake of change and their own careers, run down Sweden and Switzerland as second-rate and describe them as the 'negative countries', whereas the British Communists call them the 'dead countries'. To some extent the suicide statistics do not bear out the theory of my Polish friend; that is, if high suicide figures indicate unhappiness. For example, Sweden which is certainly prosperous, comes sixth in the list of European suicide statistics after Denmark, Austria, Switzerland, Germany, and Finland and has 18·6 per 100,000 people compared with England and Wales for which the figure is only 11·4. These figures of the World Health Organisation do *not* include the European countries behind the Iron Curtain, where in Hungary the suicide rate is known to be very high. On the other hand, suicides are not caused entirely by unhappiness or boredom. Climate and inbreeding also have their effect.

German suicide figures were comparatively high in 1955, but not really high for a nation which in 1945 seemed to have lost everything.

During my last visit to Germany in May, 1958, Munich was about to celebrate the 800th anniversary of its foundation and a labour fource of 30,000 workers were toiling day and night to remove the last scars of its bombing. Compared with the Munich of 1947, the city was hardly recognisable. New suburbs had sprung up; the main streets had been widened; the book-shops were full of well-bound books and better paper-backs than our own; there was a magnificent new university building in place of an ancient one that had been bombed.

We British, having won the war and destroyed our currency in the process, received for our debased pound eleven marks fifty instead of twenty. In the spring of 1920 I had had a suite in the Bayerischer Hof, a car to take me to the Sempt, my favourite trout river, and all my meals with excellent Moselle included, and the whole cost per day came to just one English pound. In May, 1958, so expensive was Munich for the British that I betook myself to a small *pension*.

Although I was deeply interested in the remarkable work done by the American broadcasting-stations, Radio Free Europe and Radio Liberation, which from Munich send out news talks and information in a score of languages to the Iron Curtain countries including the Soviet colonies in Central Asia, I was eager, after my long experience of Germany and the Germans, to know exactly what was the German attitude towards the Oder-Neisse Line and the expulsion of the German-Bohemians from Czechoslovakia. Was the spirit of revenge, which began very soon after the First World War, raising its ugly head again? Were Nazi-ism and anti-Semitism wholly dead?

I had the opportunity of consulting a wide panel of experts. They included Bill Griffith, then the political expert of Radio Free Europe; Somers Cocks, the British Consul-General; Julius Firt, a former Czechoslovak member of Parliament and the publisher of my books in Czechoslovakia; Eddie Schüssel, the son of my oldest German friend, and, not least, a young German who had fought in the war, had then gone round the world, is now engaged in a public service and, for that reason, shall be nameless.

I found that nearly everyone whom I consulted was of the opinion that no German Government would ever recognise officially the Oder-Neisse line. Stalin had told the British and the Americans that his name would be eternally damned by Russians, if the West did not agree to his taking a large slice of Polish Galicia including Lvov, in addition to his rape of Eastern Poland. He was certainly no diplomatic baby, for, in addition to getting his own way with Franklin Roosevelt and Winston Churchill, he recompensed the Poles for his imperialistic robbery by giving them a large slice of German territory and thereby ensured that future Poles would hate and oppose Germans even more than they hated and opposed Russians.

One of the most intelligent Poles in Radio Free Europe put forward an interesting solution for a peaceful settlement of the Eastern European problem. The Soviet Union should give back to Poland the territory round and including Lvov, and Poland would give back to Germany part of the territory given to Poland after the Second World War. The idea is excellent. It has one insuperable drawback. The Soviet Union has passed through the worst stages of its internal strife and has become the most imperialistic state in the world.

If German-Polish relations seemed to be in a cul-de-sac, there was more reassuring information about the attitude of the *Deutsch-Böhmen* or German-Bohemians as I insist on calling them, Sudeten Germans being a word invented by the Nazis. Both from our Consul-General and from Bill Griffith, who, although not a member of the American foreign service, knows more about present-day Europe than almost any American or British diplomat, I was assured that the young German-Bohemians in Bavaria and, indeed, in other parts of Germany had no desire to return to Western Bohemia. Many of them had better jobs in the German Federal Republic than they had ever had in Czechoslovakia. The only trouble-makers, I was told, were the old and aged irreconcilables like Wenzel Jaksch and Dr Lodgman who were nuisances after the First World War. Indeed, Jaksch, an obstinate and wearisome dogmatist, who came to London in 1939, had robbed me of many hours' sleep during the last war. Both Lodgman and Jaksch will go on making propaganda till they die. Propaganda has been their life-work. They have nothing else to do.

So long as there was no great recession from German prosperity and no resurgence of a violent nationalist government in Germany after Adenauer's death, both the Consul-General and Griffith were of the opinion that the German-Bohemians would not make trouble. According to the Bavarian voting statistics over the past ten years, the students, including of course the German-Bohemians, were more democratic than their elders.

This opinion was confirmed to me by Julius Firt, a man of great intelligence and industry. As an exile after the Communist *coup d'état* in Czechoslovakia in February, 1948, he had built up quite a flourishing publishing business in the United States. For patriotic reasons he gave part of his time to helping his compatriots in Radio Free Europe. A level-headed business man not given to emotionalism or sentimentality, he had satisfied himself that, every time an old anti-Czech German-Bohemian dies, his place remains empty.

He illustrated the situation with a true story. During one of Firt's temporary sojourns in Bavaria, Černy, the former

Czechoslovak Minister of the Interior, had come to Munich, and Firt had taken him to a restaurant for dinner. They were waited on by a German-Bohemian from Reichenberg, a factory town in the German fringe of Czechoslovakia. Soon all three were speaking Czech. When dinner was nearly over, Černy, now in genial mood, expressed the hope that the German-Bohemians would come back to Czechoslovakia when the country had been liberated from Communism. The waiter shook his head doggedly, and eventually Černy pressed him hard for a spoken answer. " Well," said the German-Bohemian, " perhaps I should like to come back to Karlsbad for a holiday. But who wants to go to Reichenberg ! "

My most interesting talk was with a German who had been a soldier in the last two years of the 1939–45 war and since the war had been round the world. In 1958 he was thirty-three. I found him intelligent, level-headed and unprejudiced. His journey round the world had left him with the feeling that the domination of Europe, if indeed not of the white man, was a thing of the past.

I questioned him closely about German youth. Was it true, as I had been told, that the young Germans were more democratic and pacifist than their elders ?

He was not prepared to confirm this opinion without reservations. He divided all Germans under thirty-five into two camps. There were the young men who had served in the last year of the war. They were against war, uniforms and the *Mensur* (the German students' form of duelling) and were certainly more democratic and more pacific than their elders. They were, however, not united politically or in any other way. He thought that it was important for them to form some kind of political *Kameradschaft*.

There was, however, another group, he said, which was quite different from his age group. It was composed of the youths of eighteen to twenty who were *now* (1958) in the universities. They had vaguer memories of the war and were greatly impressed by uniforms and medals. The girls of the same age took the same view and preferred smart, military-looking young men to intellectuals with long hair and sloppy clothes. Anti-Semitism and the *Mensur* were back again, the latter with the approval of the

Government. Many students joined a crack *Studenten-Korps* partly because it made them tough—and toughness is still considered a German virtue—but mainly because membership in a crack corps, like the *Borussia* in former days, opened the way to jobs in the Government and in industry.

My blond German friend, however, was quite sure that, if there were a plebiscite to-day in Germany on the arming of the German forces with nuclear weapons, there would be a big majority against it among the whole population of the Federal German Republic. There would be an equally large majority for a United Western Europe.

Having talked with these experts and also with numerous Germans from bankers to landladies, booksellers and workers, I went to lunch with Eddie Schüssel, the son of my old German merchant friend who introduced me to Bavarian trout-fishing and the charms of Munich which brought me back so often. Eddie, who owns property in Munich and lives in the country, has all his father's gifts of hospitality and friendship. I told him frankly what I had heard and I asked him for his opinion. He said at once that he was no politician and I urged him the more to give me the opinion of a business man.

He talked mainly of the economic situation and admitted that the miraculous boom which had revived the Federal Republic was temporarily over. There was, however, no serious recession, nor did he think there would be one. He defined the then situation as a kind of ' standstill '.

He confirmed that Germans between thirty and forty were anti-war and that a large percentage of the people did not want Germany to be armed with nuclear weapons.

Ever since I first went to Germany in May, 1905, I have returned more times than I can remember and over a long period have developed the dangerous habit of comparing that country with Great Britain. Although I have never been a professional pessimist, I should be dishonest if I were not to admit that on a balance of progress the comparison is in favour of Germany.

This does not mean that I would rather live in Germany than in Scotland or Cornwall. Even if I were forced to spend my remaining days in one country on the Continent, Germany would not be in my first three choices. But over a long period of years the British as a race have tended, not to over-rate the faults of the Germans which, indeed, are glaring and which have brought both Europe and their own country to the brink of disaster, but to under-rate their national virtues.

Quite apart from the miraculous regeneration of a ruined Germany in a single decade, there are several civic virtues which give the Germans advantages over the British and, indeed, many other nations. The first two virtues are cleanliness and immense capacity for hard work.

I think that anyone who has had experience of industrial towns in Britain and in Germany will admit that the German worker has a higher standard of cleanliness than his British counterpart. As for diligence, German offices and shops open an hour earlier and close at least an hour later than their British counterparts. The first impression of the Germans on almost every foreigner is their zeal for industry and their mania for organisation. Having done a full five days' work, the Bonn or Frankfurt banker or merchant is quite prepared to go to other capitals to discuss business or to close a deal. There is one capital which has been closed to him ever since the First World War because the heads of its firms are not available during the week-end. Everyone on the Continent knows which capital it is ; only the British do not realise that it is London.

Hard work brings to the Germans its own reward in progress and prosperity. There is, too, a higher standard of intellectual culture which is reflected in a much more serious Press than the British Press. There is no German newspaper as well-printed as *The Times* ; on the other hand there is no German newspaper so frivolous as the British popular daily and evening newspapers. There is, too, a higher standard in the German book-shops, which are well-stocked with German and international literature. Moreover, the German book-shops compare very favourably with the British book-shops which are so rapidly becoming the monopoly of the big firms that both in England and Scotland people are as interested in stationery and fancy goods as they are in books. Nor do the German publishers need sensational covers displaying horror, sex and violence in order to sell paper-backs to the German public.

The Germans leave nothing neglected and are always trying new ideas. They have a system of roads which leaves us far behind. While we let our canals rot, the Germans make extensive use of theirs and have recently invented river steamers which push the barges forward instead of tugging them. As for shipping, Germany had virtually none in 1945. To-day she leads the world in ship-building.

If Germany is not to outstrip us altogether in the next decade or two, we shall have to give more attention to work and less to pleasure.

What do the Germans think of Britain ? Opinions differ, mostly because of the break of the war years, and partly because the Germans have been very busy in re-building their own country and since the war go more to Paris than to London. But on return from my last visit to Germany I dined with an old friend, a leading British chartered accountant, and an Austrian who came to England between the two wars and has made a brilliant career for himself as a commercial scientist. As an Austrian who lives in Britain he is well entitled to give an unbiased opinion on England and Germany.

The British accountant and I urged him to give us his views on Britain, and, once launched on this subject, he went ahead with great frankness. Britain, he said, was well to the fore in science, but in other respects she had great weaknesses, and was in decline. The destroyers of Britain in this century were (1) Lloyd George who corrupted politics ; (2) the Webbs who put across the long-outmoded economics of Marx ; and (3) Maynard Keynes who believed that a nation could spend more than it earned.

My host insisted on the Austrian's answers to three questions : What would happen (1) to Israel ; (2) to Germany ; and (3) to Britain in the next ten years ? The Austrian's replies were that, if no outside Power interfered in the Middle East, Israel, by her own strength and superior military skill, would overwhelm the Arabs from Kuwait to Cairo. As for Germany, her armies would be dictating terms to France in five years' time.

Only a miracle could save Britain. He hoped it would come. But the decline of a nation was clearly marked when its intellect begins to atrophy. Britain had to-day no great men and its laws were idiotic. If a nation wishes to remain great or to become great, it must look after its future generations. It must protect the family. In Catholic countries the government taxes charity and gives relief to the families. In the British so-called welfare state the Government gives relief to charity and taxes the family so heavily that everyone is reduced to the same low level of unenterprising mediocrity.

This is, I think, an accurate precis of this brilliant Austrian's conversation, for I wrote the record of it that same evening. It is the view of a highly intellectual and modern-minded capitalist. Gloomy prophecies about Britain have been made before and have proved to be wrong. Nevertheless, there is as much truth in what the former Austrian said as there is in the French proverb : ' *Tant va la cruche à l'eau qu'à la fin elle se brise.*'

I am no pessimist. I expect the views of our ex-Austrian friend to be confounded, but in all forms of life the strong increase and the weak go to the wall. By reducing all to one level we reduce the strong and increase the weak.

CHAPTER EIGHT

Perceptive Pole

The deep, unutterable woe which none but exiles feel.'

FEW, if any, British citizens have had to face the choice between exile and serving or living under a totalitarian government which they dislike. Such dilemmas were frequent under the Tsarist régime in Russia, and to-day they haunt the existence of many people in the Communist-ruled countries.

It is the worst choice in this world, for one has to make it entirely alone. Many faced with the decision settle it by suicide, for there is nothing so sour as the bread of exile. Others resign themselves to existing circumstances and gradually accept the régime. Others again pretend to accept the régime and work clandestinely against it. Yet others—and they are the worst—pretend to work against the régime and yet serve it.

In the West these last are called agents-provocateurs or stool-pigeons. This designation, however, does not cover all the shades of man's weakness. Boris Savinkov, whom I knew well, was a violent anti-Tsarist and anti-Communist who fought against both Tsarism and Communism by terror and assassination. After years of exile he went back to the Soviet Union either to join the régime or to work against it secretly. The Communists did not trust him, and after a short time he was found dead on the ground below the window of his prison in the Kremlin. He may have thrown himself out of the window in despair. More likely he was 'helped to die', as so many Muscovites said later of Stalin's death.

Boris Savinkov, in his earlier days, wrote a fascinating book called *What Never Happened*. It was the portrait of a man who was a revolutionary and who also served the Tsarist police. In performing this double role he reached a point where he could not decide on which side he was.

During my seven years in Russia from 1912 to 1918 I met several Russians of the Left who fitted exactly Savinkov's portrait. There have been numerous agents-provocateurs both under Tsarism and under Communism. In Tsarist days Savinkov himself employed Azev as a terrorist, and, although many Russian revolutionaries believed him to be the most honest of men, Savinkov himself describes him as the most banal of traitors who betrayed merely for pleasure and money. In 1918, when I was head of the first British Mission to the Bolshevik Government, scarcely a week passed without an agent-provocateur coming to see me and to pretend to seek my support for plots against the Bolsheviks. In the hotel in which I lived, Blumkin, a member of the Che-ka, was only a few doors away from me. On July 6, 1918, he took part in a plot against the Government and assassinated Mirbach, the German ambassador.

The most interesting, however, of all Soviet agents-provocateurs was Malinovsky who for many years was a close friend of Lenin. He had a good brain and an excellent knowledge of Marxism and was able to render many services to the underground Bolsheviks. From time to time rumours were spread that he was working for the police. One of the informants against him was Troyanovsky, then a Tsarist officer, but also a secret member of the Communist Party and a friend of Lenin. Later Troyanovsky became Soviet ambassador in Washington. Doubtless, he knew the treachery of Malinovsky, but Lenin was obdurate and would believe no ill of this undoubtedly gifted man. In her memoirs Krupskaia, Lenin's widow, writes : ' At the beginning it never entered anyone's mind that Malinovsky could be an agent-provocateur.'

After several years, irrefutable proofs of Malinovsky's dealings with the police were laid before Lenin and forced him to brand his friend as a traitor. Fortunately for himself, Malinovsky was abroad at the time. Then came the First World War and the two Russian Revolutions of 1917, and to the astonishment of all Malinovsky came back to the Soviet Union, confessed his guilt voluntarily and asked for punishment. I do not know whether he expected mercy, but I doubt it. I believe he returned because he was a convicted Communist and because he wished to see the new Russia. Mercy not being one of the Communist virtues, he was executed. He introduced Stalin to the Party !

There is yet another type, a nobler type, of Eastern European, which the violence of our times has created. It is the exile who goes back to his country, not only to serve it honestly but also to do his best honestly to soften and reduce the asperities of its ruling dictatorship.

Such a man was my friend, Stefan Litauer, a Pole of Jewish extraction and a true Anglophile, who died in London on April 23, 1959. A man of great erudition who had studied both law and political science at the universities of Paris and Heidelberg, he came to England in 1929 after ten years in the Polish diplomatic service. Short and plump with a long face and high forehead, he was a brilliant linguist, but in all languages, including Polish, he spoke slowly enough to give his listeners the impression that he weighed his words carefully.

The job which kept him in England for fifteen years was in the Polish Telegraph Agency, an official office, of which he was the Chief London Correspondent. His wit, his reliability, and his kindness to all who came into contact with him made him popular in many quarters. He enjoyed the confidence of the Foreign Office. Above all, he was a good Samaritan to all journalists, including the foreign correspondents in London. For six years he held the rare distinction of being President of the Foreign Press Association in London.

He had a rich fund of stories, but it was his unselfish help to all lame dogs which endeared him to everyone. In the 'thirties there was one foreign correspondent whom we both knew well, but who was addicted to the bottle. Stefan Litauer and I found a doctor who said he could cure any alcoholic patient by some medicine which made the patient sick if he or she touched alcohol. We persuaded our friend to undergo the treatment. Then I went to the Balkans for three months. When I came back, I rang up Stefan : " How is X ? "

" Back in a home again," said Litauer.

" How do you mean ' back in a home ' ? When I left for Belgrade, he was in that special nursing-home where the doctor said he couldn't touch alcohol without retching."

" Yes," replied Stefan gravely. " You are quite right. But, you see, X didn't mind being sick."

Stefan Litauer's greatest public effort in England took place just over two months after the Munich tragedy of September 28, 1938, a tragedy which had depressed deeply not only Czechoslovakia, but all the small nations of Europe. On December 13 the Foreign Press Association celebrated its fiftieth Jubilee by giving a large dinner in Grosvenor House. All the leading ambassadors were invited. The toast list contained only two speakers : The President of the Association, that is Stefan Litauer, and the Prime Minister of Britain who was going to make his first big public speech since Munich.

Stefan Litauer knew beforehand that for the first time Neville Chamberlain was going to criticise the Germans, and copies of the speech had been sent in the afternoon to the Press and to the ambassadors. An hour or so before the dinner Herr Dirksen, the German ambassador, sent a telephone message to say that he would be unable to be present. Fortunately Stefan was at Grosvenor House inspecting the arrangements. The head-waiter was about to remove the German ambassador's chair from the high table. " Leave it where it is," said Stefan. " Everyone will understand."

Five hundred guests assembled. Neville Chamberlain, never a good speaker, roused a mainly anti-German audience by criticising the Nazis for their attacks on Baldwin and by his friendly references to the United States and France. But the triumph of the evening was the empty chair of the German ambassador. A battery of camera-men photographed it over and over again, and the numerous foreign correspondents present saw to it that both photograph and their own comments went round the world.

When the war came, I still saw a good deal of Stefan Litauer who, when the Polish Government was set up in London, became head of the Press Section of the Polish Ministry of Information, a post which he held until May, 1944.

In a speech in the House of Commons after the Potsdam Conference, Mr Churchill said : " There are few virtues which the Poles do not possess and there are few errors they have ever avoided." There is some truth in the remark. The Polish Government in London was not a happy Government, especially after the unfortunate death of General Sikorski. It failed in pulling together, and the strong Conservative element in it was unbelievably intransigent. On the other hand, the Poles, who fought magnificently for the Allies, received a very raw deal both from President Roosevelt and to some extent from Mr Churchill. President Roosevelt was convinced that he understood Russia and that Soviet co-operation could be won for the future by concessions at the expense of other nations and, as Mr Churchill clung—very rightly—to the American alliance, he, too, must bear some responsibility for the Polish tragedy.

I knew that Stefan Litauer was unhappy during the war. In his views he was considerably to the Left of the Polish generals and, in September, 1943, he was close to Mikulajczik, then Polish Prime Minister. Both Mikulajczik and Stefan made it clear to me that there was a big gulf between the Polish political Parties and the military policy as represented by General Sosnkowski. Both were very gloomy about the future. I made notes of their views at the time, and what the two men said was wonderfully prophetic. In a few weeks or months the Russians would be in Poland. There would be no agreement between the Russians and the Anglo-Americans. What were the Poles to do then? They expected nothing from the meeting of the Big Three or of the Foreign Secretaries and were even sceptical of any real meeting ever taking place. Only two things could happen. Russia and Germany might make a separate peace and divide Poland. Alternatively Russia might make her own new Poland. Either way it would be death for the Poles.

I asked them what would the Poles do if at a Conference the Anglo-Americans and Russians were to agree on the original Curzon Line as the new Russo-Polish frontier.

To my astonishment they replied firmly : " Poland must keep Vilna and Lvov." At this time neither Mikulajczik nor Litauer had travelled nearly far enough along the *via dolorosa* of their country. But they were well to the Left of their Polish political and military leaders.

I was therefore not surprised when in May, 1944, Stefan Litauer left the Polish emigré Government and for over a year became the special foreign correspondent of the *News Chronicle*. In October, 1945, he joined the new Polish Government in Poland and was appointed Polish Minister-Counsellor in Washington.

I had a long talk with him in March, 1946, when he was here on his way back to Washington after a short leave in Warsaw.

He again gave me remarkably prophetic information. Poland was not yet entirely under the Communists. Politically the internal situation was still built round Mikulajczik, who, however, was playing his cards badly. He had a real following among the peasants, but, inevitably, he had become the political centre for all the discontented classes and was thereafter in great danger of being drawn to the side of reaction. His position had thus become very difficult. He might easily peter out altogether. Mikulajczik, Stefan said, also did himself great harm by constantly running round to the British and American Embassies which were centres of reaction. By way of contrast Lebediev, the Soviet ambassador, was very tactful and did not show himself much.

Litauer's view was that, if the Big Three could still reach agreement, the Polish situation would be easier. If the relations among them became tense, the tension would be felt even more in Poland.

At this stage Stefan Litauer himself was in a most unpleasant situation. In Poland the Stalinists were on top and were deeply suspicious of a Pole who had spent so many years in the West. The anti-Communist Poles in the West and, indeed, most of his British friends regarded him as a traitor. His British wife refused to go to Poland with him. The kindest criticism of him was that he was a slick opportunist.

After a spell of diplomatic service in Washington he was appointed Minister in Canberra, but never took up the appointment, partly because of his marriage and partly because of difficulties made by the Australian Government. He therefore remained in Warsaw, taught political science at the university, and became a prominent broadcaster on the Polish Radio.

In at least one broadcast he attacked me personally. I bore no grudge, for I realised that we were now on opposite sides of the Iron Curtain. But I never expected to see him again.

Then came the triumph of Gomulka and a new era of limited liberties in Poland which, after years of Stalinism, seemed almost like freedom. Soon I began to hear from British journalists and B.B.C. officials who had visited Poland of the great help and good advice they had received from a Pole called Litauer. It was of course my Stefan.

On February 8, 1957, I arrived in London from Cornwall and

spent a busy, but unhappy day, because Vansittart, whom I admired above most men, had collapsed with a heart attack and I felt that he would not recover.

In the evening I had promised to go to Moura Budberg's flat and take her out to dinner. When I arrived, there was Stefan Litauer. He greeted me with a joy so natural that there seemed to be no bar between us and no change in our friendship. Indeed, I felt far more embarrassed than he was, for he was now all for Gomulka and was confident that Poland would go farther towards freedom and would do so more wisely than Hungary by going slower.

He had changed greatly since I had last seen him in 1946, mainly because his scalp had become bald and, when he spoke, the skin on the top moved forward and backwards in the most extraordinary manner. I was fascinated, and any thought of criticism of his conduct that may have lurked in my mind disappeared at once and for ever.

Just over two years later I was called to the telephone in my Cornish refuge. The speaker was Stefan. He had come to Cornwall for ten days' holiday with his second wife, an attractive Pole who had been born and brought up in Russia and whom Stefan had married only in 1956. He was quite close to us and wanted to see much of me. I asked them both to luncheon the next day, and they spent the afternoon with us.

This was the beginning of several outings and of a long talk with Stefan when his charming wife was absent, having contracted a chill. When we were four, my wife talked to Stefan, while I had to talk Russian to the wife who spoke virtually no English. She was a most patriotic Pole and, in spite of her Russian upbringing and perfect knowledge of the language, spent most of the time persuading me that Poland was different from, and better in every way than, the Soviet Union.

Stefan refrained from any severe criticism of either Poland or the Soviet Union, but was full of wisdom, still had a wonderful memory, and created the impression of a very careful man who in the Communist world was living on a razor's edge. He had been in London for nearly a year as representative of the Polish Radio and showed real delight when he told me that his assignment had just been prolonged for another year.

Although he was guarded in his comments, he gave us a brilliant picture of Gomulka, of whom he had a high opinion, and said with concern that Gomulka was in poor health as the result of long terms of imprisonment under both the Pilsudski and Polish Stalinist régimes. Sadly he told me that there was no one in Poland worthy to succeed him. Stefan also made no hesitation in saying that life in Poland was very different from that in the Soviet Union and in the other satellites and that he himself would not be allowed to exist for more than twenty-four hours in Moscow.

He was interesting, too, on the British Labour Party, many of whose members he knew well. He had been seeing Mr Bevan shortly before his Cornish visit and expressed great surprise on finding that Nye had lost much of his interest in politics and was more interested in farming than in making speeches. This made him more attractive to his friends, but was not good for his political career. Stefan did not think Labour would win the general election, but was of the opinion that, even if it did, Nye Bevan would not make a great Foreign Secretary. He had, Stefan said, no real understanding of foreign affairs.

Stefan also talked of Dick Crossman whom he regarded as outstandingly the most brilliant man in the Labour Party. He said, however, that there would be no place for Crossman in the Foreign Office. He had too many enemies in the Party.

Stefan, too, was pessimistic about Europe and commented on the old men who ruled it. In the East, he said, this was inevitable. The losses among the young men in the Second World War had been terrible in Poland and in the Soviet Union.

On Russia he was very guarded, but gave me one piece of information. In spite of M. Khrushchev's assurances that all was well between China and the Soviet Union, Moscow was very frightened of China and had been going slow for some time in helping her. He added that on this particular subject his information was a hundred per cent accurate.

On Germany he was more explicit. His view was that the Germans who range to-day from thirty-three to forty-three and who fought in the war are a good generation. The older and younger generations are dangerous. As a successor to Adenauer, Ehrhard would be more or less safe ; Strauss would be a disaster.

Like most Poles, and especially Jewish Poles, Stefan was much more anti-German than anti-Russian.

During the ten days of his stay in Cornwall I noticed that Stefan was not only very abstemious but was on a strict diet. He told me he was taking off weight and was making marvellous progress by walking four to six miles a day during his holiday.

As he was sixty-eight years old I marvelled and, indeed, envied him, for, although Cornwall has no mountains that a Scot would call even a hill, its roads are the steepest in any European country except Montenegro !

When the Cornish holiday was over, we parted as if we had never been separated, and luncheons and dinners were laid on for our visit to London at the beginning of May.

On opening my *Times* of Saturday, April 25, 1959, I looked at the obituary column and to my horror read the words ' Dr Stefan Litauer. Polish Journalist and Diplomat.' His name was the top of the list and was followed by a long, brilliant and kindly notice of a man who, though highly tried by the storms of his time, remained throughout a good and true friend to the country in which he spent the best years of his life. He had died suddenly two days before the notice appeared.

I felt sad and almost bitter. I had no idea that he had a bad heart and had previously had a thrombosis. Had he told me I should have done my utmost to stop those dreadful switchback walks in Cornwall.

BOOK III

THE LAND I LOVE

*' That old lonely lovely way of living in
Highland places.'*

DOUGLAS YOUNG

CHAPTER ONE

Old Highland Worthies

' Hard was their lodging, homely was their food.'

FOR most of my life I have been a wanderer on the face of the earth. Only twice in the long years have I had a house with my own furniture, and then only for a short time. For the traveller the golden rule is never to go back, for he or she is likely to be disappointed. Inevitably I have broken the rule, for rules are made to be broken, and to one little corner of these islands I have returned regularly either to assuage my sorrows or to celebrate the rare successes of my life. Now that I cannot afford to travel abroad I return to it with the ardour of a first love. As soon as the turn of the year is past, my thoughts turn northwards and, like the salmon, I feel the urge to return to the Spey which in the beauty of its setting and in its changes of mood is the loveliest as well as the swiftest river in Europe.

The magnet which draws me irresistibly northwards is that corner of the Central Highlands where Inverness-shire, Moray-shire and Banffshire meet. The centres of my yearly sojourn are Cromdale, once a Royal Burgh, but now a tiny village, Grantown-on-Spey, and Tomintoul, the highest village in the Highlands. All three lie close to the Spey and its tributary, the A'an. All three look out on the glory of the Cairngorms and the softer, heathery beauty of the Cromdale Hills. Here were the homes of my Macgregor forebears. Here, too, was the playground of my boyhood.

In my own life there have been great gaps, for I first went abroad in 1905 and, apart from a few short furloughs, I saw little of home and motherland until 1929. Since the last war, however, there has never been a single year in which I have not visited Strathspey, and now my wife and I spend most of every summer there.

Since my childhood there have been many changes, most of

them alas ! changes of decay rather than of progress. In the days of my boyhood Balmenach, the famous distillery, still belonged to my mother's family and was run by my grandmother and my mother's eldest brother. In the summer holidays my grandmother usually took a shoot somewhere in Strathspey, and at an early age I learnt both to shoot and to fish. Game was plentiful and hares and rabbits were almost a plague. As for fishing, the local burns were full of good trout, and my brother and I had more or less a free run of the Castle Grant water of the Spey.

For three generations the Macgregor women had borne large families, and during August and part of September our relations came to Strathspey from all corners of the world. It was almost like a clan gathering, and there must have been at times thirty or forty of them in the district at the same time. To-day there are only two distant Macgregor relations left in Cromdale and the surrounding country, and both are in the late autumn of their lives.

In those days existence was hard for the local community which lived almost entirely by farming. Rents were low, but profits were even lower, and the farmer eked out his tiny income by letting his house to summer visitors and by sending his boys to collect a shilling or two per day as beaters on the grouse moors, most of which were let to Sassenachs.

Porridge was the staple food, and big families were common. For the superfluous population emigration was the only chance of survival, and in every generation it was the cream that went. These hardy Highlanders, who were unused to any luxury, were just the people that Canada and New Zealand needed for the development of their virgin lands. It was tough going, especially in Canada, and no townsman was of any use for the job. Only the crofters could stick the hard work, the loneliness and the cold.

Many of them succeeded and lived to write their names into the history of the Commonwealth. Indeed, the area which forms a triangle with Inverness and Banff as its base and Aviemore as its apex has probably produced per head of population more famous self-made men than any other part of Britain. To Canada it gave Lord Strathcona and Lord Mountstephen ; to the United States it gave James Gordon Bennett, the founder of the *New*

York Herald, and to London Ramsay MacDonald, the first Labour Prime Minister of Britain. The list could be prolonged indefinitely, and up to 1914 there were few large families which did not receive help from some far-off son who had made good abroad. Thrift, plain living, a belief in God and in good education and, above all, determination were the ingredients of success.

To-day, after two world wars, the changes have been depressing. In many a village there are now more names of the dead on the local war memorial than there are living males of all ages. The First World War bled the Highlands and, indeed all Scotland, white. Between the two wars the increased facilities of transport brought cinemas and football to Strathspey, but took many of the men away from the district to the towns. The Second World War forced many of the women away to do war work not only in Scotland, but also in England. The outside world had now touched the Central Highlands, and the young people were eager to leave the barren North. Their thirst was now for amusement, speed and excitement. They were both unable and unwilling to live the life of simple fare and hard living of their forebears.

These changes are inevitable and are not confined to the Highlands. In most West European countries there is a pull from the country to the towns. In many respects Strathspey is a better, richer country than it was in my youth. Before the First World War the farmers were hardly able to make the barest living. To-day they thrive. There is not one who has not his motor-car or his motor-cycle. He earns much more and works less. On the other hand, the richer the farmer is the more tractors he buys and the fewer men he employs. There is therefore still the urge for emigration.

Inevitably, nearly everyone I knew as a boy has either died or left the district. Curious accidents happen to the successful emigrants who come back either to visit the old home or to spend their years there. Only two years ago I met an affluent Canadian senator in a Strathspey hotel. He had come back to see a brother who had a tiny farm in one of the loneliest spots in the district. I also know two brothers, whose father had made a fortune in the Argentine. Both father and sons wished, I think, to spend their life in Scotland. But in order to inherit the father's fortune the sons had to become Argentine subjects.

Thrift, once regarded in Strathspey as the noblest virtue, no longer exists. In my youth it was ingrained in its victims, for thrift, carried to excess, seems to have a barren end. I can remember a lonely croft, some nine miles from Grantown-on-Spey, in one of the coldest and most barren parts of the district. Apart from a keeper's cottage there was no other habitation near it. As boys my brother Rufus and I called it the abomination of desolation.

Here lived a crofter who spent all his life there. He saw no one and bought nothing. He understood sheep and once or twice a year he walked into Grantown to sell his lambs. He left £7000 which was dispersed among his various relations. The croft is now desolate. As in so many parts of the Highlands to-day a bigger farmer leases the grazing, and the crofter's cottage soon becomes a ruin. All over the bleaker areas small green patches on the hill-sides are the only signs of what has been. When man leaves the soil, the heather reclaims its own.

Not very far away from the same district there is a farm on the main Grantown road to Nairn. It is just beyond Lochan Tutach, a tiny tarn where as boys my brother and I used to catch great baskets of small trout. In my youth it was farmed by a Grant who was an expert on sheep and a great saver of money. He went frequently to the sheep and lamb sales in Grantown which was just over ten miles away. He always walked. He was often asked why he did not take the train at Dava station which was only two miles from his farm. In those days a return ticket to Grantown would have cost him about sixpence. His reply never varied : " Why should I spend my money on trains when the Lord has given me a grand pair of legs ? " He, too, left money, half of which went to his son who carries on the farm to this day and has plenty of sheep, but does not follow literally in his father's footsteps, for he has a motor-car.

The thriftiest man that I remember was ' Johnnie Gordon ' who lived in a little house in Cromdale at the corner of the road leading up to Balmenach, the Macgregor distillery. As a small boy I was afraid of him, partly because the local boys teased him and roused his anger and partly because he seemed to me the embodiment of Ebenezer, Laird of Shaws, in Stevenson's *Kidnapped*.

Johnnie came from the Cabrach about a hundred years ago. He was always a good worker as a tacksman or ploughman and was the first man in the district to get a rise in wages, namely £2 for six months. This was not the amount of the rise! This was the total wage for six months! He had of course free board and lodging, and there was little to spend on in those days except whisky at half-a-crown a bottle, and Johnnie was no drinker.

When I knew him, he had a little shop and some hens and a patch of corn. He never spent a penny. If anyone broke one of his windows, he mended it with paper. Gradually exaggerated rumours spread about his wealth. We were told or we believed that he had property in Edinburgh and walked there and back to collect his rents. This was not true. He did, however, acquire property in Fraserburgh. When he went there, he took the train, and for all food for the two-day trip he had only a ' piece ' and a bottle of milk.

He also dealt in meal and walked every week-day with his heavy wheel-barrow to Grantown and back, seven miles in all.

He used to go to Cromdale Parish Church, but never put even a half-penny into the collection bag. When it came round, he merely nodded to the church-warden to move on. When Advie was included in the Cromdale parish and through the Advie vote the minister chosen was not the one whom my grandmother wanted, she left the church and helped to set up another within a mile of the old one. As she was almost the only employer in the district, Johnnie Gordon sided with her. But he did not join the new church. He never went to church again, thus denying to it not only his contribution, but also his bodily presence.

His wife was completely illiterate and, when Johnnie was away in Fraserburgh, a neighbouring woman-friend had to sleep with her.

Johnnie died in 1908. All his Cabrach relations came to Cromdale and stayed there till the will was settled. A will was found, but rumour said its legality was doubtful. However, everyone was satisfied except in one respect. Johnnie left far less money than the whole community had expected. The reason was his mania for legislation. He went to law on countless foolish occasions. I remember a law-suit in which he accused a neighbour of allowing his sheep to interfere with Johnnie's hens.

In his whole life he never won a single case.

Aberdeen, one of the most hospitable cities in Europe, makes both propaganda and money by inventing stingy stories about its own citizens. But for real thrift the outlying farms in the Grantown area of sixty years ago had no equal.

One of the worthies whom I have described got engaged to a local girl and, to show the depth of his love, he took her to Elgin to buy an engagement ring. After long inspection she chose one and handed it to him.

He looked at it carefully, asked the price, and shook his head. " Maggie," he said, " this'll no do. Ye could buy a stirkie [a small stirk] for yon."

Maggie walked out on him straightaway—and for good.

CHAPTER TWO

Into the Big World

' Our deeds still travel with us from afar,
    And what we have been makes us what we are.'

THE reader must not think that all our folks in Strathspey spent their time in counting their pennies. There is no Englishman more hospitable than the Highlander and no European readier to take a risk. Both Grantown-on-Spey and tiny Cromdale have their celebrities both of the past and of the present. Sir James MacGrigor, the real creator of the Army Medical Corps and a firm favourite of the Duke of Wellington, was born at Cromdale in 1771. His great-grandson was the late Admiral Sir Roderick MacGrigor.

Another distinguished medical man, Air Marshal Sir Andrew Grant who in 1946 was appointed Director of Medical Services, Royal Air Force, is a son of the late A. C. Grant who in my youth built up in Grantown a tailoring business which was known all over the world, mainly because King Edward VII had his shooting clothes made there.

In the nineteenth century Highland education was at its best, partly because the dominies, all local men, were dedicated to their task and partly because the parents prized education not only for its advantages but also for itself. Discipline was as severe at home as in the school, and no boy ran howling to his mother to complain of having been beaten with the tawse, because he knew that he would have to tell why he was beaten and that he would get another beating from his father.

Thanks to the enthusiasm of the dominies, the small town and village schools of Morayshire and Inverness-shire turned out a remarkable number of men who right up to the First World War won eminence all over the world as medical men, astronomers, professors, and, not least, bankers, of whom the two most successful were the two Harveys. Alexander Harvey became manager of Rothschild's Bank in London and his cousin George became head of the Capital and Counties Bank, now Lloyd's Bank, London. Both were Grantown men and Grantown-trained. They flourished towards the end of last century.

As for the Cromdale and Grantown men who made fortunes, their number was legion. My uncle Alister Macgregor, born at Balmenach, was one of the pioneers of plantation rubber in Malaya, made a fortune and, like many other Highlanders, did not keep it. The most picturesque adventurer of the fortune hunters was Peter Geddes who was also born in Cromdale. Trained in a Grantown bank, he went to Chicago to act as clerk to an Aberdeenshire man called James Smith who was a builder. Smith made a huge fortune after the 1870 fire which destroyed nearly the whole city. Geddes, who realised quickly the vast possibilities of becoming rich, went to New York and became a most prosperous financier combining banking with stock-broking and looking after ' Chicago ' Smith's empire of investments.

Do the Central Highlands breed the same men to-day ? Are the same opportunities available ? The answer is " yes " to both questions, but there are many changes. In some respects life is much easier both for the middle-aged and the children. All people are better clothed and none need go hungry. But in this mechanised age there are not many openings for the young men and, until the Highlands can start some kind of industry of its own, adult youth will go South and, if they are wise, emigrate to the Commonwealth. They will have to work harder than they do at home, but if they show the same grit as their forebears did in a country like Canada they will go ahead far more quickly than they could ever advance in Scotland or England even if they obtained a good opening.

The grit is still there, although life is softer. Television and radio have softened the grim, dark afternoons and evenings of the Highland winter, and though the programmes could be greatly improved, imagination is fired. Sunday is no longer a day of wrath when it was a sin to play ' ducks and drakes ' with stones across the Spey. Indeed, people go to church only to have their children christened, to be married, and to be buried, although a really good preacher can still fill his church and attract visitors from afar.

The people are still the same kindly folk who welcome you when you come back yearly, and ambition is certainly not dead. Only last summer I came across two remarkable examples in which I might call my own kailyard. There is the Burgess family. The grandfather was born at Balmenach in my grandfather's time and is now high up in the eighties. To-day he still looks hale and in good spirit. He ascribes his health to the fact that he went ' canny ' after a heart attack in 1943. He gave up women and dancing. He still drinks whisky. He thinks that there are various kinds of whisky. He longs for the Balmenach malt of his youth, but still believes that there is no whisky too bad to drink. His son is the local tailor and, after taking life rather easily, began to work harder and harder until to-day he has established a very good business in tartans. The reason why he suddenly took to hard work and long hours was the best of all reasons. He had a son who the local schoolmaster said was remarkably clever. In order to send him to Glasgow University and give him a real chance, the father doubled his output. For once virtue was rewarded, for the boy, now a young man, took the highest honours in science at Glasgow University. A big oil company at once took an interest in him, and, when the young man has taken his doctorate in geology, he has a secure future before him.

Whisky, I have often said, kills those that make it, but Balmenach has produced quite a number of successful men. Within half a mile of Balmenach I went to see a charming old lady, a widow called Bell, who knew more about my Macgregor relations than I did myself. But what I was most interested in was her two sons, one of whom, James Bell, would make an epic and, indeed, is mentioned as a hero in the present Lord Tweedsmuir's book *Hudson's Bay Trader*. About thirty years ago Jimmy Bell went out from Cromdale to Canada to join the Hudson's Bay Company. Most of his time was spent in different posts in the lonely Eastern Arctic, mainly on Baffin Island.

When the last war started, he was the manager of his Company's post at Arctic Bay at the North-West end of Baffin Island. During the Second World War the Canadians and Americans set up a radio station there which was kept secret and was manned by four Canadians. As there were never more than six whites in Arctic Bay, it will be obvious that newcomers were dependent on Jimmy Bell, a giant of a man both in stature and in ability and knowledge. He weighed nearly twenty stone. He could speak Eskimo and, what was more, he won the complete confidence of the Eskimos and knew exactly how to handle them.

As a handy man he would have been a god-send to R. M. Ballantyne and other writers who wrote Arctic and Antarctic adventure stories, for there was almost nothing that he could not do. He was first and foremost a trapper and a trader for his company, but in the life of Arctic Bay he was also doctor and dentist, interpreter, culinary chef, and law-giver. As doctor he performed not only such minor operations as setting bones, but also serious and sometimes life or death amputations.

The climate in the North-West of Baffin Island is one which in winter can never be ignored, but must be faced with furs and everything in the way of clothing that a human being can carry. With the temperature at thirty below zero the cold can penetrate the slightest chink. Frost-bite is as dangerous as a deadly snake. The flesh turns gangrenous and the bone rots. Jimmy Bell became an expert in amputating useless limbs.

The Eskimos not only worshipped him. They trusted him and came to him with all their troubles. His job was to feed them and sell them consumer goods and to buy their furs. It was because he treated them so fairly that he was able to get the best out of them. One Scottish custom he never forgot in his isolated post. Like most Scots, he celebrated St Andrew's Day if there was any living soul to celebrate it with him.

This genial giant, known to the Canadians as the King of Baffin Island, would have gone far in the service of his company, but death came to him before he was fifty.

As I was leaving Mrs Bell's house, I ran into her second son who was home on leave from Rhodesia. He, too, was a fine, strapping man, but not the giant Jimmy had been. He was doing well in Rhodesia, but was fully aware of the serious problems which trouble the future of the white man in Africa.

On my way home I passed the Cromdale school, on whose benches my uncles had sat before going to Merchiston. I wondered if in any part of Britain there was any other village as small as Cromdale that had sent out so many people to so many parts of the world.

CHAPTER THREE

A Scottish Gauguin

'It is a common-place that the artist needs the stimulation of frequent change of scene.'

ACCORDING to John Masefield, the five travellers of the world who have seen wonders are Herodotus, Gasper, Melchior, Balthazar and Marco Polo. By this list I imagine that the Poet Laureate assumes that there are no wonders in modern travelling.

I do not agree. Of all Europeans the Scot, and particularly the Highlander, is the great traveller. Mostly he goes abroad to better himself, but once or so in a century a far-off wonder calls him into permanent exile. One such starry-eyed Highlander roused my curiosity when on September 25, 1956, I read the following entry under *Deaths* in *The Inverness Courier* :

' *Macdonald*—at Pao-pao, Ile de Mourea, French Oceania, on the 11th of August, 1956, William Alister Macdonald, Artist, aged 96, late of the Temple, London, and Tahiti.'

I felt at once that here was a wonder or perhaps a tragedy. Slowly I gathered the strings of a story which, far from being a tragedy, was indeed a wonder. I have called the story 'A Scottish Gauguin ', but my Highlander bears no likeness to the Frenchman apart from the fact that both men were in the financial world and were impelled by some inward fire to give up everything in order to paint.

William Alister Macdonald was born at Brora, the attractive Scottish town which lies at the mouth of the salmon-river of the same name. Like so many famous Scots, he was a son of the manse. His father, the local Free Church minister, and his mother died when the son was still a boy, and William Alister was brought up by an uncle and educated in Caithness.

As far as I can discover, none of his forebears had any leaning towards art, but he had a brother who was a well-known architect. As a young man William Alister went to London and joined the

Westminster Bank. Had he been a Lowland Scot he would doubtless have plodded along steadily until, like many Scots, he would have become a general manager. Being Highland, he had two loves : the sea beside which he had been brought up and painting in water-colours. He knew the fishermen of the North Sea and, to indulge his love of painting, he went on free passages in their boats. These early voyages brought him his first success as a painter and led to an exhibition in London. Every moment of his spare time was devoted to lessons at the Slade School, and he made rapid progress. With success came enough money to enable him not only to give up banking but also to travel. There were visits to the art galleries in Paris, Florence, Rome and Venice, visits long enough to enable him to learn fluent French. And there was always the sea.

In his youth he had sailed his dinghy round the sea-lochs in the Highlands, and now in a tramp steamer, he made his way round the world. Between journeys he painted scenes of old London and to-day many of them can be seen in the Wakefield Collection in the Guildhall.

His travels had shown him landscapes that were not to be seen under European skies, and sun and colour now shaped the destiny of his life. In 1919 he went to Tahiti and made his home in Papeete. He was then nearly sixty, but youth was still in his heart, and in painting there was always more to learn.

What manner of man was this Scottish Gauguin ? He was no Bohemian. Tall and slenderly built with the face and hands of an aristocrat, he was erect and graceful. For a while in Tahiti he grew a beard which made him look rather like Sir Compton Mackenzie as he is to-day. But mostly he wore only a moustache. Certainly he looked what he was—an artist dedicated from his early years, and as an artist he wore his fair hair long and flowing. But he was restrained in his dress and always immaculately tidy. His only exotic fad was a flowing tie which was threaded through a gold ring. In all, he was a very handsome man with a distinguished presence and might easily have passed for a Highland chieftan of ancient lineage. He was widely known as a brilliant raconteur, and there was always a humorous expression in his eyes. He had, too, the beautiful manners of a Highland gentleman, but on the subject of art he was capable of saying outrageous things and was no respecter of persons. He was exceptionally fond of music and was a great reader and an admirer of Joseph Conrad and, indeed, of nearly all writers of the sea. This was a natural choice, for the sea and painting were his life. He was also a good linguist, speaking easily both French and Tahitan and, like many Scottish artists, was very fond of the French people.

His life on Tahiti was no holiday. Always he painted and always he was fascinated by the Southern sky and seascape. His countrymen and, indeed, all Europe forgot him, but to Tahiti came Americans and Canadians who eagerly bought his pictures, and returned home with stories of the Scottish genius in the South Sea islands. Among his American friends was the late Zane Grey with whom he liked to fish for tunny.

After sixteen years in Tahiti he came home in 1936, was caught by the war, and suffered. His only son, who was preparing to be an archaeologist, lost his life as the result of an accident. In 1946 his wife died, and he was left alone. Highlander born and bred, he stayed on, but every day he pined for the blue skies, the sunshine of the South Seas, and, above all, for ' colour, colour, colour ' ! In 1953 he could stand Scotland no longer and at the age of 93 left again for French Oceania and this time settled down in a little house on the bay of Pao-pao about three hours' sail from Papeete. Again he painted without rest and without haste until he died in August, 1956, in his 97th year.

Americans, who have studied his pictures, state that he was unequalled in catching the colours of the lagoon, and it is clear that, as so often happens to British painters, his reputation as an artist is far higher abroad than in his own country.

By the courtesy of his relations in Inverness I have been shown a cutting from a German illustrated paper whose correspondent had been visiting the South Sea islands a year before Macdonald's death. There is a picture of William Alister Macdonald sitting in a chair by the sea. His features are those of a man more like fifty-six than ninety-six. The picture taken in profile shows the aristocratic nose and the firm, long hand. He is smoking a pipe and his eyes are fixed on some far-off piece of sky and water.

The German correspondent lets himself go in the text below the picture :

' *The Dreamer.* Did I have a vision ? He looks as if Gauguin could have painted him. Smoking his pipe and barefooted, the ninety-five years old English (!) painter Alister Macdonald looks over the sea and dreams. Millionaires come to him in their yachts. Unmoved he paints his much sought pictures. What called you to the South Seas ? He answers : the colours.'

Is William Alister Macdonald a genius or merely a story ? But what a life ! What persistence ! It may not be genius, but it is the stuff from which art is created. Remembering my student days in Paris when Dorgeles and, I think, Francis Carco triumphantly fooled the jury of a Dadaiste exhibition by having a picture accepted which had been painted with a brush fixed to a donkey's tail, I feel that if Alister Macdonald had been a Frenchman, his name would be on the lips of the world.

As things are, he is a Scot, and, according to his relatives, there are none of his pictures in Scottish galleries. Why not ? Has the Edinburgh Festival so infected Scottish intellectuals with the bug of foreign artistic superiority that there is no place for Scottish talent of what seems an exotic and original kind ?

CHAPTER FOUR

Golden Hours

'But mak' me, Lord, aince mair a boy—
Yon barefit boy who long ago
We' little airt, but muckle joy
Fished at the back o' Ben-y-Gloe.'

Barclay Fraser

WHEN I was a boy at the turn of the century Strathspey was still feudal. In every farm-house there was a portrait of the Dowager Countess of Seafield who both in manner and in physical resemblance was very like Queen Victoria. According to her upbringing she was conscientious in doing what she thought was her duty. She visited her tenants, kissed their children, looked after the sick and aged, and regarded all who lived on her vast estates as her subjects. If not exactly loved, because the gulf between the Castle and the croft was too wide, she was highly respected.

To-day all is changed. There can be no feudalism without respect, and the respect is gone.

In my boyhood, deer, grouse and salmon were plentiful, and a moor or a fine stretch of the Spey could be had for the tenth of what has to be paid to-day. This is no story of the 'good old days'. During my whole boyhood my parents were very poor. In the summer holidays they hired a farm-house for the six weeks from August 1 to September 14. It was always somewhere on a lonely moor and beside a burn which ran into the Spey. My brother Rufus and I fished from dawn till dark. The small streams were full of trout, and the never-to-be-forgotten Delliefure burn yielded pounders with sufficient frequency to sustain the adventurous spirit to the last. Best of all was to go down in the evening to the mouth where the burn runs into the famous March Pool of the Castle Grant water of the Spey, and watch the big trout rising. In the eerie gloaming which conjures in the mind kelpies and other wizards of the running water, great battles would be fought and won, but more often lost. More than once a salmon would take our small trout-fly and for a few moments hope rose from a fiercely beating heart. Our cheap casts were too weak ; our small reels carried too little line and no backing.

To-day I doubt if the best fisher in the world could get a basket of trout from the Delliefure or the Cromdale burns. I rarely see even a boy trying his luck. Mechanical transport and the thread-line fixed-spool reel have brought thousands of anglers where formerly there were only a few dozen, and the preservation of our game fish is already a critical problem.

Shooting and fishing in the Highlands are to-day highly commercialised. Almost every big land-owner lets every moor and every stretch of river that he possesses. Both moors and rivers are taken by syndicates or by a single individual who runs a big shoot, hires the beaters, and lets out guns at £200 to £300 a week. Beaters to-day are hard to get, and in the autumn of 1959 little schoolgirls of thirteen or fourteen were getting thirty shillings a day for walking a few miles through the heather. In these circumstances it is no wonder that virtually every brace of grouse and all salmon are sent off to London to be sold.

Very few of the good land-owners remain. The present Earl of Moray is doing a first-rate job in improving the stock of trout on his lochs. Sir Ewan Macpherson-Grant of Ballindalloch is another land-owner who does his best to improve his estate not only for himself, but for all who live on it.

But of the old famous characters of my youth hardly any are left. The only one whom I know is Colonel Oliver Haig, the nephew of Field-Marshal Lord Haig of Bemersyde. As he is one of the biggest shareholders in the Distillers Company Limited, he has had plenty of fishing and shooting and stalking in his life. For many years now he has spent the summer and autumn at Inchrory, his lodge which lies below Ben A'an nine miles from Tomintoul. The river A'an, faster even than the Spey, clear as gin in low water, and dangerous to man and beast in a flood, runs past his door.

In its loneliness, its silence, and its grandeur, Inchrory has no rival on the Scottish mainland. One sees not a living soul the whole day. The Colonel, as straight and as slim as a young sapling, likes the solitude. He is now an old man, but up to the last war he was an ardent stalker, and stalking on and around Ben A'an is no baby's toddle. Since the war he shot his moors up to 1957 and, as he lives in quite a small lodge, he finds most of his guns among the local community in and around Tomintoul. Since 1946 his moors have nearly always produced the biggest bag on the Twelfth.

The Colonel still retains an excellent memory and remembers best of all his experiences in the Boer War in which he fought. In the winter of 1958–9 he went to South Africa partly for the sunshine, but mainly to see again the battlefields which remain only in old men's minds. At an even older age Somerset Maugham has the same ambition to tread again the far-flung paths of his youth. I think I prefer Negley Farson's dictum ' never go back '.

In his younger days the Colonel was a strict disciplinarian and, like other colonels of his time, could fly into a rage if he were crossed. He was particularly angered by poachers, not so much by those who fished or fired a shot for the sport as by the gangs who came to make wholesale slaughter of game and salmon for profit. He was also not very fond of tramps.

At the time of his best stalking days he built himself a lodge at Inverlaal at the head of Loch Broom, in West Ross-shire. The lodge was quite a small affair made of wood, but the Colonel made it very comfortable and stocked it with tinned food, wines and choice cigars. When the stalking season was over, he locked the place and went away South leaving the food, the wines, the cigars and also several pairs of knickerbockers which were made of a special kind and colour of tweed and which he always wore.

The winter set in early in lonely Inverlaal, and a wretched tramp, passing by, spotted the new lodge. He was not long in forcing a window, and once inside his heart rejoiced. All he had to do was to find some wood. This done his winter was made for him, for, as the French say, he had ' *grande chere* and *beau feu* '. Not until he had eaten all the stores, drunk all the wine and smoked all the cigars did he think of moving.

When the Colonel came back to the lodge the next autumn, he registered in quick succession astonishment, disappointment and finally black anger. As one might expect, the tramp's sanitary

habits had been far from correct and, after removing such of
the furniture as had not been ruined, the Colonel set fire to the
building. There was, indeed, little else to be done.

Having dismissed Inverlaal from his mind, the Colonel did
not take any particular trouble to track down the thief. Slowly
but surely, however, justice ensnared the wrong-doer. The
tramp had moved far away from the area of his delinquency,
but he carried with him the clue to his guilt. One day the Colonel's
keeper spotted a man wearing a pair of knickerbockers of the
same special tweed which only the Colonel wore. They were,
in fact, Haig's knickerbockers.

In his old age the Colonel has become like a stately ship that
has passed out of rough seas into calm water. He has always
been hospitable and kind to those who approach him properly.
He still goes to Inchrory; still writes an excellent letter in his
own hand.

He has been particularly kind to me, for he has always allowed
me to fish his long stretch of the A'an. I owe him very much.
On the Colonel's water my son, then a boy, caught his first
salmon before the Second World War. It was a twenty-pounder.

As regards myself, I have fished his water many times and
have to thank him as long as I live for the happiest day of my
life. And here is the story of it. In July of 1958 my wife and I
went to Argyllshire. It was my first visit to this county since I
was a boy of eight. The main reasons for going there were two.
Having reached three-score and ten I was living on extra time,
and my wife considered that the small rivers of the West Highlands were more suited to my age than wading the Spey in breast
waders. Secondly, I like small rivers and I prefer a light rod and
light tackle to a two-handed salmon-rod.

Normally the West has a high rainfall, but if there is no rain
there is no water and the salmon remain tantalisingly in the sea
estuary. July of 1958 chose to be one of the rare dry summers of
the West. We never tried the rivers, because they were empty.
The lochs, too, were unkind, for they were feet below their
normal level.

We made no complaints. We enjoyed the superb sunshine,
explored the islands, and were thrilled by the rich bird life and
especially by the gannets which were in profusion and whose

diving from a great height at immense speed has always seemed to me the most wonderful movement in bird-life.

For August we went to Perthshire, hoping to fish the Earn. It was virtually unfishable, because rain fell almost every day and the river was too high and too dirty for fly-fishing. August is not a good fishing month in most places, but by now we were perturbed by doubt and disappointment. Were we to return to our Southern winter-quarters without having caught a fish?

Back we went to Strathspey for September. Normally the salmon season is actually but not legally over, and generally in September there are numerous red and black fish and even a late-running fresh salmon or grilse will take a fly before going up the burns to spawn. But in that summer all the rivers which ran North had a drought, and all the rivers South of the Drumochter Pass were almost perpetually in flood. Wading Pollawick, one of the most rewarding pools on the Spey, I fished till I could cast no more. Fish of all sizes ranging from ten pounds to one or two hoary, red monsters of forty pounds hurled themselves out of the water as if they were thirsting for rain, but not one looked at my fly. My son had a similar blank day a few days later.

As the last days of our holiday drew near, despair made me think of Colonel Haig. I wrote to him, and at once he replied inviting us to fish his water on the Friday and Saturday of September 19 and 20. As we were going South on the Sunday, we prayed for rain. On the Thursday night there was a sharp shower which made no difference to the rivers, although it may have freshened the water. On the Friday morning we set off in good time on the eighteen mile trek to the house of Colonel Haig's keeper. For once the morning sky was dull, and our hopes rose only to be shattered when we reached Macfarlane's cottage. He was waiting for us with bad news. The river was at its lowest and was as clear as crystal. There were some fish in the river, but they would not look at anything, unless perhaps after sundown.

He came with us to Dailchaoil, a pool which had served me well in former years. It was lower than I have ever seen it, but it was probably the only holding pool in the river. It was easily fished. On the right bank there was a nice stretch of gravelly

stone. The left bank was a sheer cliff of considerable height.
On this side the water ran deep and the fish lay halfway down
beside a large protruding rock. After one look I said to my
wife : " Away with the grilse rod and the big reel. Get out your
little trout rod and little reel. It's our only chance." Up went the
little eight-foot-six fibre-glass rod with a three-x cast and a
number 10 tiny Blue Charm. The trout reel had a tapered line
and fifty yards of backing. My wife made me go down first to
show her how to fish the pool. The rod, little more than a wand,
cast beautifully and halfway down the pool I touched a fish.
I felt our only chance was gone.

The day grew very warm. The clouds were beginning to break
up, and it looked as if we were going to have another Mediter-
ranean sky. Fortunately, the sun, our greatest enemy, was still
well hidden. Down the pool I went again and just off the rock
below the cliff I was into a reddish cock-salmon of about thirteen
pounds. With the light rod and tackle he took some time to land.
We had only a toy kind of gaff, and my wife had never gaffed
a fish before. She got the gaff well in the right place at the very
first attempt and all was well. The fish was quite firm and would
kipper well, and we sent it off that evening from Tomintoul to
Aberdeen to be smoked. I have caught quite a number of salmon
on trout-rods, but never on such a tiny wand as this.

After a rest my wife went down the pool and in her fourth
cast she hooked a clean-run silver grilse. It put up a magnificent
fight and was out of the water at least five times. I have reached
a stage when I get more enjoyment out of seeing someone else
catch a fish than out of my own captures. My wife played the
fish very well, but I was so excited that I made a boss-shot with
the toy-gaff. However, no damage was done. The grilse was
safely landed. Out came what properly should have been a bottle
of Haig, but was, in fact, pure malt whisky, and the little rod
was christened in white Glen Grant.

Having done well by Dailchaoil, we drove up to another pool
a mile or two higher up the glen. The road was atrocious and
fit only for a Land-rover. Here we crossed a narrow sheep
bridge, because there was a pool in which we had seen another
fresh-run grilse jump, and which could be fished only from the
other side. Here I had an unpleasant adventure because on the

other side we had to creep along a narrow and slippery sheep-path which ran across a steep greasy cliff running sheer down to the river. Halfway across I lost my nerve through exhaustion and vertigo and could not go either forward or back. However, I pulled myself together, and both my wife and I went down the pool several times and, although we saw the grilse jump twice, he wouldn't look at any of our flies.

We decided to go down-stream again, but I was determined not to go back across the cliff path. We decided to wade across the river in our Wellingtons. My wife is not a dwarf, but she is not very tall and her neat Wellingtons were much shorter than mine. Moreover, the depth of the A'an is notoriously difficult to gauge, as the local rhyme says :

> ' The A'an, the A'an, it rins sae clear
> Twould beguile a man o' a hundred year.'

I led the way with my wife following a yard or two behind. The fording place was a little deeper than I expected, and I shipped a little water in my boots. Halfway or more across the river, I heard a yell from my wife. I turned round and saw her like an hysterical hen standing still in the river and refusing to go forward or back, while the water flowed in and out of her short Wellingtons. She was half-crying and half-mad with rage.

I went back to her at once and we crossed over without more ado. She was very wet and downcast.

I felt sorry for her and guilty myself. Nevertheless, I had to pull her up. What sort of fisherwoman or fisherman had never been wet ! What sort of angler ever went out without spare stockings ! I had an extra pair of long thick woollen socks. She must take off her stockings, dry them on the radiator of the car, put on my socks and her own spare shoes, and all would be well.

All these things she did, and soon she was laughing. By now the clouds had vanished, and the sun came into his full glory. So back we drove to Tomintoul and pulled up at Ross's Central Stores to send off my red thirteen-pounder to Aberdeen to be smoked. In the superb evening sunlight two men were sitting on the seat outside the store. One of them recognised me and

said to me : " It's some time since you were here." While I was
in the shop arranging for the despatch of the fish, my wife, who
stayed in the car, heard the man who remembered me say to
his friend on the seat : " He writes bits for the papers."

We had a marvellous drive back to Grantown, with a haunting
picture of Tomintoul in the sunlight, and a view of the Cairngorms with Strathspey a riot of colouring made up of the fir
trees, the silver birches, the golden cornfields and Loch Garten
glistening like a jewel in the strath.

I have fished in many lands ever since I was a boy, but this
was *the* day. From morn till evening, while we were in the glen,
the only people we saw—and then only for a few moments at
the start and at the end—were the keeper and his wife. It was
a very precious day which, I felt, selfishly, might never come
again ; not because I am old or afraid of dying, but because
I knew instinctively that when Oliver Haig's * time was over,
Inchrory would be sold or split up. Helicopters would bring
anglers from all parts to fish the river at week-ends. The loveliness
of yet one more lonely place would vanish.

* Colonel Haig died in November, 1959.

CHAPTER FIVE

Queen of Fishers

' Give me mine angle, we'll to the river there.'

IN my time I have seen much of fishers and fishing gillies, but very little of lady anglers. Indeed, the patron saint of fishers is St Peter, and in Catholic countries anglers greet one another on setting out to fish with the words ' Petri Heil '. In the books of quotations, too, fishers are almost invariably masculine. Cleopatra is a notable exception, when in a mood of boredom she asks for her angle and betakes herself to the river.

Yet there are numerous lady anglers and they seem to be on the increase. Some of them have been very successful and others have had the lucky hand. The late Duchess of Bedford, grandmother of the present Duke, once landed seventeen salmon on the Tay in one forenoon. Lady anglers, too, have been fortunate in grassing big fish. Lady Alexandra Haig, daughter of the Field-Marshal and now Lady Alexandra Trevor-Roper, caught a forty-six pounder on the Tweed. As a child of thirteen, Miss Phyllis Spender Clay, now wife of Sir Philip Nichols, our former ambassador to Czechoslovakia, was fishing the Alt Beag pool near Fochabers on the Spey. The river was high and still a little brown after a spate. Fishing from the bank with a large two-inch fly, she hooked a monster. Fortunately she had a gillie with her for, while she was playing the salmon, the backing to the line stuck and broke. Luck was with her from the start. Like most big fish, the salmon went down deep and sulked, and while Miss Spender Clay hand-lined the fish the gillie mended the break. The fish was hooked deep under the jaw, and after a long, dour struggle the young girl brought it to the side for the gillie to gaff.

The fish was too heavy for the local butcher's scales, and Miss

Spender Clay had to take it up to Fochabers Castle, where the
Duke of Richmond had a wonderfully accurate balance which
registered up to fifty pounds. The fish weighed just over forty-
seven pounds and was nearly as big as the girl herself. The
Duke was so impressed by this remarkable capture that he gave
his beautiful scales to her as a memento. The year was 1919,
and the fish was then claimed to be the largest salmon ever
caught by a woman in these islands.

Coming down to ordinary women anglers as distinct from
record-holders, my wife caught her first salmon within ten
minutes of having had a salmon rod in her hands. The fish was
caught at a time when experienced male fishers were getting
nothing. My wife owed much to the keeper who, when I
suggested he might take her to a famous pool, said at once :
" Na, na, the ithers have been thrashing yon pool for days on
end. By your leave I'll take Her Ladyship to some pools that
hae nae been touched."

I believe that women anglers get a greater emotion and delight
from fishing or at least from catching fish, than men fishers.
There is a difference between fishing and catching fish, and it is
best illustrated by the story of the high Chinese dignitary who,
during the Manchu dynasty, fell from office and had to leave
Peking. As the Mandarin took leave of his friends, he said :
" I leave you to go to my country estates. There I shall fish,
but, pray, send me no baits or lures because I do not desire to
catch fish."

Personally I can understand this type of fishing, but lady
anglers, and many men, tire very quickly unless they are catching
fish. But when they do catch fish women anglers tend to shake
and tremble with emotion. In the summer of 1957 I watched a
lady angler catching her first salmon on one of the Tulchan
beats of the Spey. The keeper was with her and, very properly,
did not interfere with the rod. Quietly he told her what to do,
and she needed much telling. Fortunately, her husband was
on the opposite bank and, perhaps irritated by having not
seen a fish all day, kept on casting as if he were not interested
in what was happening on the other side. Be this as it may,
it was undoubtedly the right, but not very easy thing to do.
Had it been my wife, and I myself had been in the same position,

I should have been roaring unheard and quite useless instructions across a wide stretch of noisy water.

Only once in my life have I seen greater ecstasy on an angler's face, than when she brought the fish to the edge, and the gillie had it on the bank in one flash of the gaff. It was not a large salmon, certainly not more than eight pounds. It was also rather red. But such was the delight and glowing satisfaction of the angler that it might have been her first baby.

The other exhibition of uncontrolled emotion also took place on the Tulchan water, but higher up the Spey where it comes close into the road on the right bank of the river. My wife and I were driving to Ballindalloch when we saw for the first time a man heavily engaged in a fish at this very suitable spot which I must have passed on literally hundreds of occasions. We stopped the car and had an unimpeded close-up view of the operations. I could see at once that the angler was a novice. He had a dangerously long line out. It was even more dangerously slack. Moreover, the keeper, who was not in waders, was on the other side of the river and trying to give instructions across a broad stretch of the Spey. Presumably the angler had crossed the river in the shallow, smooth water in order to land his fish more easily, the opposite bank being high and steep. Fortunately, the fish was safely in the slack water, for below were fierce rapids, and if the angler had allowed his fish to drift down into them, the battle would soon have been over in the fish's favour.

We realised from the exchange of shouting that the angler was an American fishing for the first time. The fish must have been destined to die at this hour. It was nearly tired out, but more than once it fell down nearly into the rapids. The angler would not reel in. At last the gillie crossed the river and, with his trousers wringing wet, made the angler reel up. The fish came in dutifully and was soon lying on the gravelly stones on which the angler was standing. He went mad with delight. He shrieked and yoicked. He clapped his hands. Then he picked up the fish and clasped it to his breast. The embrace over, he laid the salmon back on the stones and performed a mixture of an Indian dance and a can-can round it. What the dour gillie thought I never discovered, for suddenly we realised that we had spent nearly half an hour by the riverside and were already late for our own appointment. As we started up the car, the angler spotted us for the first time. He beamed with delight, took off his hat and held it out, the opening upwards, as if begging a contribution for the wonderful performance which we had watched from a front seat.

Apart from these fortunate novices there is a lady angler who by her character, her courage and, not least, her skill has won the admiration of all who know her or who have seen her fish. She has several records to her credit. She has caught more salmon than any other lady angler now living. She has fished the Spey regularly for more years than any other living angler, male and female. The total is now over seventy years. It should be added that she began fishing at the age of nine and in her long fishing life has never used any other lure but fly. Of all the famous anglers who have fished the Spey she is and will remain the greatest figure. Her name is Mrs J. L. Wood, M.B.E. of The Hoo, Hemel Hempstead, and of Dalchroy Cottage, Advie.

In my boyhood there were two rich families which leased the famous Tulchan grouse moor and salmon fishings on the Sea-field Estates. Normally the moor and fishings went together, but the Sassoons, who lived at Tulchan Lodge and to whom came King Edward VII and the Duke of York, afterwards King George V, to shoot their grouse, were not interested in fishing. The Tulchan beats were therefore let to a Mr George McCorquodale, a partner in the famous paper firm and the most fanatical salmon-fisher the Highlands have ever known. Gradually he acquired most of the Spey salmon beats from Abelour to the old Grantown Bridge. He also had water on other salmon rivers, for his ambition, never realised, was to catch a thousand salmon in one season. The Spey was his paradise, and he built on Seafield ground a splendid lodge called Dalchroy with one of the grandest views in Scotland.

George McCorquodale was a stern, but generous man. He disliked lazy and unpunctual workers. When the painters were doing some work for him, he found them smoking while they were working. " Put those pipes away," he said. " You can smoke in your own time, but not in mine." He was violent on poaching which he regarded as the greatest sin after murder. He pro-secuted a Mr Lawson, father of the best local angler on the Spey to-day, and had his poaching gear set up in Dalchroy as a warning to others. On another occasion he had a poacher fined. The case was printed in the local paper, and George McCorquodale had the cutting framed and hung it in the passage leading to the gun-room. Yet he was more than kind to those who served him faithfully. When his retainers retired, he gave them a thousand pounds each and a cottage for life. In those days it was exceptional generosity.

Mrs J. L. Wood was the daughter of George McCorquodale. She inherits her father's passion for salmon-fishing and his love of Dalchroy and the Spey which at this point is at its most beautiful. She had, however, a gentler nature and she conceived and carried out one of those quixotic and charming acts that spring only from Celtic blood. Her father lived in the sternest competitive age and, doubtless, had built Dalchroy as a rival to Tulchan Lodge. When Mrs Wood succeeded her father, Tulchan had fallen into some disrepair and was already doomed to demolition. Gradually Mrs Wood developed the idea—local legend says after a dream—that she should give Dalchroy to the Countess of Seafield if the Seafield trustees would agree to change the name to Tulchan. Her father, she felt, would have approved, and forthwith she sent in her most generous offer.

The Countess of Seafield is a gentle and benevolent land-owner, but Scottish factors and Scottish lawyers are the last people on this earth to look a gift horse in the mouth. They want to get it securely locked up in the stable.

The conditions on which the Seafield Estates consented graciously to accept this queenly gift were approximately as follows : ' (1) that Mrs Wood should take down the old Tulchan at her own expense ; (2) that she should continue to pay the feu duty on the new Tulchan.' She carried out the provisions, and the Seafield Estates received a superb free lodge. As Mrs Wood is as eager a fisher as her father, the Estates were generous enough to give her the C and D beats of the Tulchan fishings for April and May for life and also a charming little house called Dalchroy Cottage which lay close to the river. She pays the full price for both fishing and house.

In spite of her age, Mrs Wood, who is a widow, is mar-vellously vigorous. Like her father she is very kind to those

of his former staff who are still alive. One of these old servitors
was her father's handy man. He is still a great character and is
called ' Charlie ' by everyone, his surname being Grant like most
surnames in the district. In the middle of the severe Highland
winter of 1955 Charlie Grant fell seriously ill and was moved
into hospital in Grantown. Mrs Wood was informed and without hesitation she took the night-train from London to Aviemore.
There she was met by ' Dash ' Grant, the chauffeur and handy-
man of the Palace Hotel in Grantown-on-Spey, who with great
courage and some good fortune drove her the twenty-four
miles along the ice-surfaced road from Aviemore to the Grantown
hospital.

After having cheered Charlie Grant by bringing him a new
radio, she thought she would like to see her keeper. Again the
faithful ' Dash ' had to drive her the seven miles from Grantown
to beyond Advie at a point just opposite Dalchroy Cottage.
The weather was so bad that from this point they had to walk.
A real blizzard started, and ' Dash ' tried to persuade Mrs Wood
to stay at the end of a wood and let him go ahead and bring the
keeper to her. But no ; she was so eager to look at her rods and
to hear about the prospects for the spring salmon season that she
battled on to the keeper's cottage. When ' Dash ' and she got
there, the keeper was away in Grantown.

Nevertheless, St Peter rewarded her pluck without delay.
The two C and D beats which she has for April and May are
among the best stretches of the Spey, and May is the best month.
In that May of 1955 Mrs Wood and her guests broke the record
—at least the post-war record—with a catch of 267 salmon.

She is a great fisher and a most generous benefactress. She
permits only fly and, when she says fly, she means decent,
respectable salmon flies, and not monstrous lures masquerading
as flies, and any guest fisher of hers who breaks this rule is never
asked again.

She is also deeply interested in the Aberlour Orphanage
which her father helped to finance. In her house she has a salmon
collecting-box, and every friend or guest who fishes her water
must put a half-crown into the box for every salmon he or she
catches. The charge may be higher to-day than the original
half-crown, but, whatever the amount may be, the money goes

to finance a new bed in the Orphanage. Each bed costs £500. There are now seven beds. This is in itself a tribute to the skill of Mrs Wood's rod and to the excellence of the waters which she fishes. There is not a Highlander in Speyside who does not think her the grandest woman in all broad Scotland.

CHAPTER SIX

To-day and To-morrow

' I have passed many landes and many yles and contrees, and
cherched many full strange places. . . .
Now I am come home to reste.'

Sir John Mandeville

LIKE everyone over sixty-five I have lived in three totally
different worlds and, like many of my generation, have passed
through cycles of success and misfortune. Although my parents
were far from rich, I felt no insecurity of any kind in the years
before the First World War. I was unhappy during my first two
years at Fettes. Later, like most of my family, I wasted precious
years on games. But it never occurred to me that I should be
unable to earn my bread. If I could not make the Indian Civil,
there were other openings. The travel bug was in my blood
and, after happy years of learning in Germany and France, I
went East to see the world and to make riches as a rubber
planter. There was fever instead of riches, but in the East I read
ravenously and began to write. I owe much to my parents, to
my mother who sent to me in Malaya a serious book every
week and to my father who guided my wayward steps to the
straight path of government service. In 1911 I passed into the
Consular Service and, after three months in the Foreign Office,
went to Moscow.

The First World War destroyed what was an interesting and
pleasant life. History jumped forward with a rapid spring. As
a young man I rose to giddy heights and fell sharply because,
as happens so often in the foreign service, the man on the spot
gave unpleasant information to his masters at home ; in my case
the news was that the Bolsheviks were on top and that, if the
Allies were bent on intervention, they would have to send vast
armies of their own people.

The 'twenties were a period of disillusion and of profligacy
in which the men who had fought and had survived spent their

gratuities in night-clubs and then walked the streets looking
for jobs. In Central Europe I did much the same with less excuse.
I resigned from the foreign service, went into banking, made
debts, and in September, 1928, I entered the service of Lord
Beaverbrook, who had been amused by my standing up to the
Government over Russia in 1918. I became a journalist and, to
escape from journalism, I began to write books. They sold well,
and in June, 1937, I left Fleet Street to live what I thought
would be an idyllic life of five months in the Highlands, five
months abroad, and two months in London. The dream did not
last long. The yearly trips to Europe convinced me early of two
things : that Hitler would go on grabbing until he was stopped
and that, so long as Chamberlain was Prime Minister, there
would be no stopping. The Munich disaster affected me tragically.
The home in the Highlands was abandoned. I could not rest.
Two days after Munich my book, *Guns or Butter*, was published.
It said with bitterness that Britain would not fight. Paradoxically
it sold the best of all my books in England—but not anywhere
else. In the same month I engaged myself to go back to the Foreign
Office in the event of war.

After the Second World War history again leapt forward
violently and continues to advance with a speed unparalleled.
Invention has already justified even the wildest dreams of the
most modern writers of imaginative fiction. It has made nonsense
of a prophet like H. G. Wells who in 1918 wrote that German
imperialism had been defeated and abolished and that, although
our world was feeble and unstable, it was cured of its fever for
war. If the dead of the Second World War were to come to life
to-day, they would not recognise the world which they had
left less than twenty years ago.

Western Europe, for so many centuries the centre of civilis-
ation, is in decline. Democracy is in danger from the growing
seduction of dictatorships. Worst of all is the insecurity which
Western youth has now to face. I can well understand that the
young men of Western Europe are angry and are unwilling to
listen to the advice and experience of older men. Why should
they listen? Europe has committed self-murder, and their fathers
and grandfathers are responsible for the suicide—not, indeed,
the men who fought, but the politicians of all parties who, after

the slaughter of the First World War, remained idle while a lunatic re-armed Germany.

To-day the young men of Western Europe live in a world which moves so quickly that they cannot prepare themselves for the uncertain future. Before the First World War there was a multiplicity of safe careers which were open to diligence and prudence. To-day all this is gone. Every career is full of risks, and none, except perhaps science, seems worth the long years of study. Thrift is out of fashion, for a Government which spends billions on weapons which are out of date even before they come into production, takes all savings away in taxation. In my generation youth had great hopes and therefore great disillusion-ments. To-day it is natural and perhaps even wise that youth should be aware of the difficulties and dangers of a harder era.

In my ripe age I am often asked two questions. The first is probably asked of most old people. What in your opinion are the biggest changes in your lifetime ? My invariable first answer is the decline in the prestige of Parliament. Sixty years ago the chief newspapers gave in full the daily proceedings of both the House of Commons and the House of Lords. In the early 'nineties I have vague recollections of being taken to a wayside station merely to see Mr Gladstone's train pass through. The prestige of members of Parliament was high. To-day it has sunk to a low level. Members of Parliament are regarded more with suspicion than with admiration, and the ablest young men prefer industry or banking to the House of Commons. Apart from *The Times*, the *Daily Telegraph* and one or two provincial newspapers the proceedings of Parliament are mentioned only when there is something of a crisis or a rumpus of unruly behaviour.

The second change which impresses me is the fact that the world to-day is ruled by old men at a time when the speed of political life since Queen Victoria's death has increased in the same ratio as a motor-car to a dog-cart. Mr Macmillan and M. Khrushchev are sixty-five. Mao Tse-Tung is sixty-six. General de Gaulle and President Eisenhower are sixty-nine and Dr Adenauer is eighty-three !

It was Disraeli who wrote in *Coningsby* that ' almost everything that is great has been done by youth '. Yet Disraeli, who first became Prime Minister at the age of sixty-three, found ample time to dine out in private houses and to write his letters of thanks to his hostesses in his own handwriting. To-day so severe is the strain on heads of state and Prime Ministers that, like Consuls in unhealthy countries, two years of service count as three.

I do not say this gerontocracy is a proof of decadence. The Greeks looked to their Nestors for wisdom. What I believe is true is that modern British youth has little or no respect for old age, and I therefore do not exclude an era or generation which will introduce euthanasia for the over-sixties. Indeed, I feel this possibility almost as strongly as my belief that Communism will be extinguished, not by capitalists, but by ex-Communists.

During the past fifty years life has undergone numerous transformations, but the change which saddens me most is the decline of the private bookseller. Edinburgh, where I spent some of my childhood and most of my boyhood, was a fairy-land of bookshops, each of which was run by an expert owner, who nine times out of ten was himself a lover of books. Books were cheap, and in 1905 and 1906 Nelson's and Collins's six-penny Classics and Dent's Everyman's Library provided many a poor Scottish boy with a library which would take him into the Indian Civil Service without the expense of a crammer. I was then under twenty and for five pounds I had a library of over a hundred volumes including ancient and modern history, philosophy, and all that was best in English and classical literature.

To-day the private bookshops are rapidly disappearing before the inroads of three great monopoly groups. But mono-poly, noxious though it be, is far from being wholly responsible. The decline in serious reading is caused partly by the increasing cost of books, but mainly by the changing taste of the public. When *John O' London's Weekly* died for lack of subscribers in September, 1954, Webster Evans, its last editor, gave as his last message : ' People prefer to read trash. They are just not interested in the world of literature and arts.' Writing on a similar subject, G. M. Trevelyan stated that ' education has pro-duced a vast population able to read, but unable to distinguish what is worth reading.' Christina Foyle, who ought to know, has expressed very much the same opinion, and there are some younger pessimists who believe that in time books will disappear altogether. It is easy to say that the bulk of British people prefer looking to reading, yet here perhaps is hope. In the United States there has been a decline in television and an increase in reading. In countries like Russia which have reached a high percentage of literacy only in recent years, reading is on a very large scale, and authors, so long as they conform with the prevailing dogma, are on the very summit of the privileged class.

The second question which is always put to me is in the form of a statement followed by two questions which run usually as follows : ' You have had a wonderful life ! How did you manage to see so much and to change your profession so often ? Did you inherit money or did you earn it ? '

The answer is that I have neither inherited nor made any large amount of money. In my early career I received some useful help from a rich grandmother and a well-to-do uncle. But, apart from a rather wild period in the 'twenties, I have earned my own living by hard work. The reasons why I changed jobs so often were, partly, because I liked to be my own master, but mainly because twice in twenty-five years war interfered with my career. In the 'thirties my books sold well so that by the end of 1937 I was free. In 1939 I was back in the Foreign Office on a meagre salary. During the war I spent all my savings. Throughout this period I did not write a line, but, after the war, I still preferred freedom to an embassy and went back to write for a new public. It has been hard work, and, like many other people to-day in various walks of life, I shall have to go on working till I drop.

Except for a few early follies I have no regrets. My second marriage has been very happy. I enjoy my work and believe that some occupation or hobby is essential to contentment in old age. Since 1947 I have written a weekly political commentary for the European Service of the B.B.C. I also review books as well as write them. The writing now takes longer, but since the war I have nine books to my credit. Most of all I enjoy the weekly fishing article which I write for the *Glasgow Herald* from May to October. Since the war, too, I have seen most of Western Europe, though not so much or as often as I should like.

With these reservations, I can say truthfully that I have had an interesting life, though in a sense the curious chances that I have missed stick in my mind more than the minor achievements of my official career. In this respect 1936 was a vintage year.

In February I had negotiations with Geoffrey Faber, who made me an offer to write a book on King Edward VIII to be published in time for the Coronation in 1937. The terms were most generous and would have taken me out of Fleet Street at once. I was sorely tempted. I had known the new King well enough to write an interesting book, but on reflection I refused. I already had the feeling that there would be no Coronation. Almost exactly ten months later the King abdicated.

In the autumn of 1936 I had three curious offers in four months. In August the boss of the Hearst magazines telephoned to me to say that the Editor of *The Cosmopolitan* wanted me to write a series of spy-stories in conjunction with Phillips Oppenheim on a basis of one spy story for each country. The Hearst man told me I could ask a big fee and it would be paid. I do not know whether Phillips Oppenheim was approached or would have collaborated, for I went no farther in the matter. I realised that the editor of *The Cosmopolitan* had assumed from the wretched title of my most successful book, *Memoirs of a British Agent*, that I was a spy or a secret-service man, whereas I was merely an official sent to do a job in a country which we did not recognise. Lord Kitchener was at one time British Agent in Cairo and more recently Sir George Cunningham was British Agent in Afghanistan. I knew nothing of spying and very little about the secret service except its existence.

A month later I had another American offer to write a series of secret service stories in collaboration with Paul Gallico. I was told that what was wanted was my name on the title-page and that Mr Gallico would write the stories with some expert advice from me! Mr Gallico, of whom I had then never heard, was described to me as a sports writer. To-day his name is known in every country, and I imagine and hope that he has made lots of lolly. Again I refused for the same reason as before. I knew nothing about the subject.

In November another offer, again from America, promised

no quick road to money, but was flattering to my ego. In the afternoon of Friday, November 27, I received a visit at my house from Mr Campbell Lee of the Council of Anglo-American churches. The Council, he informed me, sent a speaker every year to the United States. The speaker's task was to deliver a series of addresses in twenty important pulpits in the United States. This year, he informed me with a winning smile, the choice had fallen on me. For a moment I was dazzled and sorely tempted. My brother had always said that I should have been a music-hall comedian ; but I had fancied myself as a preacher. Fortunately I remained silent for a moment or two until Campbell Lee broke the interval by saying that it would be very important to win Lord Beaverbrook's sympathy for the cause.

Cold reason cooled quickly the momentary heat of my ambition. I remembered rapidly that I had been baptised a Presbyterian, that I had nearly become a Mohammedan in Malaya, that I had been confirmed as an Anglican in Moscow and that I was now a Catholic. Lord Beaverbrook was a firm Presbyterian. Whatever he might or might not do for the Anglo-American Council of Churches, he would not have recommended me as a preacher ! It had been rather a giddy day. I had lunched with Willie Maugham at Claridge's and had heard him speak eloquently on prison reform and on the Devil's Island which French prisoners, he said, preferred to other prisons.

Campbell Lee had called on me soon after luncheon and, while he was with me, Alexander Kerensky burst in upon me with a copy of André Gide's book, *Retour de l'U.S.S.R.* Gide had been the principal speaker at Gorki's funeral in Moscow in June of that year and was regarded as a one hundred per cent Bolshevik. Kerensky's eyes were alive with excitement. The book, he said, was woolly, but was full of disillusionment and would make first-class material for the anti-Communists. Then he told me the story of the funeral. While Gide was speaking, Stalin turned to Alexei Tolstoy. " Who's that foreigner ? "

" Oh ! That's Gide—our latest conquest and very important for us in France."

" Hm," said Uncle Joe with displeasure. " I don't trust these Frenchmen."

2

Inevitably the speed of these days has declined, and in old
age the tempo drops gradually. But long ago I had learnt from
my remarkable Fettes form-master, Kenneth Plumpton Wilson,
that in his declining years man must learn to enjoy loneliness,
to get rid of his possessions, and to live entirely for others. It
is a good philosophy.

During the winter I work seven days a week and enjoy my
work. I keep abreast of all that is happening in the Slav world
generally and in the Iron Curtain countries in particular. For
my work I read Russian and Czech and for pleasure I read mostly
memoirs and history. My main pleasure, however, is the summer
sojourn in the Highlands and, although I now prefer watching
my wife fish to fishing myself, Highland rivers and burns and
Highland mountains mean more to me than anything else in
life, and, as the Spey flows down from the hills to the Moray
Firth I see the beginning and end not only of myself but of my
Highland forebears. ' The virtuous,' Confucius said, ' take
delight in mountains ; the wise in rivers.' I am neither virtuous
nor wise, but I understand what the sage means.

The loss of friends brings sorrows, but, although I have not
the competitive spirit of my father who lived to nearly ninety-
two and who gained extra strength and vigour from the knowledge that he had outlived this or that contemporary, age softens
the blow of death. Moreover, I have been fortunate in making
new friends, partly fortuitously and partly through fishing.

During the war, especially during the Blitz, quite a number
of Ministers, of Members of Parliament, officials and members
of White's Club, used to visit Heppell's chemist shop—now
defunct—at 146 Piccadilly in order to have a pick-me-up after
the whizz-bangs of the night. Sitting there always was a fine-
looking old general who had served gallantly in the First World
War, had been Commandant of Woolwich, and in his day had
been the finest whip of a four-in-hand coach in Britain. His
name is Geoffrey White and, at the time of writing he is in his
ninetieth year. He became the president of Heppell's Club,
kept a book in which members, some of them famous both as

authors and artists, wrote their contributions. Geoffrey himself was and still is quite an artist who in his day drew and painted horses in action better than any famous painter alive or dead.

He is probably the last living man who was one of the officers imprisoned in Pretoria at the time when Winston Churchill, then a war correspondent, was also a prisoner, but escaped. Geoffrey White, whose memory is quite remarkable, affirms that the rumour that Winston Churchill let down the other officers who were plotting an escape is quite untrue and was, indeed, conceived long after the event.

With the late Lord Rosslyn, Geoffrey White produced the prison magazine called 'The Gram' which Harry Rosslyn edited and Geoffrey White illustrated. Geoffrey still has its only three numbers, the third being started to the sound of the British liberating guns. The copies must be rare.

The type of humour of the British officer in 1900, in what Geoffrey calls 'the last gentleman's war', can be gauged from the following item in the first number :

CHAMPAGNE ! !

Krug(er) 1900. The fashionable vintage.

This is a natural wine with a good deal of body. When first introduced to the public it was full of gas, which, however, is fast evaporating. Unlike other champagne wines Kruger 1900 should be sent to a warm place and kept there. In a month's time we expect to be able to sell this wine at a merely nominal price.

Roberts, Kitchener & Co., Wine Merchants.

Geoffrey White * is a charming old gentleman who is loved by everyone who knows him.

A fishing friend, of whom I see too little, is Peter Reiss, a great airman, a superb games-player, a skilful dry-fly fisher, and a member of Lloyds. He has a strong independent mind of his own and has the kind of airman's courage which conquers all fear. In his long flying life he has covered every corner of Europe and, twenty-five years ago, made a pioneer flight to Moscow and then by stages to Odessa and homewards via Rumania. It was, I think, the first private flight to the Soviet Union.

* Major-General Geoffrey White, C.B., C.M.G., D.S.O., died in December, 1959.

We met over fishing, and I gave him introductions to fishing friends in Yugoslavia, Czechoslovakia and Austria, for he always took a rod with him when flying. In 1937 he was flying in the East with a comparative beginner who had a private plane. While the beginner was flying the machine, it crashed, and Peter Reiss was very badly injured. When he came back to London, still on crutches, I never thought he would fly again. But I had misjudged Peter. He was determined to get up in the air again, even if he had to be lifted in and out of the machine. He felt that, if he didn't do so as soon as possible, he might lose his colossal air nerve. So up he went while still an invalid.

To-day he has a charming week-end cottage close to the Test at Wherwell and has a private aeroplane in which he goes everywhere. Indeed, I have a photograph of him, dressed in morning coat and silk hat, driving his plane to Lloyds in London.

Perhaps because it is the contemplative art, angling appeals to old people who have never fished before. Lord Beaverbrook has become a big-game angler and in his now annual winter sojourn in Nassau takes to sea in his splendid motor-ship, named of course *John Calvin*, and goes after such powerful fish as shark, tunny, barracuda, dolphin and, best of all to eat, king-fish. He thinks the dolphin the best fish for sport. If he does not kill his fish in ten minutes or so he hands the rod to someone else. Quarter of an hour of holding a big fish, he says, takes all the strength out of an old man. He also says that the shark, the enemy of other fish, is attacked violently by them when they see he is fairly hooked, and by the time the shark is landed he is in a terrible mess.

It would seem that, in relation to sharks, there is more justice in the sea than there is on land.

The B.B.C. has a habit of asking some aged great man to leave a message of wisdom for posterity. I do not think that the message has much value, partly because contemporary observers are more often than not blind to the events of their own time, partly because for every prophet who happens to be right there are probably twenty who have prophesied something exactly the opposite, but mainly because old people are not or should not be listened to very seriously by the young people on whom the future depends. Old people change their views almost as quickly as young people.

Between January 1917 and January 1918 I heard Chaliapin sing *God Save The Tsar*; *the Marseillaise* (for the Lvov-Kerensky régime); and *The Internationale* (for the Bolsheviks). He sang all three with the same fervour. An artist, however, is a privileged person. In Oxford I heard Bertrand Russell tell a Foreign Office Conference that we must arm. A few years later he was saying we must throw away our arms and lie down to Communism. On the first occasion the atom bomb was, as far as he knew, the exclusive possession of the Americans. On the second occasion both East and West had the more destructive hydrogen bomb.

On the whole I agree with Harold Nicolson that the old should not brow-beat the young. From the beginning of history there have been prophets of woe, and I do not think that they have affected the course of events in any way.

In 1875, after the Franco-Prussian War, Dostoyevsky prophesied the end of Europe's ascendancy. To-day it looks as if he may be right. In 1896 Solovyov, a Russian saintly visionary, prophesied that a Japanese-Chinese Empire would over-run Russia and would conquer Europe. This, too, seems more like a forecast than the wild prophecy of a semi-crazy Christian seer.

We know that nothing on this earth is eternal. To-day some dream of world government. Others dread the extinction of the white man. After the First World War there was a universal belief in democracy. To-day it looks as if democracy and small nations are on the way out.

And not only small nations. The Great Powers of Western Europe appear to have lost not only their strength, but also their prestige, and the recovery of their greatness seems improbable.

But nobody knows anything for certain. Indeed the only knowledge is the awareness that we know nothing, and even this one does not realise until one has learnt everything. If therefore a scientist, old in years but still wise in mind, has a discovery, let him put it in writing, for poets die young while scientists reach maturity late in life, but let him not try to dictate to youth.

As Schopenhauer said, from the standpoint of youth life is an endlessly long future ; from the standpoint of age a very short past. Moreover, youth is the period of unrest and age the period of rest.

Youth will see the realities of the future without the help of white-haired prophets. The happiness of old age lies in the ability of the aged to make peace with themselves.

I have lived in an age of immense change and, in spite of the bloodiest wars in history, have never been bored or uninterested, and my old age, though full of financial troubles, has so far been happier than my turbulent youth. I hope and believe that the new generation of to-day will be wiser and do better than mine.

INDEX

INDEX